The Workbook on
Lessons from the Saints

The Workbook on
Lessons from the
Saints

MAXIE DUNNAM

UPPER
ROOM BOOKS®
NASHVILLE

Library of Congress Cataloging-in-Publication Data
Dunnam, Maxie D.
    Workbook on lessons from the saints / Maxie D. Dunnam.
        p. cm.
    Includes bibliographical references.
    ISBN 0-8358-0965-X
        1. Spiritual life—Christianity. 2. Christian saints—Biography. I. Title.
BV4501.3 .D86 2002
248.4—dc21

                                                                2001045445

To
Sheila Lovell, Linda McDonald,
and Ginny Proctor—
saints without portfolio,
who by their research and clerical support
have enabled me to tell the story of other saints

OTHER BOOKS BY MAXIE DUNNAM

The Workbook on Living Prayer (20th Anniversary Edition)

The Workbook on Becoming Alive in Christ

The Workbook on Christians Under Construction and in Recovery

The Workbook on the Christian Walk

The Workbook on Coping As Christians

The Workbook on Intercessory Prayer

The Workbook on Loving the Jesus Way

The Workbook on Spiritual Disciplines

The Workbook on the Seven Deadly Sins

The Workbook on Virtues and the Fruit of the Spirit

The Workbook on Keeping Company with the Saints

CONTENTS

INTRODUCTION

Eugene H. Peterson, a widely respected writer and professor of theology who wrote *The Message*, a helpful paraphrase of scripture, says that the growing interest in spirituality in America today is "more likely to be evidence of pathology than health. . . . The interest itself is not sick, but sickness has provoked the interest." Although considerable confusion exists about the cure, he notes that there is widespread agreement about the diagnosis: "Our culture is sick with secularism" (*Subversive Spirituality*, 32).

It's true, isn't it? We Americans have tried to live without a spiritual center. The result is that we are spiritually empty and relationally hollow. We are utterly incapable of healing our souls' deepest hungers, hurts, and fears. We don't know where to turn. We have this strong notion of what is missing—something "spiritual." So everywhere you turn these days, folks are talking about spirituality. Yet, too often this spirituality is reduced to the lowest common denominator, and more confusion results. We find no deep, abiding meaning.

The value of this workbook will be enhanced if you study it with a group of 8 to 12 persons. Group meetings are designed to last for 1 1/2 hours.

Eugene Kennedy, a Roman Catholic psychologist, has said that a lot of what floats around under the label of spirituality is little more than "McSpirituality, junk food for the soul." Commenting on Kennedy's observation, my friend James A. Harnish says,

> My own spin on Kennedy's colorful phrase is that "McSpirituality" is quick. Who has time these days to dig around in old recipe books, shop for quality food, and spend hours in the kitchen preparing a full-course meal? Fast-food spirituality doesn't get in the way of all the stuff that fills our calendars.
>
> McSpirituality is cheap; it can be purchased with pocket change. Unlike the preparation of a gourmet dinner, it never competes with our payments on the really important things, like the latest gadget from "The Sharper Image." (*Passion, Power and Praise*, 89)

I wrote this workbook and its predecessor, *The Workbook on Keeping Company with the Saints*, in response to this "McSpirituality." Throughout the ages there have been persons who diligently sought for God. These individuals share some common characteristics:

- They saturated themselves in scripture.
- They attempted to imitate Christ in their everyday lives.
- They bore others' burdens in order to live a kingdom lifestyle.
- They saw Christianity not merely as theory but as a practical way of living.

- They were ordinary people who became extraordinary in their witness and model of true spirituality because they sought to live not for themselves but for God alone.

Saint Thérèse of Lisieux, a young French nun who lived from 1873–1897, is an example of an ordinary person who became extraordinary. Early in her autobiography Thérèse reflected on the way God's grace works in different persons. She remarks, "God seems to pour out such extraordinary graces on great sinners like St. Paul, St. Augustine and so many others, forcing His grace on them, so to speak. . . . Also I wondered why so many poor savages die without even hearing Our Lord's name."

The revelation that came to Thérèse is an inspiring challenge:

> Jesus chose to enlighten me on this mystery. He opened the book of nature before me, and I saw that every flower He has created has a beauty of its own; that the splendour of the rose and the lily's whiteness do not deprive the violet of its scent, nor make less ravishing the daisy's charm. I saw that if every little flower wished to be a rose, nature would lose her Spring adornments, and the fields would be no longer enamelled with their varied flowers.
>
> So it is in the world of souls, the living garden of the Lord. It pleases Him to create great saints, who may be compared with the lilies or the rose; but He has also created little ones, who must be content to be daisies or violets nestling at His feet to delight His eyes when He should choose to look at them. The happier they are to be as He wills, the more perfect they are. (Thérèse of Lisieux, *The Story of a Soul*, 6)

So it is possible for even ordinary people like us to become extraordinary in our witness and model of meaningful spirituality when we seek to live not for ourselves but for God alone.

In the introduction to *The Workbook on Keeping Company with the Saints*, I shared how my vocational calling forced me to give attention to the saints. In 1973 The Upper Room invited me to join their staff to direct a ministry, primarily to call people to a life of prayer, providing direction and resources to encourage growth in the practice of prayer and developing a structure for united expression of prayer by people around the world. I told Dr. Wilson Weldon, then editor of *The Upper Room* daily devotional guide, that the fact that The Upper Room invited me to assume this responsibility indicated they were desperate, since I was such a novice in this area of prayer life and its development.

My new position forced me to become even more deliberate and disciplined in my prayer life, and it introduced me to a wider dimension of spirituality than I had previously known. During those days, I knew no one within the Protestant tradition who talked of spiritual formation. Roman Catholics, on the other hand, have known the importance of this aspect of Christian growth and have used formation language for centuries.

Soon we at The Upper Room began talking about spiritual formation and seeking to provide resources for a broader expression of spirituality than we had known before. Among The Upper Room's responses to this calling were The Weekend Adventure in Living Prayer, the Emmaus movement, the Academy for Spiritual Formation, the journal *Weavings*, and the children's magazine *Pockets*.

Later, as part of The Upper Room's mission of providing resources for spiritual formation, I wrote *The Workbook on Keeping Company with the Saints* to introduce readers to the writing of four individuals who are giants in their contribution to spiritual writing and their role in shaping spirituality: William Law, Julian of Norwich, Brother Lawrence, and Teresa of Avila. At the time I wrote that workbook, I intended to follow it with another workbook to introduce four more saints, thus inspiring readers to continue a deliberate and ongoing journey of "keeping company with the saints."

I tentatively selected four other saints for the second workbook. But as I sought to pinpoint my focus for this book, it became clear that I needed to move in a different direction. As I continued to keep company with the saints, I noticed ten characteristics they have in common. Other dimensions of their lives may deserve notice, but these traits seem to be central:

- They passionately sought the Lord.
- They discovered a gracious God.
- They took scripture seriously.
- Jesus was alive in their experience.
- They practiced spiritual disciplines, with prayer at the center of these disciplines.
- They were convinced that obedience was essential to their life and growth.
- They did not seek ecstasy but surrender of their will to the Lord.
- They thirsted for holiness.
- They lived not for themselves but for God alone.
- They knew joy and peace that transcended all circumstances.

So, rather than focusing on four particular saints, as I had done in the first workbook, I decided to focus on these ten characteristics of the saints and to use writings from a variety of persons to further explain these characteristics.

The term *saint* means different things to different people. One of my mentors, Douglas Steere, provides a definition I want you to keep in mind as you use this workbook.

> What is an "apostle," or if you like, a "saint?" Either term is so alien to our ordinary habits of thought that it needs definition and clarification and illustration. If a "saint" or an "apostle" were defined as a religious genius, the modern mind would be better able to understand it. . . . [However] the apostle or saint . . . is not a genius. . . .
>
> He is an apostle only as whatever capacities he possesses are wholly open to use for the purposes of God. He is an apostle by reason of the totality of his abandonment to God. . . . An apostle is "just a human being released from the love of self and enslaved by the love of God," and [the apostle] rejoices in it. The life of an apostle is one where "God and [God's] eternal order have more and more their undivided sway." The only difference between an apostle [saint] and ourselves is that [the apostle] has faced and accepted without condition the quiet demand, "Who chooseth me must give and hazard all he hath," and we have not. (Steere, *On Beginning from Within*, 33, 35)

I pray that this workbook will help you understand, accept, and integrate these characteristics of the "saints" into your life and that you may become far more of a "saint" than you ever thought possible.

NOTES ON QUOTED MATERIAL

Excerpts in this book have not been edited for inclusive language but retain the original language, which uses male pronouns for references to humanity and God. Quotations from sources other than scripture are identified in parentheses at the end of each selection. The citation includes the author's name, book title, and pages where the quotation is found. These citations are keyed to the Bibliography at the back of the book. There you will find complete information for each book, should you wish to read certain works more fully.

HOW TO USE THIS WORKBOOK

This workbook is designed for individual and group use. Let's look at the process. It is simple but important.

From my years of teaching and ministry with small groups, I have learned that six to eight weeks is the most manageable and effective time frame for group study. Also, people can best digest content and truth in small doses. That is why this book is organized in daily readings.

> *A saint is just a human being released from the love of self and enslaved by the love of God.*
>
> —*Douglas Steere*

The plan for this workbook calls for an eight-week commitment. I ask you to devote about thirty minutes each day to each reading so that you can inform, enhance, and shape your faith and life. Some individuals will find their thirty minutes at the beginning of the day. However, if setting aside this much time in the morning is impossible, find another time in the day. The important thing is to devote time *regularly*. This study is not only an intellectual pursuit but also a spiritual journey; its purpose is for you to incorporate the content into your daily life. Even though this journey is personal, I hope that you will share it with some fellow pilgrims who will meet together once a week during the eight weeks of the study.

The workbook is arranged into eight sections, each designed to guide you for one week. Each section contains seven readings, one for each day of the week. Each day's reading has three major aspects: (1) reading, (2) reflecting and recording ideas and thoughts about the material and your own understanding and experience, and (3) practical suggestions for incorporating ideas from the reading material into your daily life.

Each day's reading includes scripture, a selection from the writings of a saint, and my commentary. The content is not too much to read, but it will be enough to challenge you to think and act.

Throughout the workbook you will see this symbol: ✥ ✥ ✥. When you come to the symbol, please stop. Do not read any further. Think and reflect as you are requested so that you can internalize the ideas shared or the experience reflected upon.

REFLECTING AND RECORDING

A time for reflecting and recording follows each day's reading. This section asks you to record some of your thoughts. The degree of meaning you receive from this workbook depends largely on your faithfulness in practicing its method. You may be unable on a particular day to do precisely what is requested. If so, then simply record that fact and make a note of why you can't follow through. This exercise may give you some insight about yourself and help you grow.

On some days you are asked to reword the quotations from the saints. This is an important exercise. The language and style of the saints' writing is dated. Sometimes, to really understand them, we have to paraphrase them into our everyday speech. The paraphrasing is a helpful exercise within itself, so I urge you to respond.

Also, on some days there may be more suggestions than you can do in the time you have available. Do the activities that are most meaningful, and do not feel guilty about the rest.

Finally, always remember this pilgrimage is personal. What you write in your workbook is your private property. You may wish not to share it with anyone. For this reason, do not attempt to share workbooks. The importance of what you write is its meaning for you, not for anyone else. Writing, even if we jot only brief notes or single-word reminders, helps us clarify our thoughts and feelings.

The significance of the reflecting-and-recording dimension will grow as you move along. Even beyond the eight weeks, you will find meaning in looking back to what you wrote on a particular day in response to a particular situation.

SHARING THE JOURNEY WITH OTHERS

In the history of Christian spirituality, the spiritual director or guide has been a significant person. To varying degrees, most of us have had spiritual directors—individuals to whom we have turned for support and direction in our spiritual pilgrimage. There is a sense in which this workbook can serve as a spiritual guide, for you can use it as a private venture without participating in a group. Also, in a very real way, you will meet and keep company with individuals who have guided many others in their spiritual journeys.

The value of the workbook will be enhanced, however, if you share the adventure with eight to twelve others. (Groups larger than twelve tend to limit individual participation.) In this way, group members can profit from one another's insights. Each week's section concludes with a guide for the group meeting.

If studying the workbook is a group venture, everyone should begin the workbook on the same day so that when the group meets, all of you will have dealt with the same material and will be at the same place in the text. Having an initial get-acquainted group meeting to begin the adventure will be helpful. This introduction contains an outline of what to do in the initial meeting.

Group sessions for this workbook are designed to last for one and one-half hours (with the exception of the initial meeting). Group members should agree to attend all sessions unless an emergency prevents attendance. There are eight weekly sessions in addition to this first get-acquainted time.

GROUP LEADER'S TASKS

One person may lead the study for the entire eight weeks, or leaders may be assigned from week to week. The leader's tasks are:

- Read the Group Meeting directions at the end of each week and determine ahead of time how to handle the session.

- It may not be possible to use all the suggestions for sharing and praying together. Select those you think will be most meaningful and for which you have adequate time.

- Model a style of openness, honesty, and warmth. Do not pressure anyone to share. Usually, as leader, be the first one to share, especially personal experiences.

- Moderate the discussion.

- Encourage reluctant members to participate; do your best to avoid letting a few group members dominate the discussion.

- Center the sharing in personal experience rather than academic debate.

- Honor the time schedule. If it appears necessary to go longer than one and one-half hours, gain the group's consensus for continuing another twenty or thirty minutes.

- See that everyone knows the meeting time and place, especially if meetings are held in different homes.

- Make sure that the necessary materials for meetings are available and that the meeting room is arranged ahead of time.

If possible, hold weekly meetings in group members' homes. (Hosts or hostesses can make sure there are as few interruptions as possible from children, telephones, pets, and so forth.) If the group meets in a church, find an informal setting. Invite participants to dress casually so they can be comfortable and relaxed.

If refreshments are planned, serve them after the formal meeting. In this way, those group members who wish to stay longer for informal discussion may do so, while those who cannot stay may leave, having had the full value of the meeting time.

SUGGESTIONS FOR INITIAL GET-ACQUAINTED MEETING

Read the entire introduction before the meeting. Since the meeting is for the purpose of getting acquainted and beginning the shared pilgrimage, here is a way to get started.

- Ask group members to tell their names. Address everyone by first name or nickname. If name tags are needed, provide them.

- Let each individual briefly describe a happy, exciting, or meaningful experience during the past three or four weeks.

- Ask each person who is willing to share expectations of this workbook study. Why did he or she become a part of this study? What does each person expect to gain from it? What are his or her reservations?

- Review the introduction to the workbook, and ask if anyone has questions about how to use the book. If group members have not already received copies of the workbook, distribute books now. Remember that everyone must have a workbook.

- Day 1 in the workbook is the day after this initial meeting; the next meeting should be held on Day 7 of the first week. If the group must choose a weekly meeting time other than seven days from this initial session, adjust the reading assignment so that the weekly meetings are always on Day 7, and Day 1 is always the day after a meeting.

- Nothing builds a sense of community more than praying for one another. Encourage group members to write everyone's name in their workbooks and commit to praying daily for each individual by name during the eight weeks.

- After being sure that everyone knows the time and place of the next meeting, close with prayer, thanking God for each person in the group, for the opportunity to grow, and for the possibility of growing through spiritual disciplines.

God bless you as you continue this workbook journey.

WEEK 1

THEY PASSIONATELY SOUGHT AND FOUND A GRACIOUS GOD

DAY
1

Thirsting for a Gracious God

Martin Luther King Jr. lives in the memory of people around the world, especially in the United States. His birthday is a national holiday in America, a day when U.S. citizens celebrate his commitment to civil rights and nonviolence. It bothers me that when we recall King's contribution to American life, we forget that his commitments were rooted in his deep personal faith in God. In *Pilgrimage to Nonviolence*, he wrote, "I have . . . become more and more convinced of the reality of a personal God." King said there was a time when God was little more to him than an interesting topic for theological or philosophical debate. That all changed. He experienced God personally, and the reality of God's presence in his life was validated in the everyday pressure and tension of the struggle in which he engaged. King wrote:

Two lessons from Martin Luther

1. *The saints passionately sought God.*
2. *They found a gracious God.*

> In the midst of outer dangers I have felt an inner calm and known resources of strength that only God could give. In many instances I have felt the power of God transforming the fatigue of despair into the buoyancy of hope. I am convinced that the universe is under the control of a loving purpose and that in the struggle for righteousness man has cosmic companionship. (King, *A Testament of Hope*, 40)

In his sermons and speeches, almost without fail, King affirmed the presence of God and our need for more intimate companionship with God. Along with Christians throughout the ages, I seek that companionship.

I often punctuate my devotional life with this prayer: "Oh Lord, give me the grace to be wholly yours." Psalm 42 expresses the same yearning:

As a deer longs for flowing streams,
*   so my soul longs for you, O God.*
My soul thirsts for God,
*   for the living God.*
When shall I come and behold
*   the face of God? (Psalm 42:1-2)*

I wonder if Martin Luther was thinking of the psalmist's passionate prayer when he wrote:

I am seeking, searching, thirsting for nothing else than a gracious God.
     Yet God continuously and earnestly offers himself as a God of grace, and urges even those who spurn him and are his enemies, to accept him as such. (*Daily Readings with Martin Luther*, 48)

In his soul yearning, Luther vividly expressed two lessons I have identified that we might learn from the saints:

1. They passionately sought God.

2. They found a gracious God.

We will live with those two lessons this week.

All the saints with whom I have kept company passionately sought God. They constantly worked at knowing God better and deeper. When Thomas Aquinas entered the monastery, he desired only to think, to speak, and to hear of God. He dedicated all his works and actions to God. On one occasion he said that God asked him what reward he wanted for the many works he had written. He replied, "No other but Thyself alone, my Lord and my Love!" (*A Year with the Saints*, 358).

Francis de Sales, a French Jesuit who lived from 1567–1622, expressed the same desire for God:

We must begin with a strong and constant resolution to give ourselves wholly to God, professing to Him, in a tender, loving manner, from the bottom of our hearts, that we intend to be His without any reserve, and then we must often go back and renew this same resolution. (*A Year with the Saints*, 2)

REFLECTING AND RECORDING

One way to internalize the lessons of the saints is to put their sayings into our own words. I would reword de Sales's admonition like this:

The beginning of a serious relationship with God is a commitment of my will. I must give myself wholly to God, and this must be my ongoing resolution. I surrender my will to Him in love—determined to give myself to Him, holding nothing back. I know that I will need to renew this commitment regularly.

Disregarding what I have written, put de Sales's quotation into your own words. Use the space above (beside de Sales's quotation) to record your "translation."

(When you see this symbol, do not proceed
until you have followed the previous instructions.)

Pray the following prayer:

Lord, give me the grace to be wholly yours.

DURING THE DAY

Pray the above prayer three or four times a day. You may want to cut out this prayer from page 243 and carry it with you.

DAY
2

Our Only Resource

Again, the kingdom of heaven is like a merchant in search of fine pearls; on finding one pearl of great value, he went and sold all that he had and bought it. (Matthew 13:45)

The saints often used the parable of the pearl of great price to illustrate our need to passionately seek God. Merchants seeking for riches do not take into account what they have already acquired. They forget the fatigue they have borne as they put all their thought and care into seeking new acquisitions. Past achievements and possessions are also forgotten in their quest for the treasure they now seek.

Sooner or later, a passionate search for God leads to the recognition that we cannot depend on our own resources.

The saints used another comparison for seeking God. They challenged us to act like travelers who do not regard the road they have traveled or the distance they have come but look only to what lies ahead. Likewise, we must keep our destination before our eyes, even to the journey's end.

In passionately seeking God, the saints acknowledged this foundational truth: Always and ultimately, God is our only resource.

Jean-Pierre de Caussade contended that God wants to destroy in us any confidence we get from depending on ourselves so that God becomes our only resource. He expressed this idea in a letter to someone he was counseling spiritually.

The loss of hope causes you more grief than any other trial. I can well understand this . . .

Allow me, with the help of God's grace, to set this trouble in its true light and so to cure you. What you want, my dear sister, is to find support and comfort in yourself and in your good works. Well, this is precisely what God does not wish and what he cannot endure in souls aspiring after perfection.

What! Lean upon yourself? Count on your works? Could self-love, pride and perversity have a more miserable fruit?

It is to deliver them from this that God makes all chosen souls pass through a fearful time of poverty, misery and nothingness.

He desires to destroy in them gradually all the help and confidence they derive from themselves so that he may be their sole support, their confidence, their hope, their only resource. (*The Joy of the Saints*, 353)

Sooner or later, a passionate search for God leads to the recognition that we cannot depend on our own resources or count on our own works to achieve meaning or to help us grow closer to God. De Caussade continued his counsel in this fashion:

Why is it that in spite of your attraction to give yourself entirely to God, and your pious reading, you seem to remain always at the entrance of the interior life without the power of entering? I will tell you the reason, my dear sister, for I see it very distinctly; it is because you have misused this attraction by inordinate desires, by overeagerness, and a natural activity, thus displeasing God, and stifling the gentle action of grace.

Also, because in your conduct there has been a secret and imperceptible presumption which has made you rely on your own industry and your own efforts. Without noticing it you have acted as if you aspired to do all the work by your own industry, and even to do more than God desired.

You who would have taken yourself to task for any worldly ambition, have, without scruple, allowed yourself to be carried away by a still more subtle ambition, and by a desire for a high position in the spiritual life. But, be comforted; thanks to the merciful sternness of God's dealings with you, so far nothing is lost; on the contrary, you have gained greatly. God punishes you for these imperfections like a good father, with tenderness; and enables you to find a remedy for the evil in the chastisement he awards you. (*The Joy of the Saints*, 263)

REFLECTING AND RECORDING

De Caussade suggested two reasons his friend remained "always at the entrance of the interior life without the power of entering":

1. She responded to the attraction of the spiritual life with inordinate desires and overeagerness.

2. She relied on her own industry and efforts.

Spend some time examining your own spiritual journey. Has either of these dynamics kept you at the entrance of "the interior life without the power of entering" or hindered you from the intimate relationship with God you have desired?

Read again de Caussade's last paragraph above. Spend a few minutes reflecting on God's "merciful sternness" in dealing with you. In what ways have you experienced the merciful sternness of God? Make some notes describing your experience.

DURING THE DAY

Continue to say this prayer throughout the day: "Lord, give me the grace to be wholly yours."

DAY
3

Every Right to Be Lord

When they found him on the other side of the sea, they said to him, "Rabbi, when did you come here?" Jesus answered them, "Very truly, I tell you, you are looking for me, not because you saw signs, but because you ate your fill of the loaves. Do not work for the food that perishes, but for the food that endures for eternal life, which the Son of Man will give you. For it is on him that God the Father has set his seal." Then they said to him, "What must we do to perform the works of God?" Jesus answered them, "This is the work of God, that you believe in him whom he has sent." So they said to him, "What sign are you going to give us then, so that we may see it and believe you? What work are you performing? Our ancestors ate the manna in the wilderness; as it is written, 'He gave them bread from heaven to eat.'" Then Jesus said to them, "Very truly, I tell you, it was not Moses who gave you the bread from heaven, but it is my Father who gives you the true bread from heaven. For the bread of God is that which comes down from heaven and gives life to the world." They said to him, "Sir, give us this bread always." (John 6:25-34)

You may recall that this encounter took place after Jesus' miraculous feeding of the thousands on the mountainside by the Sea of Galilee. The crowd had gathered to hear Jesus teach. When he looked and saw the great multitude coming toward him, he said to Philip, "Where are we to buy bread for these people to eat?" (John 6:5). Philip replied, "Six months' wages would not buy enough bread for each one of them to get a little!" (v. 7).

The nearer the soul approaches the perfect purity of divine love, the more its thoughts and reflections are turned away from itself and fixed on the infinite goodness of God.

—*Jean-Pierre de Caussade*

Then follows one of the most beautiful stories in scripture. Andrew—Simon Peter's brother, the one who had brought Simon Peter to Jesus—knew that in the crowd was a boy with five small barley loaves and two fish. Andrew mentioned the boy and his lunch to Jesus but asked how far this meager amount of food would go among so many people—about five thousand. Jesus replied, "Make the people sit down." Jesus took the loaves, gave thanks to God, and distributed food to everyone. When the crowd had eaten, the disciples gathered up what was left, and the leftovers filled twelve baskets.

Many people who had witnessed Jesus' miraculous multiplication of the loaves and fishes followed him the next day to the other side of the sea. He confronted them with the stern fact that they paid little attention to him until he fed them. "You are looking for me," Jesus said, "not because you saw signs, but because you ate your fill of the loaves" (v. 26).

What motivates us to seek God? Our motives are an ongoing issue in our spiritual journey. Do we seek God to obtain "food that perishes" or "food that endures" (John 6:27)? Is our desire for God a desire for a relationship of love or for material blessings? Why do we practice spiritual disciplines?

Margery Kempe, an English religious writer who lived from about 1373 to 1438, experienced an exchange in prayer that addresses these questions.

> Lord, you are my joy and happiness, the only treasure I have in this world. I do not wish for material goods but think only of you. My dear Lord and my God, do not leave me.
>   [God answers]
>   "Rejoice and be happy! If you knew how much pleasure I get from speaking to you, you would never do anything else."
>   "If you said the Lord's Prayer a thousand times a day, it would not make me as glad as when you remain silent and let me speak to you."
>   "You can be as sure of the love of God, as God is God. Your soul is more secure in the love of God than in your own body. Your soul will leave your body but God will never leave your soul." (*The Joy of the Saints*, 116)

Jean-Pierre de Caussade described the nature of pure love, which should be our motive for practicing spiritual disciplines.

> It is true that love, even the purest, does not exclude in the soul the desire of its own salvation and perfection.

But it is equally incontestable that the nearer the soul approaches the perfect purity of divine love, the more its thoughts and reflections are turned away from itself and fixed on the infinite goodness of God.

. . . .

This love, which includes the love of ourselves but is independent of it, is what theologians call pure love; and all agree in recognizing that the soul is so much the more perfect according to the measure in which it habitually acts under the influence of this love, and the extent to which it divests itself of all self-seeking, at any rate unless its own interests are subordinated to the interests of God.

Therefore total renunciation without reserve or limit has no thoughts of self-interest—it thinks but of God, of his good pleasure, of his wishes, of his glory. (*The Joy of the Saints*, 44)

REFLECTING AND RECORDING

In the space beside de Caussade's quotation above, paraphrase the second and third paragraphs in your own words.

Spend time reflecting on the following statements and their meaning for your life. To what mind and heart changes do they call you?

- "You can be as sure of the love of God, as God is God."

- "Your soul is more secure in the love of God than in your own body."

- "Total renunciation without reserve or limit has no thoughts of self-interest—it thinks but of God, of his good pleasure, of his wishes, of his glory."

DURING THE DAY

Reflect on this word from God, which you read earlier:

> Rejoice and be happy! If you knew how much pleasure I get from speaking to you, you would never do anything else.

Cut this message from page 243 and carry it around with you. Three or four times during the day, whenever you can find some privacy and silence, read God's message to you.

Continue praying, "Lord, give me the grace to be wholly yours."

DAY
4

Grace: The Gift of God's Self

On Day 2 we looked at a quotation from de Caussade in which he referred to "the merciful sternness of God's dealings with you." Many people perceive that God always deals with them sternly. Rarely do they see their situation as God's *merciful* sternness.

I can't recall any saint who didn't acknowledge experiencing dark nights of the soul. Few of us, if any, escape the tragic aspects of life. Even the Gospel writer Matthew viewed a life in which no one is spared God's diverse offering in a fallen world:

> *[God] makes his sun rise on the evil and on the good, and sends rain on the righteous and on the unrighteous. (Matthew 5:45)*

Was Matthew perhaps recalling the story of Job, one of God's most righteous persons? The Almighty described Job like this: "There is no one like him on the earth, a blameless and upright man who fears God and turns away from evil" (Job 1:8). Yet no one suffered like Job.

Seeking to shape Job's response to his suffering, Bildad, one of Job's friends, talked about God in this fashion:

> *Dominion and fear are with God;*
> *he makes peace in his high heaven.*
> *Is there any number to his armies?*
> *Upon whom does his light not arise? (Job 25:2-3)*

Perhaps Matthew had Bildad's words in mind when he wrote "[God] makes his sun rise on the evil and on the good, and sends rain on the righteous and on the unrighteous."

The lessons we can learn from studying the characteristics of the saints inspire us. Yes, the saints passionately sought God. And how encouraging and hopeful for us—*they discovered a gracious God.*

The great reformer Martin Luther had a transforming perspective of grace:

All the many countless blessings which God gives us here on earth are merely those gifts which last for a time.

But his grace and loving regard are the inheritance which endures throughout eternity . . .

In giving us such gifts here on earth he is giving us only those things that are his own, but *in his grace and love towards us he gives his very self.*

In receiving his gifts we touch but his hand; but in his gracious regard we receive his heart, his spirit, his mind, his will.

Man receives grace immediately and fully. In this way he is saved. Good works are not necessary to assist him in this: they follow. It is as if God were to produce a fresh, green tree out of a dry log, which tree would then bear its natural fruit. (*Daily Readings with Martin Luther*, 49, italics mine)

Luther shared these convictions in a letter to a man whose wife had died:

I have been urged by friends of yours to write to you. Please receive this letter kindly. They tell me that since the death of your dear wife, who departed this life at peace with God, you have been trying to help the repose of her soul with good works and services.

First, I beg to remind you of what Job says: "The Lord gave, and the Lord has taken away; as it seemed good to the Lord, so has he done." You should sing the same song to God, a loving and faithful God who gave you a loving and faithful wife. . . . She was his before he gave her; she was his after he had given her; and she still remains his (as we all do). . . .

Although it hurts us when he takes his own from us, his goodwill should be a greater comfort to us than all his gifts, for God is immeasurably more than all his gifts. Although we cannot perceive God's will as clearly as we can see a wife, yet we can perceive and apprehend his will by faith.

Cheerfully give back to God what is his, and accept this proper exchange, this strange barter whereby, instead of a dear, kindly wife, you have a dear, kindly will of God. Nay, more! God himself. Truly, God's goodness and mercy extend beyond this life. (*The Joy of the Saints*, 284)

What a heartening understanding Luther had of God's grace:

I am seeking, searching, thirsting for nothing else than a gracious God.

Yet God continuously and earnestly offers himself as a God of grace. . . .

In his grace and love towards us he gives his very self. (*Daily Readings with Martin Luther*, 48–49)

Therefore, Luther could say that the man who had lost his wife eventually would receive kindly the will of God, but more than that—he would receive God's self.

REFLECTING AND RECORDING

Saint Thomas Aquinas insisted that the surest way to "attain to the love of God is to dwell on his mercies." In other words, the more we acknowledge God's mercies, the more we appreciate them, and the more we love God.

> *In his grace and love towards us [God] gives his very self.*
>
> —Martin Luther

What mercies of God have you experienced during the past few months? Write them in the left-hand column below.

God's mercies   **My sins, misdeeds, and failures**

_____   _____

_____   _____

_____   _____

_____   _____

_____   _____

Francis de Sales said, "Nothing can so humble us before the compassion of God as the abundance of his mercies." Your above reflection should confirm this. De Sales also said, "Nothing so humbles us before [God's] justice as the abundance of our misdeeds." Spend just five minutes recording some of your sins, misdeeds, and failures toward God in the right-hand column.

Do not try to balance the two columns; merely reflect on all God has done for you and all you have done against God. Spend the time you have left pondering those subjects.

DURING THE DAY

Move through this day seeking to confirm the truth that "in his grace and love towards us [God] gives his very self." Reread three or four times the message from God that you cut out yesterday. Also, continue using the prayer "Lord, give me the grace to be wholly yours."

DAY
5

The Mercies of God

Paul, an apostle of Christ Jesus by the will of God, and Timothy our brother,
*   To the church of God that is in Corinth, including all the saints throughout Achaia:*
*   Grace to you and peace from God our Father and the Lord Jesus Christ. Blessed be the God and*
Father of our Lord Jesus Christ, the Father of mercies and the God of all consolation, who consoles us in
all our affliction, so that we may be able to console those who are in any affliction with the consolation with
which we ourselves are consoled by God. For just as the sufferings of Christ are abundant for us, so also
our consolation is abundant through Christ. (2 Corinthians 1:1-5)

Paul begins his Second Letter to the Corinthians much like his other letters (see 1 Cor. 1:1-3; Gal. 1:1-5; Eph. 1:1-2). He carefully presents himself as an apostle "by the will of God" (v. 1). Paul makes clear that the church is God's church (v. 2). The church is God's idea and thus is accountable not to apostles or elders, but to the Almighty. Always Paul offers the grace and peace of "God our Father and the Lord Jesus Christ" (v. 2). He crowns his greeting to the Corinthians with this illuminating, encouraging, and challenging word:

Blessed be the God and Father of our Lord Jesus Christ, the Father of mercies and the God of all consola-
tion, who consoles us in all our affliction, so that we may be able to console those who are in any affliction
with the consolation with which we ourselves are consoled by God. (2 Corinthians 1:3-4)

Because of their circumstances, the Corinthians may have doubted God's compassion, as it is easy for us to do. Paul wanted them to keep that truth alive in their experience. The Father of mercies and the God of all consolation comforts us in our troubles, he said. That enables us, in turn, to extend to others the mercies we have received.

Saint Thérèse entered the Carmelite convent in Lisieux, France, at the young age of fifteen. Her mother had died when she was four. Thérèse lived only to age twenty-four. She wrote her autobiography out of obedience to her mother superior. Not until after her death was the decision made to "let it [Thérèse's autobiography] pass beyond the walls of the Carmel."

My dearest Mother, it is to you, to you who are in fact a mother twice over to me, that I now confide the Story of my Soul. The day you asked me to do it, I thought it might be a distraction to me, but afterwards, Jesus made me realise that simple obedience would please Him best. So I am going to begin singing what I shall sing for ever, *"the mercies of the Lord."* (Thérèse of Lisieux, *The Story of a Soul*, 5)

Though we may not be aware of it, our spiritual journeys begin at birth. God's prevenient grace, God's "going before us," is a dynamic factor of which we become aware only in retrospect. Thérèse was unusual in this respect. Perhaps her parents' ardent Christian commitment—their intimate involvement in the devotional life prescribed by the church—captured her attention as a child. But there seems to be much more to her recognition. Her spiritual inclination and intuition were present in a remarkable way even in her preteen years. In her autobiography, she wrote:

> At fourteen my thirst for knowledge had become so great that God thought it was time to season the "fine flour" with the honey and oil of Fr. [Father] Arminjon's conferences on "The End of this World and the Mysteries of the World to Come." As I read, I experienced that joy which the world cannot give, something of what God has prepared for those who love Him. All our sacrifices seemed quite petty compared with this reward and I wanted so much to love Jesus with my whole heart and prove it in a thousand ways while I still had the chance. (*The Story of a Soul*, 68–69)

Thérèse discusses how, in this time before she made her life commitment to the monastic life, she became sure that grace was being poured into her soul.

> For God, as the *Imitation* says, "sometimes gives Himself to us in radiant light, sometimes veiled in symbols and in shadows."
>
> It was veiled in this way that He showed Himself to us, but the veil was so light that we could almost see through and there was no room for doubt. Faith and hope gave way to love; we had found already the One we were seeking. (*The Story of a Soul*, 69)

Thus Thérèse would write her autobiography as a song of "the mercies of the Lord," about which she would sing forever. She echoed the psalmist,

> *I will sing of your steadfast love, O Lord, forever;*
> *with my mouth I will proclaim your faithfulness to all generations.*
> *I declare that your steadfast love is established forever;*
> *your faithfulness is as firm as the heavens. (Psalm 89:1-2)*

The saints connected God's mercy with their awareness of God's presence in their lives.

I like *The Living Bible*'s rendering of Psalm 107:1-2a: "Say 'thank you' to the Lord for being so good, for always being so loving and kind. Has God redeemed you? Then speak out!"

The saints did not measure God's graciousness by their life circumstances. Many of the individuals who suffered the most were also some of the most ardent in praising God. They connected God's mercy with their awareness of God's presence in their lives.

One of Thérèse's favorite ways to describe herself was as "a victim to the merciful love of God." For her the word *victim* carried no negative connotation. It meant a positive act of the will, a free response of submission, a willingness to suffer and to offer that suffering as a sacrifice to Christ. The apostle Paul also understood suffering: "We suffer with him so that we may also be glorified with him" (Rom. 8:17).

Because she had found a gracious God, Thérèse could offer herself as a "victim of love." Her attitude is revealed in these words:

Why fear to offer yourself as a victim to the merciful love of God? You might have reason to fear if it were to His divine justice, but the merciful love will have pity on your weaknesses and treat you tenderly. (*The Story of a Soul*, 197)

REFLECTING AND RECORDING

While praying, Margery Kempe received this word from the Holy Spirit:

Go in the name of Jesus. I will go with you to help and support you in all you do. Trust me, you have never found me wanting. I will never ask you to do anything that is unacceptable to God.

   I am your God and I delight in you, we shall never be parted. All the promises I have made to you will come true at the right time. (*The Joy of the Saints*, 51)

Reread the above quotation slowly and receive it as the Spirit's word to you.

DURING THE DAY

The Holy Spirit's word to Margery Kempe is printed on page 243. Cut it out, carry it with you, and read it three or four times each day for the next few days. Claim the truth and promise of this message, and notice how it affects your life.

DAY
6

God from the "Bottom Upwards, Not from the Top Downwards"

In his bestseller *Tuesdays with Morrie*, Mitch Albom tells the story of Morrie Schwartz, a Brandeis University professor who was dying of Lou Gehrig's disease. When Mitch discovered that his former college professor was terminally ill, he reconnected with his mentor and began visiting him regularly. During one of their visits, Mitch asked Morrie if he had any regrets or wished he had done anything differently in his life. Morrie responded,

"Mitch," he said, "the culture doesn't encourage you to think about such things until you're about to die. We're so wrapped up with egotistical things, career, family, having enough money, meeting the mortgage, getting a new car, fixing the radiator when it breaks—we're involved in trillions of little acts just to keep going. So we don't get into the habit of standing back and looking at our lives and saying, Is this all? Is this all I want? Is something missing?" . . .

"Everyone knows they're going to die," he said again, "but nobody believes it. If we did, we would do things differently." . . .

"The truth is, Mitch," he said, "Once you learn how to die, you learn how to live." (Albom, *Tuesdays with Morrie*, 64–65, 81–82)

What persons say or pray as they are dying reveals a great deal about them. Some of John Wesley's last words were, "The best of all is, God is with us!" On his deathbed, Martin Luther prayed:

O heavenly Father, God of all comfort, I thank thee that thou hast revealed to me thy beloved Son, Jesus Christ, in whom I have believed, whom I have preached and confessed, whom I have loved and praised. . . .

I pray thee, dear Lord Christ, let me commend my soul to thee.

O heavenly Father, if I leave this body and depart this life, I am certain that I will be with thee for ever and ever, and that I can never, never tear myself out of thy hands.

So God loved the world that he gave his only-begotten Son, Jesus Christ, that whosoever believeth in him should not perish, but have eternal life. [Luther repeated this verse three times.]

Father, into thy hands I commend my spirit. Thou hast redeemed me, thou true God. Amen. (*The Joy of the Saints*, 341)

John Wesley and Martin Luther had found a gracious God, the One revealed in Jesus Christ.

Luther said, "If you want to escape from despair and hatred of God, let speculation go. Begin with God from the bottom upwards, not from the top downwards." He was reflecting the truth of the Incarnation as the Gospel writer John expressed it:

And the Word became flesh and lived among us, and we have seen his glory, the glory as of a father's only son, full of grace and truth. (John testified to him and cried out, "This was he of whom I said, 'He who comes after me ranks ahead of me because he was before me.'") From his fullness we have all received, grace upon grace. The law indeed was given through Moses; grace and truth came through Jesus Christ. No one has ever seen God. It is God the only Son, who is close to the Father's heart, who has made him known. (John 1:14-18)

God the Father longs for you. God the Son wishes to be your Saviour, your liberator.

—*Martin Luther*

Luther's calling for a bottom-upward, rather than a top-downward, view of God was grounded in his teaching about doubt and despair:

God is invisible, inscrutable, incomprehensible, and so on . . . Give up all such speculation, which is utterly unrelated to the word of God anyhow. God is saying to you, From the unrevealed God I shall become your own revealed God: I shall incarnate my own beloved Son. . . . What Christ says and does, you may be sure of. 'No man cometh to the Father but by me.' 'He that hath seen me hath seen the Father.' What God is saying to you is this: "Here in Christ you have me, here in Christ you will see me."

If you want to escape from despair and hatred of God, let speculation go. Begin with God *from the bottom upwards, not from the top downwards.* In other words, begin with Christ incarnate, and with your own terrible original sin. There is no other way. Otherwise, you will remain a doubter for the rest of your life.

At all costs cling to the revealed God. Allow no one to take the child Jesus from you. Hold fast to Christ, and you will *never* be lost. God the Father longs for you. God the Son wishes to be your Saviour, your Liberator. (*The Joy of the Saints*, 260)

In his book *The Authoritative Word*, William Bouknight notes that Christians don't need to address God as "Your Highness" or "Your Holiness." Jesus used the Aramaic word *Abba*, which means Daddy, to address God. Therefore, since we Christians have been adopted into God's family, we have the wonderful privilege of calling God "Daddy."

Bouknight shares a wonderful story about two first-grade boys who were brothers. As the children were introducing themselves on their first day of school, one boy said, "Me and Jack are brothers. One of us is adopted and one is not, but I can't remember which is which."

So it is with us Christians. We don't have to worry about "which is which"—all of us are adopted. God invites us to be members of his family. That adoption happens when we respond in faith and God gives us new birth. (William Bouknight, *The Authoritative Word*, 101)

John Wesley, the founder of Methodism, offered this definition of the witness of the Spirit:

> An inward impression on the soul, whereby the Spirit of God directly witnesses to my spirit, that I am a child of God; that Jesus Christ hath loved me, and given himself for me; and that all my sins are blotted out, and I, even I, am reconciled to God. (*The Works of John Wesley*, vol. 5, 115)

Reflecting and Recording

Focus your mind for a few minutes on Jesus Christ. As Luther said, Jesus is a picture of God "from the bottom upwards." What characteristics of God did Jesus reveal to us? Write them in the space below.

Other than Father, what are your three favorite names for God? Why do you think this is so?

Think of someone you know who has faced death well. What kind of attitude—what spirit— did this person reflect? How did he or she respond to personal circumstances? How did he or she treat loved ones? What do you remember this person saying? Make some notes here.

DURING THE DAY

Three or four times during the day, read the Holy Spirit's word to Margery Kempe, which you cut out yesterday. Claim the truth and promise of this message, and think about how it affects your life.

DAY
7

The Fragrance Exhaled
by the Life of Jesus

The language of scripture is often sensual and visceral, appealing to our physical senses as well as our intuitional and rational capacities. Here is an example in which Paul presents a daunting challenge to the Corinthians:

> When I came to Troas to proclaim the good news of Christ, a door was opened for me in the Lord; but my mind could not rest because I did not find my brother Titus there. So I said farewell to them and went on to Macedonia.
> But thanks be to God, who in Christ always leads us in triumphal procession, and through us spreads in every place the fragrance that comes from knowing him. For we are the aroma of Christ to God among

those who are being saved and among those who are perishing; to the one a fragrance from death to death, to the other a fragrance from life to life. Who is sufficient for these things? For we are not peddlers of God's word like so many; but in Christ we speak as persons of sincerity, as persons sent from God and standing in his presence. (2 Corinthians 2:12-17)

What a picture! Followers of Christ in procession being seen, but more than that, exuding a fragrance that comes from knowing Christ. What a designation! The *aroma* of Christ—the fragrance of life for those who are being saved, the fragrance of death to those who are perishing.

The saints also used this kind of language. Thérèse of Lisieux wrote about "the fragrance exhaled by the life of Jesus."

> Since the Lord is in heaven I can only follow him by traces full of light and fragrance which he has left behind him. When I open the Gospels, I breathe the fragrance exhaled by the life of Jesus, and I know which way to run.
>
> It is to the lowest that I hasten. I repeat with all confidence the humble prayer of the publican. Most of all I imitate the behavior of Mary Magdalene, for her amazing—or, rather, loving—audacity which delighted the heart of Jesus, has cast its spell upon mine. (*The Joy of the Saints*, 204)

How tragic it is when Christians don't exude Christ's aroma. *Angela's Ashes*, Frank McCourt's classic modern memoir, paints a contrasting picture of Christians. The church plays a dominant role in the life of McCourt's poverty-bound family in Limerick, Ireland. Despite their rags and hunger and pain, McCourt gives witness to the fact that love and strength often come out of misery. He describes a seven o'clock Mass on Ash Wednesday.

> The alarm clock shocks us out of our sleep. Aunt Aggie calls from her bed, The three of ye are to get up and go to Mass. Do ye hear me? Up. Wash yeer faces and go to the Jesuits.
>
> Her backyard is all frost and ice and our hands sting from the tap water. We throw a little on our faces and dry with the towel that's still damp from yesterday. Malachy whispers our wash was a lick and a promise, that's what Mam would say.
>
> The streets are frosty and icy, too, but the Jesuit church is warm. It must be grand to be a Jesuit, sleeping in a bed with sheets blankets pillows and getting up to a nice warm house and a warm church with nothing to do but say Mass / hear confessions / and yell at people for their sins / have your meals served up to you and read your Latin office before you to go to sleep. I'd like to be a Jesuit some day but there's no hope of that when you grow up in a lane. Jesuits are very particular. They don't like poor people. They like people with motor cars who stick out their little fingers when they pick up their teacups. (Frank McCourt, *Angela's Ashes: A Memoir*, 244–45)

They join with others in the crowded church, waiting for the climax of the service when the priest will make the sign of the cross on their foreheads with ashes.

> *The aroma of Christ is the fragrance of life for those who are being saved, the fragrance of death to those who are perishing.*

> Malachy whispers that Michael shouldn't get the ashes because he won't be making his First Communion till May and it would be a sin. Michael starts to cry, I want the ashes, I want the ashes. An old woman behind us says, What are ye doin' to that lovely child? Malachy explains the lovely child never made his First Communion and he's not in a state of grace. Malachy is getting ready for Confirmation himself, always showing off his knowledge of the catechism, always going on about state of grace. He won't admit I knew all about the state of grace a year

ago, so long ago I'm starting to forget it. The old woman says you don't have to be in a state of grace to get a few ashes on your forehead and tells Malachy stop tormenting his poor little brother. She pats Michael on the head and tells him he's a lovely child and go up there and get your ashes. He runs to the altar and when he comes back the woman gives him a penny to go with his ashes. (*Angela's Ashes*, 245)

The contrast between Frank's perception of the Jesuits and the old woman's actions can serve as a challenge to Christians. If we "breathe the fragrance exhaled by the life of Jesus," we will become the aroma of Christ, and certainly those around us will receive his life-giving spirit. That life-giving spirit is the transforming power of Christ's mercy and love.

Thérèse continues her witness:

It is not because I have been preserved from serious sin that I lift up my heart to God in trust and in love. I am certain that even if I had on my conscience every imaginable crime, I should love nothing of my confidence, but would throw myself, my heart broken with sorrow, into the arms of my Saviour.

I remember his love for the prodigal son, I have heard his words to Mary Magdalene, to the woman taken in adultery. No—there is no one who could frighten me, for I know too well what to believe concerning his mercy and his love. (*The Joy of the Saints*, 204)

REFLECTING AND RECORDING

Call to mind a person you believe breathes "the fragrance exhaled by the life of Jesus." Name that person here: _____

Write six to eight sentences describing this person. How can you tell he or she breathes "the fragrance . . . of Jesus"? How does this person's life reflect Christ?

Thérèse says that when she opens the Gospels, she breathes "the fragrance exhaled by the life of Jesus." Spend some time examining the importance of scripture to you. What kind of influence and power do the Gospels have in your life?

DURING THE DAY

Call or write a note to the person you named on the previous page, and explain that you believe he/she breathes "the fragrance exhaled by the life of Jesus." Clarify what you mean.

Reread the Holy Spirit's word to Margery Kempe (see page 243), on which you have focused for the past two days. Claim its truth and promise, and note how it affects your life.

Group Meeting for Week 1

Leader: You will need a chalkboard or a large piece of paper for this session and a Polaroid camera, if one is available. If a Polaroid camera is not available, bring a regular one.

Introduction

Group sessions are most meaningful when all participants share their experiences. This guide is designed simply to facilitate personal sharing. Therefore, you need not be rigid in following these suggestions. The leader especially needs to be sensitive to what is happening in participants' lives and focus the group's sharing of those experiences in light of that knowledge. Ideas are important; we need to wrestle with new ideas as well as with ideas with which we disagree. It is important, however, that the group meeting not become a debate. Emphasize individuals—their experiences, feelings, and meaning. Content is important, but applying content to our individual lives and to our relationship with God and others is more important.

As the group comes to the point where all can share honestly and openly what is happening in their lives, group meetings will be more meaningful. This does not mean that group members share only the good or positive; they can also share their struggles, difficulties, and negatives.

This process of group sharing is not easy; it is deceptive to pretend it is. Growth requires effort. Francis de Sales expressed this truth clearly:

> Observe that perfection is not acquired by sitting with our arms folded, but it is necessary to work in earnest, in order to conquer ourselves and to bring ourselves to live, not according to our inclinations and passions, but according to reason, our Rule, and obedience. The thing is hard, it cannot be denied, but necessary. With practice, however, it becomes easy and pleasing. (*A Year with the Saints*, 10)

I repeat my above assertion: Growth requires effort. Don't be afraid to share your questions, reservations, and "dry periods," as well as meaningful times.

Sharing Together

1. Begin your time together by allowing time for each individual to share his or her most meaningful day with the workbook this week. The leader should begin this sharing. Tell why that particular day was so meaningful.

2. Now share your most difficult day with the material, describing what you experienced and why it was so difficult.

3. Turn to the Reflecting and Recording section of Day 1. Read Francis de Sales's word and invite two people to read their rewording of de Sales's instruction.

4. Invite two or three persons to share their experience of praying "Lord, give me the grace to be wholly yours."

5. Spend eight to ten minutes discussing the two reasons de Caussade said (in Day 2) his friend remained "always at the entrance of the interior life without the power of entering": (a) inordinate desires and overeagerness; and (b) her own industry and efforts. How have these characteristics hindered you?

6. Invite a couple of persons to share their reflections on de Caussade's claim in Day 3: "Total renunciation without reserve or limit has no thoughts of self-interest—it thinks but of God, of his good pleasure, of his wishes, of his glory."

7. Spend five to eight minutes discussing Luther's understanding of God's grace (Day 4):

   In his grace and love towards us he gives his very self.

   In receiving his gifts we touch but his hand; but in his gracious regard we receive his heart, his spirit, his mind, his will.

8. Continue your discussion for five to six minutes, reflecting on Francis de Sales's insistence that "Nothing can humble us before the compassion of God as the abundance of his mercies" and "Nothing so humbles us before [God's] justice as the abundance of our misdeeds."

9. Invite group members to share their three favorite names for God, other than Father (Day 6, Reflecting and Recording). List these on the chalkboard or newsprint.

10. Now focus on Jesus. If Jesus is a picture of God "from the bottom upwards," make a list of the characteristics of God that Jesus makes known.

11. Spend a few minutes talking about how the characteristics of God revealed by Jesus harmonize with your favorite names for God.

12. Invite a couple of people to describe the person they named on Day 7 as one who breathes "the fragrance exhaled by the life of Jesus."

13. Spend the remaining time talking about how this workbook venture and your relationship with the group will help you in your Christian walk.

PRAYING TOGETHER

Each week's suggestions call for the group to pray together. Corporate prayer is one of the great blessings of Christian community. It empowers Christians, and including this dimension in a shared pilgrimage is important.

Group members need to feel comfortable during corporate prayer. No one should feel pressured to pray aloud. Silent corporate prayer may be as vital and meaningful as spoken corporate prayer. God does not need to hear our words spoken aloud to hear our prayers. Times of silence, where thinking is centered and attention is focused, may provide our deepest periods of prayer.

Verbalizing thoughts and feelings to God in the presence of fellow pilgrims can also be a powerful experience for a community on a common journey. Verbal prayers may be offered spontaneously as persons choose to pray aloud. Avoid suggesting, "Let's go around the circle now, and each one pray."

Suggestions are given each week for this "praying together" time. The leader for the week should regard these only as suggestions. What is happening in the meeting—the mood, the needs expressed, the timing—determines the direction of the group's prayer time together. Here are some possibilities for this closing period.

- Invite the group to spend a few minutes in silence, deliberately thinking about each person in the group and what that person has shared. Offer a silent sentence prayer of petition or thanksgiving for that person.

- Invite any two or three persons to offer a brief, spontaneous prayer, thanking God for the group and the opportunity to share with others in this study/learning/prayer experience.

- If someone has a Polaroid camera, take a picture of each person in the group. (If you do not have a Polaroid camera, take pictures with whatever camera is available, get pictures developed this week, and share this exercise at your next gathering.)

- Turn pictures facedown on the table and ask each group member to choose a picture. (If someone picks up a picture of himself/herself, have him/her return the photo to the table and select another one.) Ask group members to pray during the coming week for the person in their picture. Encourage each individual to talk to the person whose picture he or she selected and ask about concerns or events that could be incorporated in prayer.

- Another option is for everyone to write the names of group members in the front of his or her workbook. Everyone prays for group members each week. Saint Vincent de Paul, who founded the Congregation of Priests of the Mission (an institute of priests dedicated to evangelizing rural people) in France in 1633, became known as The Apostle of Charity. The Sisters of Charity were an outgrowth of de Paul's work. In the midst of the most distracting factors connected with his works of charity, Vincent de Paul kept alive his life with God, thus teaching us a lot about prayer. By praying for one another, the group will be following his teaching:

  > When we have to speak to others on spiritual matters, we ought first to speak of them to God in prayer, and empty ourselves of our own spirit, that we may be filled with the Holy Spirit, which alone illuminates the mind and inflames the will. (*A Year with the Saints*, 256)

WEEK 2

THEY PRACTICED DISCIPLINE, WITH PRAYER AT ITS HEART

DAY

1

To Be a Saint

The story is told that Sister Marie Bonaventura was living a relaxed life as a nun in Rome. After much encouragement, she was finally persuaded to attend a conference on the Exercises, the disciplines of the spiritual life. The first meditation was on the purpose of humanity. The meditation inspired such fervor in Sister Marie's heart that the priest giving the meditation had scarcely finished when she called him to her, and said, "Father, I mean to be a Saint, and quickly." She then went to her room at the convent, wrote the same words on a scrap of paper, and fastened it to her crucifix, where the note would be a constant reminder.

There is no quick way to be a saint.

All the saints knew that there is no way "to be a Saint, and quickly." Francis de Sales gave direction for our beginning journey.

> We must begin with a strong and constant resolution to give ourselves wholly to God, professing to Him, in a tender, loving manner, from the bottom of our hearts, that we intend to be His without any reserve, and then we must often go back and renew this same resolution. (*A Year with the Saints*, 2)

Tiger Woods is one of the most inspiring models of discipline in the sports world. At the time of this writing, he is unquestionably the best golfer in the world. He won the Masters Tournament at age twenty-one—the youngest person ever to win, and he won by a record twelve strokes. In his article "How the Best Golfer in the World Got Even Better," Don Goodgame wrote:

> For a glimpse into the greatness of Tiger Woods, look past his runaway victory in the British Open at St. Andrews last month [July 2000]. Forget his triumph—also by a record margin—in the U.S. Open at Pebble Beach in June. And set aside his prospects for stomping the field in another major tournament, next week's PGA Championship at Valhalla. Consider, instead, what Woods did right after he dominated the 1997 Masters. He studied videotapes of his performance: blasting 300-yd. drives, hitting crisp iron shots right at the pins, draining putts from everywhere. And he thought, as he later told friends, My swing really [stinks].
>
> Now let's put that in perspective. Woods had joined the pro tour only seven months earlier, at age 20, and captivated the game and its fans as no rookie ever had. He had won four of the 15 PGA Tour tournaments he entered, earning $1.8 million in prize money and some $60 million in endorsement contracts from the likes of Nike and Titleist. At the Masters, against the

best golfers in the world, he had virtually lapped the field, winning by a record 12 strokes. He was being hailed as the next Jack Nicklaus, who is considered the greatest golfer of all time.

And now, incredibly, Woods was going to risk it all by overhauling the swing that had brought him to this summit. He told his coach he wanted to make serious changes in the way he struck the ball. . . . What was Woods thinking?

"I knew I wasn't in the greatest positions in my swing at the Masters," Woods said during an exclusive interview last week. "But my timing was great, so I got away with it. And I made almost every putt. You can have a wonderful week like that even when your swing isn't sound. But can you still contend in tournaments with that swing when your timing isn't as good? Will it hold up over a long period of time? The answer to those questions, with the swing I had, was no. And I wanted to change that."

In other words, Woods, already considered the best by many of his peers, was gambling that he could get dramatically better—and was willing to do whatever he thought might help him someday surpass his idol Nicklaus as the greatest ever. (*Time*, August 14, 2000, 57–58. © 2000 Time Inc. Reprinted by permission.)

Now, that's discipline. It can serve as a challenge to serious Christians. Anyone who has read the Gospels knows that Jesus calls us to a narrow way.

Then Jesus told his disciples, "If any want to become my followers, let them deny themselves and take up their cross and follow me. For those who want to save their life will lose it, and those who lose their life for my sake will find it. For what will it profit them if they gain the whole world but forfeit their life? Or what will they give in return for their life?" (Matthew 16:24-26)

Paul also spoke of the necessity of self-sacrifice:

I appeal to you therefore, brothers and sisters, by the mercies of God, to present your bodies as a living sacrifice, holy and acceptable to God, which is your spiritual worship. (Romans 12:1)

I don't know of a Christian in all the ages to whom we turn for teaching and inspiration who did not consistently give himself or herself to discipline and devotion. It should be obvious that we need to place the disciplines for the spiritual life at the heart of the gospel. The purpose of discipline is to enhance our relationship with Christ, to cultivate a vivid companionship with him. Through spiritual discipline we learn to be like Christ and to live as he lived.

In his book *The Road Less Traveled*, psychiatrist M. Scott Peck observes:

There are many people I know who possess a vision of [personal] evolution yet seem to lack the will for it. They want, and believe it is possible, to skip over the discipline, to find an easy shortcut to sainthood. Often they attempt to attain it by simply imitating the superficialities of saints, retiring to the desert or taking up carpentry. Some even believe that by such imitation they have really become saints and prophets, and are unable to acknowledge that they are still children and face the painful fact that they must start at the beginning and go through the middle. (*The Road Less Traveled*, 77)

Sister Marie Bonaventura's commitment may have been genuine: "Father, I mean to be a Saint"—but her time line—"and quickly"—is laughable. We must, as Peck says, "start at the beginning and go through the middle." The beginning is, as de Sales said, "a strong and constant resolution to give ourselves wholly to God," and the middle often consists of going back to the beginning to renew this same resolution.

REFLECTING AND RECORDING

Test yourself. How strong is your resolution to give yourself to God?

How intensely do you feel about giving yourself to God without any reserve?

Write a prayer of commitment, expressing your desire to give yourself wholly to God, and of confession—acknowledging your reservations—asking God for the strength to overcome those.

Here are some disciplines that were common to the saints:

Scripture reading	Confession
Prayer	Submission and service
Devotional reading	Generosity
Solitude	Fasting

Put a *check mark* by the disciplines you *practice with some degree of regularity*. Put an X beside the disciplines you *know about but practice little*, and place a *star* (★) beside the disciplines you are *unfamiliar with*. What does this self-assessment say about your need for spiritual discipline? Reflect on this for a few minutes.

DURING THE DAY

As you move through the day, notice the "discipline quotient" of people around you. Observe how much discipline a particular job requires, or think about how disciplined certain individuals had to be to reach their positions in their work or avocation. Talk to one or two persons about the importance of discipline in their lives and yours.

Reread Margery Kempe's word from the Holy Spirit (see Week 1, Day 5). Claim its truth, and think about how it affects your life.

DAY
2
The Meaning of Devotion

Therefore prepare your minds for action; discipline yourselves; set all your hope on the grace that Jesus Christ will bring you when he is revealed. Like obedient children, do not be conformed to the desires that you formerly had in ignorance. Instead, as he who called you is holy, be holy yourselves in all your conduct; for it is written, "You shall be holy, for I am holy."

If you invoke as Father the one who judges all people impartially according to their deeds, live in reverent fear during the time of your exile. You know that you were ransomed from the futile ways inherited from your ancestors, not with perishable things like silver or gold, but with the precious blood of Christ, like that of a lamb without defect or blemish. He was destined before the foundation of the world, but was revealed at the end of the ages for your sake. Through him you have come to trust in God, who raised him from the dead and gave him glory, so that your faith and hope are set on God.

Now that you have purified your souls by your obedience to the truth so that you have genuine mutual love, love one another deeply from the heart. You have been born anew, not of perishable but of imperishable seed, through the living and enduring word of God. . . . (1 Peter 1:13-23)

Rid yourselves, therefore, of all malice, and all guile, insincerity, envy, and all slander. Like newborn infants, long for the pure, spiritual milk, so that by it you may grow into salvation—if indeed you have tasted that the Lord is good.

Come to him, a living stone, though rejected by mortals yet chosen and precious in God's sight, and like living stones, let yourselves be built into a spiritual house, to be a holy priesthood, to offer spiritual sacrifices acceptable to God through Jesus Christ. (1 Peter 2:1-5)

The call to Christians is clear: "As he who called you is holy, be holy yourselves in all your conduct" (1 Peter 1:15). The purpose for which we are saved and adopted into God's family is "to be a holy priesthood, to offer spiritual sacrifices acceptable to God" (1 Peter 2:5). But Peter knew that our call can become distorted, and we might forget our redemption "from the futile ways" of our ancestors and how that redemption was purchased: "not with perishable things like silver or gold, . . . but with the precious blood of Christ, like that of a lamb without defect or blemish" (1 Peter 1:18-19).

We must hold together in our minds these two things: (1) our redemption through the mercy and grace of God in Jesus Christ, and (2) God's call to holiness. If we disconnect the two, we thwart our Christian growth. Author Dallas Willard reminds us,

> Faith today is treated as something that only *should* make us different, not that actually *does or can* make us different. In reality we *vainly* struggle against the evils of this world, waiting to die

and go to heaven. Somehow we've gotten the idea that the essence of faith is entirely a mental and inward thing. (*The Spirit of the Disciplines*, x)

One reason this has happened is the mistaken association of discipline with merit.

History contains some horrible examples, especially in the monastic movement of the church, of persons distorting the meaning of the call to offer "spiritual sacrifices acceptable to God through Jesus Christ" (1 Peter 2:5). Some older Roman Catholic editions of the Bible translated the Greek word *metanoia* with the English rendering "penance." In a modern Confraternity edition of the New Testament, the strong and forceful word *repent* is used. Unfortunately, in different periods of church history, and sometimes even now, penance is connected with the mistaken notion that a person can pay for the sins of the body by causing the body to suffer. This is not a biblical teaching. An important lesson we learn from scripture and from the saints is that giving our bodies is useless if we have not first given ourselves.

An important lesson we learn from scripture and from the saints is that giving our bodies is useless if we have not first given ourselves.

Francis de Sales gives us the proper perspective on devotion.

> You wish to live a life of devotion, . . . because you are a Christian and know that it is a virtue most pleasing to God's Majesty. Since little faults committed in the beginning of a project grow infinitely greater in its course and finally are almost irreparable, above all else you must know what the virtue of devotion is. . . .
>
> A man given to fasting thinks himself very devout if he fasts, although his heart may be filled with hatred. Much concerned with sobriety, he doesn't dare to wet his tongue with wine or even water but won't hesitate to drink deep of his neighbor's blood by detraction and calumny. Another man thinks himself devout because he daily recites a vast number of prayers, but after saying them he utters the most disagreeable, arrogant, and harmful words at home and among the neighbors. Another gladly takes a coin out of his purse and gives it to the poor, but he cannot extract kindness from his heart and forgive his enemies. . . . All these men are usually considered to be devout, but they are by no means such. . . .
>
> Genuine, living devotion . . . presupposes love of God, and hence it is simply true love of God. . . . Inasmuch as divine love adorns the soul, it is called grace, . . . Inasmuch as it strengthens us to do good, it is called charity [love]. When it has reached a degree of perfection at which it not only makes us do good but also do this carefully, frequently, and promptly, it is called devotion. (*Introduction to the Devout Life*, 39–40)

Only when we surrender ourselves to God do devotion and discipline have meaning. Our acts of "self-sacrifice" mean nothing if they are efforts to prove our merit or earn salvation. This is what de Sales means when he says, "Genuine, living devotion . . . presupposes love of God." Paul also reminds us of this truth in 1 Corinthians 13:3: "If I give away all my possessions, and if I hand over my body so that I may boast, but do not have love, I gain nothing."

Yet, we must be careful that we are not satisfied simply with "being saved." The aim of Christianity is not just to get to heaven; it is to be new persons here and now. According to Paul, our ultimate purpose is to "come to the unity of the faith and of the knowledge of the Son of God, to maturity, to the measure of the full stature of Christ" (Eph. 4:13). Paul further contends that as Christians we are dead to sin (Rom. 6:11). This does not mean that we lack the natural desires that sin has twisted into destructive actions and attitudes. In Christ, we are new persons in that we have a new orientation and a new motivation for how we express our natural desires. Through disciplines such as prayer, scripture reading, confession, regular corporate worship, submission, and service, we keep ourselves beyond the grip of sin. In that way we are "dead to sin" because we discipline our wills to choose to think and act as new persons in Christ.

Paul provides a dynamic for training and exercising our wills.

> So you also must consider yourselves dead to sin and alive to God in Christ Jesus.
>
> Therefore, do not let sin exercise dominion in your mortal bodies, to make you obey their passions. No longer present your members to sin as instruments of wickedness, but present yourselves to God as those who have been brought from death to life, and present your members to God as instruments of righteousness. For sin will have no dominion over you, since you are not under law but under grace. (Romans 6:11-14)

Some translations use the word *reckon* rather than *consider* in verse 11: "*Reckon* yourselves to be dead to sin." I like this rendering better because it stops you in your mental tracks. "Reckon"—in other words, with all your conscious being, purposefully, concretely—regard yourself as "dead to sin."

Again, this requires discipline. We form habits and thought patterns and make decisions based on our interaction with Christ through devotional practices. Oswald Chambers talked about forming habits on the basis of God's grace:

> The question of forming habits on the basis of the grace of God is a very vital one. To ignore it is to fall into the snare of the Pharisee—the grace of God is praised, Jesus Christ is praised, the Redemption is praised, but the practical everyday life evades working it out. If we refuse to practise, it is not God's grace that fails when a crisis comes, but our own nature. When the crisis comes, we ask God to help us, but He cannot if we have not made our nature an ally. The practising is ours, not God's. God regenerates us and puts us in contact with all His divine resources, but He cannot make us walk according to His will. (*The Psychology of Redemption*, 26–27)

REFLECTING AND RECORDING

Reread the second paragraph of de Sales's quotation from the previous page.

De Sales identifies bitterness, calumny (defamation of character), angry and hurtful language, and lack of forgiveness as actions and attitudes that betray our devotion, that demonstrate we are not genuinely devout. Take a few minutes for self-examination. Which of your actions and attitudes might indicate that your acts of devotion and piety do not please God?

We have feelings and thoughts deep within, which only God and we know about, that do not please God and that, to some degree, nullify our expressions of devotion. We also have attitudes and actions that hinder our witness of genuine devotion.

As a result of your self-examination exercise, list two or three items in each category that betray your devotion and hinder your witness of genuine devoutness. Your workbook is personal and private, so be honest. Being explicit enough to write something down is often necessary for genuine confession and earnestly dealing with a problem.

Known to me and God	**May be observed by others**
_____	_____
_____	_____
_____	_____
_____	_____
_____	_____

Spend what time you have left reflecting on Chambers's word: "God regenerates us and puts us in contact with all His divine resources, but He cannot make us walk according to His will."

DURING THE DAY

The following word of wisdom from de Sales is printed again on page 243. Cut it out and put it in a place where you can read it two or three times during the day. Claim the meaning of grace and devotion as wisdom to guide you.

> Divine love, enlightening our soul and making us pleasing to God, is called grace. Giving us power to do good, it is called charity. When it reaches the point of perfection where it makes us earnestly, frequently and readily do good, it is called devotion. (*The Joy of the Saints,* 34)

DAY
3

Alert and Self-Controlled

But you, beloved, are not in darkness, for that day to surprise you like a thief; for you are all children of light and children of the day; we are not of the night or of darkness. So then let us not fall asleep as others do, but let us keep awake and be sober; for those who sleep sleep at night, and those who are drunk get drunk at night. But since we belong to the day, let us be sober, and put on the breastplate of faith and love, and for a helmet the hope of salvation. For God has destined us not for wrath but for obtaining salvation through our Lord Jesus Christ, who died for us, so that whether we are awake or asleep we may live with him. Therefore encourage one another and build up each other, as indeed you are doing. (1 Thessalonians 5:4-11)

Since Christians belong to Christ, we are children of light, not of darkness. First Thessalonians 5:9 (NIV) says, "God did not appoint us to suffer wrath but to receive salvation through our Lord Jesus Christ." Because of the gift that is ours—salvation, or belonging to Christ—Paul urges us in verse 6, "Let us keep awake and be sober." The New International Version translates this verse as, "Let us be alert and self-controlled."

In his Letter to the Thessalonians, Paul made clear what I contended yesterday: We must hold together our redemption through the mercy and grace of Jesus Christ and God's call to holiness. Thus Paul calls us to "be alert and self-controlled."

In his book *The Spirit of the Disciplines*, Dallas Willard reminds us:

> The general human failing is to want what is right and important, but at the same time not to commit to the kind of life that will produce the action we know to be right and the condition we want to enjoy. This is the feature of human character that explains why the road to hell is paved with good intentions. We intend what is right, but we avoid the life that would make it reality. (*The Spirit of the Disciplines*, 6)

We need to realize and accept the necessity of discipline. To be sure, the power of Christ enters our lives in many different ways:

- when we sense God's forgiveness and love
- when we discover a life-changing truth
- through Holy Spirit-infused worship that makes God's presence real
- through preaching that confronts us with judgment, yet offers grace

- through reconciliation with another
- through an unexplainable experience of the communion of saints

All of these ways are valid and make a difference in our lives. Yet it is statistically verifiable that "neither individually nor collectively do any of these ways reliably produce large numbers of people who really are like Christ and his closest followers throughout history" (Willard, *The Spirit of the Disciplines*, x).

The purpose of discipline is to enable us to be like Christ and to live as Christ wants us to. Through discipline we cultivate our awareness of the indwelling Christ and allow the Holy Spirit to shape us. Realizing this, it becomes clear that Oswald Chambers was right when he said, "The Sermon on the Mount is not a set of principles to be obeyed apart from identification with Jesus Christ" (*The Psychology of Redemption*, 34).

So when Jesus called us to turn the other cheek and go the second mile, to bless those who persecute us and give to those who ask, he was not laying down the law but instead was describing Christlikeness and what others could expect of "children of light." As Christians, our natural element is Christ and his kingdom. Paul urged the Ephesians to "put away your former way of life, your old self, corrupt and deluded by its lusts, and to be renewed in the spirit of your minds, and to clothe yourselves with the new self, created according to the likeness of God in true righteousness and holiness" (Eph. 4:22-24).

Dallas Willard appropriately reminds us,

> Our mistake is to think that following Jesus consists in loving our enemies, going the "second mile," turning the other cheek, suffering patiently and hopefully—while living the rest of our lives just as everyone around us does. (*The Spirit of the Disciplines*, 5)

The heart of our life as Christians is contained in God's word to Abraham in Genesis 17:1: "Walk before me, and be blameless." In order to walk before God, or to walk in God's presence, we must give ourselves completely to Him, and that requires discipline. Speaking to this issue, François Fénelon wrote:

> When outward distractions and a wayward imagination hinder you from having a peaceful inner life, then you must, by an act of will, bring yourself before God. Not that you can force yourself into God's presence, but even the desire to come into God's presence is, in itself, a powerful aid to your spirit. Cultivate a pure and upright intention toward God.
>
> From time to time you must stir up your deepest desires to be fully devoted to God. There need to be seasons when you think on Him alone, with a wholly undistracted love. Consecrate your senses to Him completely at these times. Don't get caught up with things that you know distract you both outwardly and inwardly from God. Once you are distracted from God it is hard to return to Him.
>
> Whenever you notice that you want anything too much, then stop yourself immediately. God does not dwell in the midst of chaos and disorder. Don't get caught up with what is said and done around you. You will be deeply disturbed if you do. Find out what God expects from you in any given situation and stick strictly to doing that. This will help you keep your inner

Make a habit of bringing your attention to God on a regular basis. You will then be able to quiet all your inner commotion as soon as it starts to be churned up.

—François Fénelon

spirit as free and peaceful as possible. Get rid of everything that hinders you from turning easily to God.

An excellent way to maintain a quiet spirit is to let go of every action just as soon as you complete it. Don't keep thinking about what you have or haven't done! And don't blame yourself for forgetting something, or for doing something you regret. You will be much happier if you keep your mind only on the tasks at hand. Think of something only when it is time to think of it. God will tell you when the time comes to deal with something. You will exhaust your mind by trying to figure out God's will before the right time comes.

Make a habit of bringing your attention back to God on a regular basis. You will then be able to quiet all your inner commotion as soon as it starts to be churned up. Cut yourself off from every pleasure that does not come from God. Seek God within, and you will undoubtedly find Him with peace and joy. Be more occupied with God than anything else. Do everything with the awareness that you are acting before God and for His sake. At the sight of God's majesty, calmness and well-being should fill your spirit. A word from the Lord stilled the raging sea and a glance from Him to you, and from you to Him, will do the same for you. (*The Seeking Heart*, 121–23)

Fénelon's instructions are clear:

- When outward distractions and a wayward imagination hinder you, bring yourself back to God by an act of your will.

- On a regular basis, stir up your deepest desires to be fully devoted to God.

- When you want anything too much, stop yourself—turn away from your desires.

- Seek to discover what God expects of you in every situation, and concentrate on that.

- Get rid of everything that hinders you from easily turning to God.

- After you complete an action, let go of it; don't fret about what you have or haven't done.

- Think only of the tasks at hand. Don't exhaust your mind by trying to figure out God's will before the right time comes.

- Make a habit of bringing your attention back to God on a regular basis.

REFLECTING AND RECORDING

Look prayerfully at the above list of instructions. Put check marks by the four statements most closely related to your desire to be more spiritually disciplined.

Now put each of the four statements you checked in your own words as a commitment, such as, "When my mind begins to wander and things around me distract me from my devotional reading or prayer, I will deliberately focus my mind and heart on God and what God is saying to me."

1.

2.

3.

4.

DURING THE DAY

Continue pondering de Sales's words on devotion on page 39. Ask God to guide you as you seek to demonstrate genuine devotion in your life.

DAY
4

Ask, Seek, Knock:
A New Perspective

And he said to them, "Suppose one of you has a friend, and you go to him at midnight and say to him, 'Friend, lend me three loaves of bread; for a friend of mine has arrived, and I have nothing to set before him.' And he answers from within, 'Do not bother me; the door has already been locked, and my children are with me in bed; I cannot get up and give you anything.' I tell you, even though he will not get up and give him anything because he is his friend, at least because of his persistence he will get up and give him whatever he needs."

So I say to you, Ask, and it will be given you; search, and you will find; knock, and the door will be opened for you. For everyone who asks receives, and everyone who searches finds, and for everyone who knocks, the door will be opened. Is there anyone among you who, if your child asks for a fish, will give a snake instead of a fish? Or if the child asks for an egg, will give a scorpion? If you then, who are evil, know how to give good gifts to your children, how much more will the heavenly Father give the Holy Spirit to those who ask him!" (Luke 11:5-13)

Somewhere along the way, I heard a story of a group of tourists traveling in Switzerland. In one of the most picturesque villages, they stopped to visit with an old man sitting beside the fence. In a rather patronizing way, one tourist asked, "Were any great men born in this village?" The old man replied, "Nope, only babies."

No one is physically born full grown. Likewise, no one is "born again"—*spiritually born*—full grown.

All the saints knew that frequent renewal of good resolutions and practice of discipline were essential elements of their growth in Christ. No matter how far along they were in their quest for perfection, they never relaxed their vigilance, and they knew discipline and self-control were essential. None of us can afford to be careless in spiritual things.

John Wesley affirmed this truth and gave us a new perspective of Jesus' call to ask, seek, and knock:

O how meek and gentle, how lowly in heart, how full of love both to God and man, might ye have been at this day, if you had only asked; if you had continued instant in prayer! Therefore, now, at least, "ask, and it shall be given unto you." Ask, that ye may thoroughly experience, and perfectly practise, the whole of that religion which our Lord has here so beautifully described. It shall then be given you, to be holy as he is holy, both in heart and in all manner of conversation.

Seek, in the way he hath ordained, in searching the Scriptures, in hearing his word, in meditating thereon, in fasting, in partaking of the Supper of the Lord, and surely ye shall find: Ye shall find that pearl of great price, that faith which overcometh the world, that peace which the world cannot give, that love which is the earnest of your inheritance. Knock; continue in prayer, and in every other way of the Lord: Be not weary or faint in your mind: Press on to the mark: Take no denial: Let him not go until he bless you, "And the door of mercy, of holiness, of heaven, shall be opened unto you." (*The Works of John Wesley*, vol. 5, 401)

> *Knock; continue in prayer, and in every other way of the Lord . . . And the door of mercy, of holiness, of heaven shall be opened to you.*
>
> —*John Wesley*

Look carefully at Wesley's instruction. It is only as we practice our faith that we will be holy as God is holy—"both in heart and in all manner of conversation." Holiness is not something we earn; it is a gift. Oswald Chambers put it this way: "We cannot grow into holiness, but we must grow in it" (*The Psychology of Redemption*, 51).

On Day 2 of Week 1, we mentioned the fact that the saints often used Jesus' parable of the pearl of great price to teach us about how to passionately seek God. The merchant in the parable was willing to search tirelessly, and when he had found the treasured pearl, he was willing to sell everything to possess it. Wesley used this image in describing how to find the pearl of great price: "peace which the world cannot give," and "love which is the earnest of your inheritance." We are to search the scriptures and meditate on God's Word; we are to fast and to partake of the Lord's Supper. These were not the only disciplines Wesley prescribed. He also called upon Christians to avail themselves of all the means of grace available, especially prayer, Christian conferencing, and what he called *prudential* means of grace: doing no harm and deliberately doing good.

In the above admonition, Wesley called us to continue in prayer—"not weary or faint in your mind," taking no denial, "let him not go until he bless you." And what is the result? The door of mercy, *of holiness*, of heaven itself will be opened to us.

Wesley was in the tradition of all the saints. While we do not grow into holiness, we grow in it. Following is one of the ways Francis de Sales talked about holiness:

> The great work of our perfection is born, grows, and maintains its life by means of two small but precious exercises—aspirations and spiritual retirement. An aspiration is a certain springing of the soul towards God, and the more simple it is, the more valuable. It consists in simply beholding what He is, and what He has done and is doing for us; and it should excite the heart, as a consequence, to acts of humility, love, resignation or abandonment, according to circumstances. Now, these two exercises have an incredible power to keep us in our duty, to support us in temptation, to lift us up promptly after falls and to unite us closely to God. Besides, they can be made at any time or place, and with all possible ease; therefore, they ought to be as familiar to us as the inspiration and expiration of air from our lungs. (*A Year with the Saints*, 272)

REFLECTING AND RECORDING

Beside the quotation above, translate de Sales's teaching into your own words.

Pay attention to the twin exercises of aspirations and spiritual retirement. Retirement does not mean rest or ceasing, but rather whatever spiritual acts issue from our concentration on God. The results of the exercises of aspiration and spiritual retirement are acts of humility, love, resignation, or abandonment. Concentrate for a few minutes on resignation, or abandonment. Spiritually, this means submission, which requires an act of the will. Submission is not just a matter of being stoically resigned to some situation or relationship that is out of your control. It is determining positively that you will yield to whatever God seeks to teach you through the experience.

Is there a situation or state of relationship to which you have been stoically resigned, about which you have thought you could do nothing? In a few sentences, describe it here:

Now offer this situation or relationship to God in prayer, yielding yourself in submission to be taught by it.

Concentrate now, for a few minutes, on abandonment. For the saints, abandonment meant surrender of self, but it also means to give up or to forsake something. What in your life do you need to give up or forsake in order to grow in holiness? Write your thoughts here.

DURING THE DAY

Continue meditating on de Sales's words as you have done for the past two days. Claim the meaning of grace and devotion in your own life.

DAY
5

Discipline and Devotion According to Our Calling

And whenever you fast, do not look dismal, like the hypocrites, for they disfigure their faces so as to show others that they are fasting. Truly I tell you, they have received their reward. But when you fast, put oil on your head and wash your face, so that your fasting may be seen not by others but by your Father who is in secret; and your Father who sees in secret will reward you.

Do not store up for yourselves treasures on earth, where moth and rust consume and where thieves break in and steal; but store up for yourselves treasures in heaven, where neither moth nor rust consumes and where thieves do not break in and steal. For where your treasure is, there your heart will be also.

The eye is the lamp of the body. So, if your eye is healthy, your whole body will be full of light; but if your eye is unhealthy, your whole body will be full of darkness. If then the light in you is darkness, how great is the darkness! (Matthew 6:16-23)

Though all the saints practiced discipline, with prayer at its heart, each of them chose practices with special meaning to them. They would never give in to the notion that "one size fits all." Saint Francis de Sales gave this warning:

To be able to advance much in perfection, it is necessary to apply ourselves to one thing by itself—to a single book of devotion, to a single spiritual exercise, to a single aspiration, to a single virtue, and so on. Not, indeed, that all other things ought to be quite rejected and passed by, but in such a way that this to which one is applying himself may usually be aimed at more in particular and as the special object of the most frequent effort, so that if one chance to turn to others, these may be like accessories. To do otherwise, by passing from one exercise to another, is to imitate those who spoil their appetite at a banquet by tasting a little of every delicacy. It is perpetually seeking, and never attaining, the science of the Saints, and so it results in losing that tranquillity of spirit in God, which is the "one thing needful" that Mary chose. (*A Year with the Saints*, 27)

The condition of our lives, the issues we deal with, our work, our relationships, and even our personalities play a role in the disciplines we practice. Daily prayer has been part of my devotional life for a long time. During the past five years, my prayers have taken a particular shape of intercession.

I came to the presidency of Asbury Theological Seminary "kicking and screaming." I did not want to come. I was happily involved in a meaningful pastorate, serving as one of the ministers of Christ United Methodist Church in Memphis, Tennessee. My work as a preacher and pastor was rewarding. I was excited about the church and its ministry, and I saw myself as remaining involved in that ministry for the rest of my active life. Through a series of circumstances, involvement, and relationships, I was confronted with the call to Asbury. Being a seminary president was completely foreign to any thoughts I had had about vocation. But, over a period of nearly a year, it became increasingly clear that God was calling me to that work. I became the president of Asbury, convinced that this was God's call. Even so, I did not go happily.

Before the beginning of each school year in September, I go away for a retreat—to center my life, to listen, and to pray for the students, faculty, staff, and the work of the coming year. Preceding my third year, on that retreat I received a special call from God. I had been generally consistent in praying for members of the seminary community, and I always prayed for particular needs that presented themselves. But God called me to be more specific in my prayers—especially for students. He gave me the plan. I divided our student body, staff, and faculty into thirty-three groups—the number of weeks during the school year. I would pray for one of those groups each week. By doing so, I would have the opportunity to pray for each person in our community for a week during a school year. Two weeks prior to the week that I will be praying for them, I write each individual a note, letting him/her know that I will be praying for him/her during a particular week and inviting each one to share joys and thanksgivings with me, as well as prayer concerns.

We need to be focused in our discipline and devotion, always involving ourselves in exercises that will address areas of our life that especially need the Holy Spirit's shaping.

This pattern of prayer has changed my life—not only my prayer life but also my relationship to the seminary community, how I do my work, the way I seek to be a pastoral presence in the community. It has brought to me the kind of joy and meaning I felt when serving as a pastor of a local congregation.

We need to be focused in our discipline and devotion—always involving ourselves in exercises that will address areas of our life that especially need the Holy Spirit's shaping. While there may be value in the practice of general penance in the Roman Catholic tradition, such as repeating the Lord's Prayer a certain number of times, the most meaningful disciplines are those that address our limitations, distortions, weaknesses, misdirections, and harmful habits—those things that prevent our growth in holiness. De Sales wrote challenging words on this issue:

> Our profit does not depend so much upon mortifying ourselves, as upon knowing how to mortify ourselves; that is, upon knowing how to choose the best mortifications, which are those most repugnant to our natural inclinations. Some are inclined to disciplines and fasts, and though they be difficult things, they embrace them with fervor, and practice them gladly and easily, on account of this leaning which they have toward them. But then they will be so sensitive in regard to reputation and honor, that the least ridicule, disapproval, or slight is sufficient to throw them into a state of impatience and perturbation and to give rise to such complaints as show an equal want of peace and reason. These are the mortifications which they ought to embrace with the greatest readiness, if they wish to make progress. (*A Year with the Saints*, 82)

Don't be put off by the word *mortification*. Certainly, the practice of mortification has been distorted, even perverted, as a spiritual discipline, but its true meaning and correct practice is essential. To mortify means to "subdue," to bring into submission for the sake of wholeness and holiness. De Sales warned against turning the means into an end. Discipline for discipline's sake has no spiritual value. All *means of grace* are to be just that—channels or avenues through which grace operates in our life. John Wesley underscored this truth when he talked about fasting.

> I am . . . to show, in what manner we are to fast, that it may be an acceptable service unto the Lord. And, First, let it be done unto the Lord, with our eye singly fixed on Him. Let our intention herein be this, and this alone, to glorify our Father which is in heaven. . . .
>
> Let us beware of mocking God, of turning our fast, as well as our prayers, into an abomination unto the Lord, by the mixture of any temporal view, particularly by seeking the praise of men. . . .
>
> . . . Let us beware, Secondly, of fancying we merit anything of God by our fasting. We cannot be too often warned of this; inasmuch as a desire to "establish our own righteousness," to procure salvation of debt and not of grace, is so deeply rooted in all our hearts. Fasting is only a way which God hath ordained, wherein we wait for his unmerited mercy; and wherein, without any desert of ours, he hath promised freely to give us his blessing.
>
> Not that we are to imagine the performing the bare outward act will receive any blessing from God. . . .
>
> . . . let us take care to afflict our souls as well as our bodies. Let every season, either of public or private fasting, be a season of exercising all those holy affections which are implied in a broken and contrite heart. (*The Works of John Wesley*, vol. 5, 357–59)

Having realized the value of specialized discipline—deliberately choosing practices to address specific needs of our life—we must not disregard the more expansive need for discipline and devotion. Similarly, de Sales called us "to a single book of devotion, to a single spiritual exercise, to a single aspiration, to a single virtue." He also said:

> We must, however, guard ourselves here from one fault, into which many fall. It is that of attaching ourselves too much to our own practices and spiritual exercises. This, naturally, makes us feel dislike for all methods not conformed to our own; for each one thinks that he employs the only suitable one, and considers as imperfect those who do not work in the same way. Whoever has a good spirit draws edification from everything, and condemns nothing. (*A Year with the Saints*, 27)

REFLECTING AND RECORDING

Recall and record here an experience when you deliberately chose to practice some discipline to meet a need or correct something amiss in your life.

Are you wrestling with some harmful habit, unhealthy attitude, or destructive relationship that needs to be addressed by adopting a particular spiritual discipline? Name the problem and decide how you are going to deal with it through a particular spiritual discipline.

Wesley warned against our "fancying we *merit* anything of God by our fasting." The warning applies to any work on our part. Spend a few minutes in self-examination, looking closely at the spiritual disciplines you practice, your works of *piety* or works of *mercy*. Do any of these reflect a desire to establish your own righteousness so that you gain merit in God's eyes?

During the Day

De Sales insisted that the mortification (subduing) of the senses in seeing, hearing, and speaking was worth much more than wearing chains or haircloth. As you move through this day, pay attention to what you see and hear and how you speak, seeking to bring these under the Holy Spirit's control.

Continue reading de Sales's words on which you have focused on the past three days; claim their explanation of grace and devotion as wisdom to guide you.

DAY
6

Our Minds Stayed on Christ

Prayer was the central spiritual discipline for all the saints. They adhered to Jesus' word "about their need to pray always and not to lose heart" (Luke 18:1). Jesus told a parable to support his call:

> He said, "In a certain city there was a judge who neither feared God nor had respect for people. In that city there was a widow who kept coming to him and saying, 'Grant me justice against my opponent.' For a while he refused; but later he said to himself, 'Though I have no fear of God and no respect for anyone, yet because this widow keeps bothering me, I will grant her justice, so that she may not wear me out by continually coming.'" And the Lord said, "Listen to what the unjust judge says. And will not God grant justice to his chosen ones who cry to him day and night? Will he delay long in helping them? I tell you, he will quickly grant justice to them. And yet, when the Son of Man comes, will he find faith on earth?" (Luke 18:2-8)

Jesus was not comparing his Father to the judge, not at all. He made clear the nature of our heavenly Father in relation to our praying:

> "Is there anyone among you who, if your child asks for a fish, will give a snake instead of a fish? Or if the child asks for an egg, will give a scorpion? If you then, who are evil, know how to give good gifts to your children, how much more will the heavenly Father give the Holy Spirit to those who ask him!" (Luke 11:11-13)

In the parable of the judge, Jesus taught the necessity of ongoing prayer. It is interesting that Luke introduces the parable with this word: "Then Jesus told them a parable about their need to pray always and not to lose heart" (Luke 18:1). Jesus closed the parable with this burning question: "When the Son of Man comes, will he find faith on earth?"

The saints knew that prayer and faith are connected. To pray without faith is useless. For faithful people not to pray is self-robbery. It is unlikely that we will know God, even moderately well, unless we pray.

Though most Christians do not need convincing that prayer is an essential part of the Christian life, most of us have not yet learned what the saints knew:

Without prayer our souls wither. Through prayer we are united with God, and our souls come vibrantly alive.

Without prayer our souls wither, but through prayer we are united with God, and our souls come vibrantly alive. Thérèse of Lisieux expressed it thus:

The power of prayer is indeed wonderful. It is like a queen, who, having free access always to the king, can obtain whatever she asks. To secure a hearing there is no need to recite set prayers composed for the occasion—were this the case, I should indeed deserve to be pitied!

Apart from the Office [the daily prayer of the Church] which is a daily joy, I do not have the courage to search through books for beautiful prayers. They are so numerous that it would only make my head ache. Unable either to say them all or to choose between them, I do as a child would who cannot read—I just say what I want to say to God, quite simply, and he never fails to understand.

For me, prayer is an uplifting of the heart, a glance towards heaven, a cry of gratitude and love in times of sorrow as well as joy. It is something noble, something supernatural, which expands the soul and unites it to God. (*The Joy of the Saints*, 112)

Francis de Sales shared a particular perspective on prayer and recommended the following:

Since prayer places our intellect in the brilliance of God's light and exposes our will to the warmth of his heavenly love, nothing else so effectively purifies our intellect of ignorance and our will of depraved affections. [Prayer] is a stream of holy water that flows forth and makes the plants of our good desires grow green and flourish and quenches the passions within our hearts.

. . . I especially recommend to you mental prayer, the prayer of the heart, and particularly that which centers on the life and Passion of our Lord. By often turning your eyes on him in meditation, your whole soul will be filled with him. You will learn his ways and form your actions after the pattern of his. He is "the light of the world" and therefore it is in him and by him and for him that we must be instructed and enlightened. . . . so also by keeping close to our Savior in meditation and observing his words, actions, and affections we learn by his grace to speak, act, and will like him.

. . . I assure you that we cannot go to God the Father except through this gate [prayer]. (*Introduction to the Devout Life*, 40)

A Collection of Forms of Prayer was John Wesley's first published work. This book was a collection of prayers for each day of the week, morning and evening, gathered and edited from a variety of sources. The following excerpt is not only a model prayer of submission; it also encompasses most of what we have considered about discipline:

To you, O God, Father, Son, and Holy Spirit, my Creator, Redeemer, and Sanctifier, I give up myself entirely. May I no longer serve myself, but you, all the days of my life.

I give you my understanding. May it be my only care to know you, your perfections, your works, and your will. Let all things else be as dross unto me, for the excellency of this knowledge, and let me silence all reasonings against whatsoever you teach me, who can neither deceive nor be deceived.

I give you my will. May I have no will of my own. Whatsoever you will, may I will, and that only. May I will your glory in all things, as you do, and make that my end in every thing. May I ever say with the Psalmist, *"Whom have I in heaven but you? And there is nothing on earth that I desire other than you."* May I delight to do your will, O God, and rejoice to accept it. Whatever threatens me, let me say, "It is the Lord; let him do what seems good to him." And whatever befalls me, let me give thanks, since it is your will concerning me.

I give you my affections. Dispose of them all. Be my love, my fear, my joy; and may nothing have any share in them, but with respect to you and for your sake. What you love, may I love; what you hate, may I hate; and that in such measures as you are pleased to prescribe for me.

I give you my body. May I glorify you with it, and preserve it holy, fit for you, O God, to dwell in. May I neither indulge it, nor use too much rigor toward it; but keep it, as far as in me lies, healthy, vigorous, and active, and fit to do you all manner of service that you shall call for.

I give you all my worldly goods. May I prize them and use them only for you. May I faithfully restore to you, in the poor, all you have entrusted me with, above the necessaries of life; and be content to part with them too, whenever you, my Lord, shall require them at my hands.

I give you my credit and reputation. May I never value it, but only in respect of you; nor endeavor to maintain it, but as it may do the service and advance your honor in the world.

I give you myself and my all. Let me look upon myself to be nothing, and to have nothing, apart from you. Be the sole disposer and governor of myself and all; be my portion and my all.

O my God and my all, when hereafter I shall be tempted to break this solemn engagement, when I shall be pressed to conform to the world and to the company and customs that surround me, may my answer be: "I am not my own. I am not for myself, not for the world, but for my God. I will give unto God the things that are God's. God, be merciful to me a sinner."
(*A Longing for Holiness: Selected Writings of John Wesley*, 15–17)

REFLECTING AND RECORDING

Write your own prayer, using the following outline. Add two or three sentences after each introductory statement.

Dear God,

I give you my understanding.

I give you my will.

I give you my affection.

I give you my body.

I give you all my worldly goods.

I give you my credit and reputation.

I give you myself and my all.

Which issue of surrender, of giving to God, was most difficult for you? Spend a few minutes reflecting on what this exercise may be saying to you about discipline. What specific disciplines might this exercise be calling you to practice?

DURING THE DAY

Continue the practice you began yesterday—paying attention to what you see and hear and how you speak, seeking to bring all these senses under the control of the Holy Spirit.

DAY
7

Evidence of the Cross

Once when Jesus was praying alone, with only the disciples near him, he asked them, "Who do the crowds say that I am?" They answered, "John the Baptist; but others, Elijah; and still others, that one of the ancient prophets has arisen." He said to them, "But who do you say that I am?" Peter answered, "The Messiah of God."

He sternly ordered and commanded them not to tell anyone, saying, "The Son of Man must undergo great suffering, and be rejected by the elders, chief priests, and scribes, and be killed, and on the third day be raised."

Then he said to them all, "If any want to become my followers, let them deny themselves and take up their cross daily and follow me. For those who want to save their life will lose it, and those who lose their life for my sake will save it. What does it profit them if they gain the whole world, but lose or forfeit themselves? Those who are ashamed of me and of my words, of them the Son of Man will be ashamed when he comes in his glory and the glory of the Father and of the holy angels." (Luke 9:18-26)

The General Conference is the supreme legislative body of The United Methodist Church; the conference convenes every four years. I remember what may have been the most significant moment during the two-week meeting in Denver in 1996. The conference was well into the second day when a delegate from Iowa, June Goldman, got the attention of the presiding bishop to ask, "Where is the cross?" There was no cross on the platform. Mrs. Goldman felt there ought to be a cross visible on the platform for the meeting of a Christian denomination whose major symbol is the cross. She had to ask that question three times that day and the next before someone finally placed a cross on the stage. Perhaps June Goldman was a prophet sent from God to ask the question of those United Methodists: "*Where is the cross?*"

The cross is central to the Christian faith, spirituality, and discipleship—Jesus' death on the cross and his call to deny ourselves, daily take up our cross, and follow him.

The saints teach us that discipline, of which prayer is the heart, gives evidence of the cross in our life. When they talked about renunciation and mortification, the cross was always in their minds. The crucifix, Jesus nailed to the cross, was the visual aid most frequently used in their devotion.

Protestant Christians replaced the crucifix in our churches with an empty cross to give witness to the Resurrection. Though we know that the death of Jesus without resurrection could never accomplish the salvation God provides, we can never ignore or diminish Jesus' passion, suffering, and death.

Early in the life of the church, especially during the fourth century, many Christians tried to escape the cares of city life in order to live a life of prayer and cultivate purity of heart. They went into the deserts of Egypt and Syria. Some became hermits, living alone; others formed communities. They discovered that even in the desert they faced the same problems they had sought to escape—concern about food and possessions, temptations of pride, wayward thoughts, and dysfunctional relationships. In their seeking to deal with these problems, the "wisdom of the desert" was forged.

John Cassian was one of the desert fathers. He lived for many years among the monks and hermits of the desert, seeking to absorb their wisdom. Then he summarized the wisdom for the benefit of Western European Christians attempting to live in community. Cassian sought to provide guidance for those who could not move geographically to the desert in order to escape distractions and responsibilities, yet wanted to love their neighbors, love their enemies, and pray without ceasing. Cassian became a "living bridge" between the desert mothers and fathers and the nuns and monks of medieval Christendom. He taught that we should learn first the actual reason for the renunciation of the world.

> Renunciation is nothing but the evidence of the cross and of mortification. You must know that today you are dead to this world and its deeds and desires. As the apostle says, "*the world has been crucified to me, and I to the world.*" Consider therefore the demands of the cross under the sign of which you should live in this life from now on. "*It is no longer I who live, but it is Christ who lives in me,*" who was crucified for you. We must therefore pass our time in this life in that fashion and form in which he was crucified for us on the cross so that (as David says), "*our flesh trembles for fear of the Lord.*" In this way we fulfill the command of the Lord that says, "*Whoever does not take up the cross and follow me is not worthy of me.*" But perhaps you will ask how anyone can carry a cross continually? How can anyone who is alive be crucified? Hear briefly how this is.
>
> The fear of the Lord is our cross. As one who is crucified no longer has the power of moving or turning his limbs in any direction he pleases, so we also ought to fix our wishes and desires—not according to what is pleasant and delightful to us now, but according to the law of the Lord. Those who are fastened to the wood of the cross no longer consider things present, nor think about their likes, nor are perplexed by anxiety and care for the next day, nor disturbed by any desire of possession, nor inflamed by any pride or strife or rivalry. They do not grieve at present injuries or remember past ones. While they still breathe in the body, they consider themselves dead to all earthly things. So we also, when crucified by the fear of the Lord,

ought to be dead indeed to all these things—not only to vices of the flesh but also to all earthly things, having the eye of our minds fixed where we hope at each moment that we are soon to pass. (*Making Life a Prayer,* 43–44)

On Day 1 of this week, in the Reflecting and Recording section, some disciplines common to the saints were listed: scripture, prayer, devotional reading, solitude, confession, submission and service, generosity, fasting. None of these stands alone, and there is a sense in which prayer pervades them all. There is also a sense in which the purpose of all discipline is to make our lives a prayer.

In my book *Alive in Christ,* I defined *spiritual formation* as that dynamic process of receiving through faith and appropriating through commitment, discipline, and action, the living Christ into our own life so that our life conforms to and manifests the reality of Christ's presence in the world.

Discipline, of which prayer is the heart, gives evidence of the cross in our life.

I also defined prayer as "recognizing, cultivating awareness of, and giving expression to the indwelling Christ." This is what John Cassian was speaking of when he insisted that our discipline must be the evidence of the cross in our lives. We are seeking to completely die to the deeds and desires of this world and vibrantly come alive to the life of Christ within us. The goal is very clear: "It is no longer I who live, but it is Christ who lives in me" (Gal. 2:20).

In *The Spirit of the Disciplines,* Dallas Willard makes a strong case that discipline is absolutely essential for the Christian life. He talks about the great leaders of the ages, and how they recognized this fact. They "met God in their practices"—and they are the result of the grace of the God they met. And that result—even when far from perfect—speaks for itself to the ages.

> The result of not practicing rigorously for the spiritual life, on the other hand, also speaks for itself. Who are the great ones in The Way, what are the significant movements in the history of the church that do not bear the deep and pervasive imprint of the disciplines for the spiritual life? If there are none, what leads us to believe that we might be an exception to the rule and might know the power of the Kingdom life without the appropriate disciplines? How could we be justified in doing anything less than practicing and teaching the disciplines Jesus Christ himself and the best of his followers found necessary? (*The Spirit of the Disciplines,* 126)

REFLECTING AND RECORDING

Spend a few minutes answering Willard's first question in your mind. How does your practice of discipline give evidence of the cross in your life?

What influential Christian witnesses—persons who have had a powerful Christian impact—have you known who did "*not* bear the deep and pervasive imprint of the disciplines for the spiritual life"?

Read again Dallas Willard's first question from the previous page.

Spend the balance of your time answering in your mind the last two questions Willard raised.

DURING THE DAY

Continue your practice of paying attention to what you see and hear or how you speak, seeking to bring those senses under the control of the Holy Spirit.

Group Meeting for Week 2

Introduction

Participation in a group such as the one studying this book involves a covenant relationship. You will profit most in your daily use of this workbook if you faithfully attend these weekly meetings. Do not feel guilty if you have to miss a day in the workbook or be discouraged if you cannot give the full thirty minutes in daily discipline. Don't hesitate to share that with the group. We learn something about ourselves when we share our thoughts and feelings with others. You may discover, for instance, that you are subconsciously afraid of dealing with the content of a particular day because its requirements might reveal something about you. Be patient with yourself, and always be open to what God may be seeking to teach you.

All the saints have known that there is no way "to be a Saint . . . quickly." Francis de Sales gave direction for our beginning journey:

> We must begin with a strong and constant resolution to give ourselves wholly to God, professing to Him, in a tender, loving manner, from the bottom of our hearts, that we intend to be His without any reserve, and then we must often go back and renew this same resolution. (*A Year with the Saints*, 2)

Your spiritual growth, in part, hinges upon your group participation, so share as openly and honestly as you can and listen to what others are saying. If you are attentive, you may pick up meaning beyond the surface of their words. Being a sensitive participant in this fashion is crucial. Responding immediately to the feelings you discern is also important. The group may need to focus its entire attention upon a particular individual at times. If some need or concern is expressed, the leader may ask the group to enter into a brief period of special prayer. But participants should not depend solely upon the leader for this kind of sensitivity. Even if you aren't the leader, don't hesitate to ask the group to join you in special prayer. This praying may be silent, or a group member may lead the group in prayer.

Remember that you have a contribution to make to the group. Even if you consider your thoughts or experiences trivial or unimportant, they may be exactly what another person needs to hear. You need not seek to be profound but simply to share your experience. Also, if you happen to say something that is not well received or is misunderstood, don't be defensive or critical of yourself or others. Don't get diverted by overly scrutinizing your words and actions. Saint Francis de Sales says that "it is self-love which makes us anxious to know whether what we have said or done is approved or not" (*A Year with the Saints*, 209).

SHARING TOGETHER

Leader: It may not be possible in your time frame to use all the suggestions provided each week. Select what will be most beneficial to the group. Be thoroughly familiar with these suggestions so that you can move through them selectively according to the direction in which the group is moving and according to the time available. Plan ahead, but do not hesitate to change your plan in response to the sharing taking place and the needs that emerge.

1. Open your time together with the leader offering a brief prayer of thanksgiving for the opportunity of sharing with the group and with petitions for openness in sharing and loving response to each other.

2. Ask a volunteer to read the prayer he/she wrote on Day 1, expressing the desire to give oneself wholly to God.

3. Spend five to eight minutes sharing about how you "checked out" in the disciplines common to the saints (Reflecting and Recording, Day 1).

4. Ask a couple of persons to share their reflection on Oswald Chambers's word: "God regenerates us and puts us in contact with all His divine resources, but He cannot make us walk according to His will" (Day 2). Allow only five or six minutes.

5. Spend eight to ten minutes discussing the claim that we must hold together our redemption through the mercy and grace of Jesus Christ and God's call to holiness. To begin this discussion, invite someone to read from the text on page 42, beginning with the words "We need to realize. . ." and concluding with Chambers's quotation from *The Psychology of Redemption* on page 43.

6. Invite each person to share one of the four commitments he or she made in the Reflecting and Recording period on Day 3.

7. Invite a volunteer to read his or her translation of Francis de Sales's word about growing in holiness on Day 4.

8. Spend a few minutes discussing de Sales's claim that our perfection depends on the exercises of "aspirations" and "spiritual retirement." What are the different understandings and expressions of those exercises by the group?

9. Invite two or three people to share their experience of deliberately choosing to practice some discipline in order to meet a need or correct something amiss in their life (Day 5).

10. Invite each person to read one of the prayers he or she wrote in the Reflecting and Recording period of Day 6.

11. Spend four to five minutes discussing which issue of surrender in these prayers you had the most difficulty with and what this says about our need for discipline.

PRAYING TOGETHER

1. Praying corporately each week is a special ministry. Take time now for a period of spoken prayer. First, be specific. On Day 4 of this week, you were asked if there was a situation or state of relationship to which you were stoically resigned, about which you have thought you could do nothing. Are there persons who want to share their responses so that the group can pray specifically? Invite a couple of persons to offer brief prayers in response to these needs.

2. Now allow each person to mention any special needs he or she wishes to share with the entire group. A good pattern is to ask for a period of prayer after each need is mentioned. The entire group may pray silently, or someone may offer a brief two-or-three-sentence spoken prayer.

3. Close your time by praying together the great prayer of the church, the Lord's Prayer. As you pray this prayer, remember that the prayer links your group with all Christians of all time in universal praise, confession, thanksgiving, and intercession.

WEEK 3

JESUS WAS ALIVE IN THEIR EXPERIENCE

DAY
1

Conformed to Christ's Likeness

Martin Luther could not have expressed his thoughts about Christianity more clearly:

He who is not *crucianus*, if I may coin a word, is not *Christianus*: in other words, he who does not bear his cross is no Christian, for he is not like his Master, Jesus Christ. (*The Joy of the Saints*, 258)

We centered on this thought yesterday (Week 2, Day 7). Jesus' death on the cross and his call to deny ourselves, take up his cross daily, and follow him are the heart of the Christian faith, spirituality, and discipleship. Luther talked about this idea in terms of "being conformed to Christ."

The cross teaches us to believe in hope even when there is no hope. The wisdom of the cross is deeply hidden in a profound mystery. In fact, there is no other way to heaven than taking up the cross of Christ. On account of this we must beware that the active life with its good works, and the contemplative life with its speculations, do not lead us astray. Both are most attractive and yield peace of mind, but for that very reason they hide real dangers, unless they are tempered by the cross and disturbed by adversaries. The cross is the surest path of all. Blessed is the man who understands this truth.

It is a matter of necessity that we be destroyed and rendered formless, so that Christ may be formed within us, and Christ alone be in us . . . Real mortifications do not happen in lonely places away from the society of other human beings. No! They happen in the home, the market place, in secular life . . . "Being conformed to Christ" is not within our powers to achieve. It is God's gift, not our own work. (*The Joy of the Saints*, 258)

Luther's reflection was a response to Romans 8:28-30:

We know that all things work together for good for those who love God, who are called according to his purpose. For those whom he foreknew he also predestined to be conformed to the image of his Son, in order that he might be the firstborn within a large family. And those whom he predestined he also called; and those whom he called he also justified; and those whom he justified he also glorified.

Luther does not limit his warning. In both our contemplative and active lives, we can be led astray. Both lifestyles are inviting, yielding peace of mind. Implicit in both is the danger of betraying our Christian vocation. Peace can be seductive and numb us to the need for a dynamic relationship and dependence on God. The cross is essential. Keeping the cross at the center of our awareness always forces us to assess the depth of our discipleship and the degree of our yieldedness to Christ.

Notice also that being conformed to the cross—Jesus' death—is not our only task; we are also to be conformed to his *likeness*. One of the lessons we learn from the saints is that Jesus was alive in their experience. They expressed their experiences of Christ in all sorts of ways. Here is one witness from Margery Kempe.

> The Lord Jesus Christ appeared to me in a vision when I was in distress; he sat on my bedside wearing a cloak of purple silk. He looked at me with so much love that I felt his strength flow into my spirit and he said, "Why have you forsaken me, when I have never abandoned you?" Blessed be Jesus who is always near in times of stress. Even when we cannot feel his presence he is close.
>
> Jesus said within my heart, "I will never leave you either in happiness or distress. I will always be there to help you and watch over you. Nothing in heaven or earth can part you from me.
>
> "When you are quiet and still I can speak to your heart." (*The Joy of the Saints*, 141)

I have shared in previous books one of the most inspiring witnesses of Jesus' promise to be with us. My brother-in-law, Randy Morris, was smitten with cancer when he was barely forty. Married and father of two children, he endured a long, hard, anguishing battle. In the midst of his battle, I was preaching a series of sermons on selected psalms, and I sent some of the recorded messages to Randy. In response, he wrote letters of gratitude, sharing the depth of his struggle and his feelings. One of my sermons was a reflection on Psalm 56. In verse 8, the psalmist says, "You have kept count of my tossings; / put my tears in your bottle. / Are they not in your record?"

In this particular psalm, it's not the tears of the psalmist that are new. The psalmist is always talking about tears. But it's the image connected with the tears in this particular petition that grabs my attention: "Put my tears in your bottle."

It is a matter of necessity that we be destroyed and rendered formless, so that Christ may be formed within us.
—*Martin Luther*

In her book *Strange Scriptures That Perplex the Western Mind*, Barbara M. Bowen provides some background on the image the psalmist may have been referring to. She describes the old custom of collecting the tears of a family and preserving those tears in bottles. When death or serious trouble occurred, each member of the family brought his or her tear bottle and collected tears from all the persons present. These bottles were sacred to the family members because they represented all the sorrows of the family. Each person was buried with his or her tear bottle. Many of these bottles have been found in ancient tombs.

In my sermon on Psalm 56, I affirmed that God not only knows our tossings and turnings, but God also cares. When Randy listened to this sermon, he had gone through a period of remission with everything looking good after the first round of heavy chemotherapy; but now the enemy had struck again, and the malignancy was raging in his bone marrow. Randy responded to the sermon with a beautiful witness about trust.

I have grown to love the Psalms during this past year. It is true that God does know of all our tossings. And now I will share with you a prayer experience that proves this to me. It was a major experience with Jesus. Father Rick said I have been touched in a way few people ever experience.

For several years I have prepared for prayer by going through a total relaxation phase to release my body and mind for prayer. After a few moments I travel in my mind to a place in the north Georgia mountains where I used to go on camping trips. There I have built an open structure, a gazebo, where I go to talk with Jesus. Normally I go in and call for Jesus and he comes in. We visit, and usually I give him my prayers of thanksgiving and intercessions. It's a conversational sort of setting.

In late August, I was completely demoralized with the recurrence of the lymphoma. I was an emotional wreck; I went into prayer. Everything went on as normal until Jesus came to the door of the gazebo. At that moment a completely unthought-of event happened that shook me to tears. I became like a camera recording the event. A little boy, me, when I was about Evan's age [five years], ran up to Jesus and hugged him. He picked me up and carried me to a seat and held me in his arms. He hugged me. I didn't say anything, but he knew my "tossings." He knew I was frightened. There were no answers and the future seemed so dim. As he hugged me he said, "Trust me. Trust me."

It was real, a personal miracle. He held me for a long time that night, until he knew I understood what he meant. I've told just a few people about this, and every time I tell it, even as I type this for you, tears come to my eyes; and the feeling I experienced that night renews itself in me. Rick said that feeling is "the same reason Moses couldn't look God in the face and why we remove our shoes on holy ground." And now I know that experience, too. We must trust Jesus as a child trusts—totally.

Because of this, whatever turns out to be the ultimate result of this disease, it's not the burden it was before. He made no promises, nor did he reveal the future, but he provided the format for living out the rest of my life with just two words. . . *Trust me.*

Randy received the same word that had come to Margery Kempe: "When you are quiet and still I can speak to your heart."

REFLECTING AND RECORDING

Recall your most vivid experience of feeling and knowing Christ's presence. Write about that experience here.

Spend three or four minutes reflecting on Luther's claim: "There is no other way to heaven than taking up the cross of Christ." What does Luther mean? Do you believe him?

Think about situations you are currently experiencing that you may designate as "crosses." Name one or two of those here.

What is the difference between your crosses and the cross Luther says we must take up in our journey to heaven? (See page 65.) How do your crosses and the cross of Christ connect?

Offer a prayer, committing your crosses to God and requesting perspective and power in bearing them. Also, pray that you will yield yourself to carrying your cross.

DURING THE DAY

John 6:35 is printed on page 243. Cut it out and place it where you will see it often during the day—for example, on your refrigerator door, on the dashboard of your car, or on your desk. Read it as often as you have opportunity. Jesus gives two directions: (1) come to me; (2) believe in me. Come to Jesus—call him to mind—as often as possible today. Believe in Christ. Affirm your faith by claiming what he promised in this scripture.

DAY
2

My Soul Stays with Christ

All the saints would join Martin Luther in testifying, "My soul stays with Christ." For Luther, the "Bread of life" passage was especially precious.

Then they said to him, "What must we do to perform the works of God?" Jesus answered them, "This is the work of God, that you believe in him whom he has sent." So they said to him, "What sign are you going to give us then, so that we may see it and believe you? What work are you performing? Our ancestors ate the manna in the wilderness; as it is written, 'He gave them bread from heaven to eat.'" Then Jesus said to them, "Very truly, I tell you, it was not Moses who gave you the bread from heaven, but it is my Father who gives you the true bread from heaven. For the bread of God is that which comes down from heaven and gives life to the world." They said to him, "Sir, give us this bread always."

Jesus said to them, "I am the bread of life. Whoever comes to me will never be hungry, and whoever believes in me will never be thirsty." (John 6:28-35)

Of these words, Luther wrote:

We must not only know but turn them to our profit and say, "With these words I shall go to bed in the evening and arise in the morning; on them I shall rely, on them I shall sleep, wake and work, and with them cross the final bridge of death into eternal life."

Seek yourself only in Christ and not in yourself; then you will find yourself in him eternally. (*The Joy of the Saints*, 315)

I think of my mother when I read these last sentences of Luther. She was eighty-nine when she died, and I still miss her desperately. During the last two or three years of Momma's life, my wife, Jerry, and I visited her in Perry County, Mississippi, about every six weeks. Without fail on all of those visits, the subject of faith would come up—my mother's faith, the little rural Baptist church she loved so much, and her pastor's faithfulness. And of course we talked about the Bible. It would not be long in any conversation before my mother would pick up her large-print edition of the Bible from the coffee table and announce, "This is my favorite scripture." It didn't matter that she had shared this passage on our previous visit, and the visit before, and the visit before that. I'm not sure she even remembered that she had shared it. She got joy and strength from reading it to

The one doctrine which I have supremely at heart is that of faith in Christ, from whom, through whom, and unto whom, all my theological thinking flows.

—Martin Luther

me. In her choppy reading style, never cultivated for public reading because she did not go beyond elementary school, she would begin Psalm 24:

> *The earth is the Lord's and all that is in it,*
>   *the world, and those who live in it;*
> *for he has founded it on the seas,*
>   *and established it on the rivers.*
> *Who shall ascend the hill of the Lord?*
>   *And who shall stand in his holy place?*
> *Those who have clean hands and pure hearts,*
>   *who do not lift up their souls to what is false,*
> *and do not swear deceitfully. (vv. 1-4)*

And always—it never failed—she would stop at that point in her reading and say to me earnestly, "Son, I've got clean hands and a pure heart." This was her way of affirming her faith and letting me know that all was well with her soul. It was one of those rituals of home and parents that strengthened my soul. And that's the reason I miss it—and hold it in sacred memory. Intuitively, Mom knew this is a great psalm, a premier piece of scripture.

I never will forget my last experience with my mother and Psalm 24. It was a couple of months before she died. When I first arrived to see her on that occasion, she didn't know me. In fact, only now and then during that visit did she seem to know who I was. Anyone who has experienced a parent not recognizing you knows how painful this is.

During that visit, I sat beside her on the sofa and asked if she would like for me to read her favorite psalm. She didn't respond. I'm not sure she understood. But I read it anyway. I leaned over close to her and began, "The earth is the Lord's and all that is in it, the world, and those who live in it." When I got to the question, "Who shall stand in his holy place?" I heard her respond in a raspy whisper, "Clean hands—pure heart."

My pain in not being known by my mother was eased by the confidence that she was known by God—and she knew God. Her desire was evident—a desire for clean hands and a pure heart. And I knew that all was well with her soul. She was testifying with Luther: "Seek yourself only in Christ and not in yourself; then you will find yourself in him eternally."

Luther continued his testimony:

> The one doctrine which I have supremely at heart is that of faith in Christ, from whom, through whom and unto whom all my theological thinking flows back and forth, day and night.
>   To preach Christ means to feed the soul, to make it righteous, to set it free and to save it, if it believe the preaching. For faith alone is the saving and efficacious use of the word of God.
>   Christ ought to be preached to the end that faith in him be established, that he may not only be Christ, but be Christ for you and for me, and that what is said of him, and what his name denotes, may be effectual in us. (*The Joy of the Saints*, 315)

Though addressing the preacher and what preaching means, Luther's word has universal application: Christ's presence must be effectual in us. He must be Christ *for me*.

REFLECTING AND RECORDING

In his Second Letter to the Corinthians, Paul wrote, "Examine yourselves to see whether you are in the faith; test yourselves. Do you not realize that Christ Jesus is in you—unless, of course, you fail the test?" (2 Cor. 13:5, NIV). He connects being in the faith with Christ Jesus dwelling inside the believer.

List five or six characteristics of a person who is in the faith, in whom Christ is present.

Test yourself. According to the characteristics you listed, does Christ dwell in you? Spend the balance of your time reflecting on the degree to which Christ lives in you.

DURING THE DAY

Continue your meditative reading of John 6:35. Consider Jesus' invitation to come to him and believe in him.

DAY
3

Abiding in Christ

A variation on the theme that Christ was alive in the saints' experience is the lesson that there is a difference between *following* Christ and *being in* Christ. This has been a major failure of Christians since the second century. We have emphasized following Jesus as the heart of Christianity. In doing so, we tend to reduce Christianity to a religion of morals and ethics, thus denuding it of its power.

Following Jesus is important. That's what we are called to do. But the point is, we cannot follow Jesus for long unless we are *in* Christ—abiding in him. We renew our strength by waiting on God, spending time in God's presence in prayer, immersing ourselves in scripture, spending time with God's people, and cultivating the presence of Christ within us, so that we act from the depths of the indwelling Holy Spirit that inspires us.

> *Those who abide in me and I in them bear much fruit, because apart from me you can do nothing.*
> —*John 15:5, NRSV*

In 1963, the atomic submarine USS *Thresher* disappeared in the depths of the ocean, killing everyone aboard (112 naval personnel and 17 civilians). Experts surmised that the submarine had gone so deep that it simply went out of control. The oxygen pressure inside the submarine would allow it to go only to certain depths. The experts decided that the vessel had gone deeper than its capability, gotten out of control, and became lost.

Some years later, submarine design was more nearly perfected. Because of technological advances, another submarine descended—a smaller one, thick-plated and highly pressurized—much deeper than the *Thresher* had been able to go. The crew in this little sub discovered the *Thresher*—a strange sight. They found that it had imploded—exploded in on itself—and this hunk of steel was like a crushed piece of cardboard. The pressure within the submarine was obviously not able to withstand the pressure outside, and the submarine had collapsed upon itself. The surprising thing about the whole situation was that around the crushed *Thresher* were all sorts of sea creatures. They had huge eyes and very thin skin, yet they swam around the *Thresher* in the extreme environment of the same pressure that had crushed a steel machine as though it were a toy. How could these sea creatures survive in that pressure? Scientists, writing about the phenomenon, told us that inside these sea creatures was an *opposite and equal* pressure to the pressure outside them.

That's a parable for us—the way it must be in our lives as Christians. We must cultivate the indwelling Christ to the point that his power prevails and gives us the strength to continue where our own strength would fail. We can survive the *doing* of our Christianity if we keep the *being* of our Christian life intact and up-to-date.

One understanding of *redemption* is the "impartation of life." Jesus said, "I came that they may have life, and have it abundantly" (John 10:10*b*). God's redemptive gift to us is a new kind of life—the life of Christ himself. The incarnation continues as Christ lives on in us. This is the amazing promise of Jesus:

> *I am the true vine, and My Father is the vinedresser. Every branch in Me that does not bear fruit He takes away; and every branch that bears fruit He prunes, that it may bear more fruit. You are already clean because of the word which I have spoken to you. Abide in Me, and I in you. As the branch cannot bear fruit of itself, unless it abides in the vine, neither can you, unless you abide in Me. I am the vine, you are the branches. He who abides in Me, and I in him, bears much fruit; for without Me you can do nothing. If anyone does not abide in Me, he is cast out as a branch and is withered; and they gather them and throw them into the fire, and they are burned. If you abide in me, and My words abide in you, you will ask what you desire, and it shall be done for you. By this My Father is glorified, that you bear much fruit; so you will be My disciples. (John 15:1-8, NKJV)*

But how do we abide in Christ? All the saints would insist that we spend regular time, daily when possible, with scripture, devotional reading, and prayer. They would call us to observe the sacrament of Holy Communion and to find frequent times of solitude to recollect and reflect on God; Christ's life and teaching; his passion, suffering, death, and resurrection. Abiding in Christ and Christ alive in them was such a part of the saints' experience that they spoke about it in many different ways.

Margery Kempe referred to *resting in God*:

In my soul I heard Jesus say, "If you will love me with all your heart then I may rest there. If you allow me to rest in your heart on earth then believe me when I tell you that you will rest with me in heaven."

"I ask no more of you than that you love me as I love you."

"You know that when you have received me into your soul you are in peace and quiet."

"I would speak to you more often than you will let me."

"I would take you by the hand so that people know that you are my friend." (*The Joy of the Saints*, 207)

François Fénelon answered the matter of distraction by "returning to His Presence":

If you are resolved to resist distraction, you will do so successfully; and whenever you discover it, you will recall your mind to God, calmly and without struggling, not delaying to raise your eyes to Him. This faithfulness, in returning to His Presence, will win for you a more abiding sense of it, and thus that Presence will become familiar to you. After a time the practice of speedily returning, the moment you are conscious of distraction, will win for you an habitual easy recollection. But do not suppose you can obtain such by your own efforts; for then you would be perpetually constrained, uneasy, and scrupulous, when you should be free and calm. You would be always fearing that you were losing God's Presence, and striving to retain it, and thus become lost amidst the phantoms of your own imagination; and that Presence, the healing light of which should illumine all around, would only serve to render you confused, and almost incapable of your external duties. (Baillie, *A Diary of Readings*, 5)

Francis de Sales summarized devotion like this:

The thoughts of those moved by natural human love are almost completely fastened on the beloved object, their hearts are filled with affection for it, and their mouths full of its praises. When it is absent they lose no opportunity of testifying to their passions by letters, and they do not pass by a tree without inscribing the name of their beloved in its bark. Thus too those who love God can never stop thinking about him, longing for him, aspiring to him, and speaking about him. If it were possible, they would engrave the holy, sacred name of Jesus on the breasts of all mankind. . . .

Since the great work of devotion consists in such use of spiritual recollection and ejaculatory prayers★ it can supply the lack of all other prayers, but its loss can hardly be repaired by other means. Without this exercise we cannot properly lead the contemplative life, and we can but poorly lead the active life. (*Introduction to the Devout Life*, 99–100, 103)

★According to *American Heritage Dictionary, ejaculatory* used in this sense means "a sudden, short exclamation, especially a brief, pious utterance of prayer."

REFLECTING AND RECORDING

Recall an experience that would have defeated you—in other words, something that would have made you collapse like the *Thresher*—if you had not had the support of your Christian faith. Record that experience here.

As you reflect on the faith that enabled you to survive, perhaps even overcome, the experience just described, what role did the presence of Christ within you play? Make some notes.

Part of my understanding of the dynamic of spiritual formation is recognizing, cultivating awareness of, and giving expressions to the indwelling Christ. In one of the above quotations, de Sales said, "The great work of devotion consists in such use of spiritual recollection [that means recognizing and cultivating awareness of God's presence and activity] and ejaculatory prayers."

Spiritual recollection makes up for deficiencies in our praying and protects us from temptations that threaten our discipleship. Ejaculatory prayers are short, spontaneous prayers.

Thinking in these terms, examine your daily effort to keep Christ alive in your experience. What role do recollection and ejaculatory prayer play?

DURING THE DAY

Your daily use of John 6:35, if practiced as suggested, is a spiritual recollection. The prayer you were asked to use as you began this workbook venture—"Lord, give me the grace to be wholly yours"—is an ejaculatory prayer. Continue to use John 6:35 as an act of recollection, but see how many times you can offer an ejaculatory prayer in your own words today.

DAY
4

The Mystery: Christ in You

Nathaniel Hawthorne once noted in his journal, "A story, the principal personage of which shall seem always on the point of entering the scene; but never shall appear." In other words, he was thinking about writing a story in which the main character never appeared! Studying the lives of the saints reminds us that too many Christians are like that—their lives are stories in which the "main character" seldom, if ever, appears.

Christianity is Christ. He came not only to save us from our sins, but to be an indwelling presence to shape us into his likeness. He is not to be an infrequent guest, one we invite only to share special occasions. Christ is not a "fix-it" person to call upon only when we need special help, but rather "a very present help in trouble" and a companion along all our ways.

Thérèse of Lisieux confessed that her final retreat, before she took her lifelong vows (made her profession) as a nun, was a time of desolation rather than a time of consolation and joy. Her soul felt dry. She said, "Complete aridity . . . was my lot. . . . Such an attitude of mind," she added, "proves that I am far from being a saint." Yet, she confessed, "The way to please God and practise virtue was being made clear to me."

> Now I must tell you about my retreat for profession. Far from experiencing any consolation, complete aridity—desolation, almost—was my lot. Jesus was asleep in my little boat as usual. How rarely souls let Him sleep peacefully within them. Their agitation and all their requests

have so tired out the Good Master that He is only too glad to enjoy the rest I offer Him. I do not suppose He will wake up until my eternal retreat, but instead of making me sad, it makes me very happy.

Such an attitude of mind proves that I am far from being a saint. I should not rejoice in my aridity, but rather consider it as the result of lack of fervour and fidelity, while the fact that I often fall asleep during meditation, or while making my thanksgiving, should appal me. Well, I am not appalled; I bear in mind that little children are just as pleasing to their parents asleep as awake; that doctors put their patients to sleep while they perform operations, and that after all, *"the Lord knoweth our frame. He remembereth that we are but dust."*

. . . I have often noticed that Jesus will not give me a store of provisions; He nourishes me with food that is entirely new from moment to moment, and I find it in my soul without knowing how it got there. In all simplicity, I believe that Jesus Himself is, in a mysterious way, at work in the depths of my soul inspiring me with whatever He wants me to do at that moment. (*The Story of a Soul*, 115–16)

Paul gave witness to Christ's presence within, which he called the great mystery of the Christian faith:

I am now rejoicing in my sufferings for your sake, and in my flesh I am completing what is lacking in Christ's afflictions for the sake of his body, that is, the church. I became its servant according to God's commission that was given to me for you, to make the word of God fully known, the mystery that has been hidden throughout the ages and generations but has now been revealed to his saints. To them God chose to make known how great among the Gentiles are the riches of the glory of this mystery, which is Christ in you, the hope of glory. It is he whom we proclaim, warning everyone and teaching everyone in all wisdom, so that we may present everyone mature in Christ. For this I toil and struggle with all the energy that he powerfully inspires within me. (Colossians 1:24-29)

At least three truths are evident in this passage. One truth is the Incarnation: God has come to us in Jesus Christ. Earlier in this first chapter of his Letter to the Colossians, Paul encapsulated the essence of God's saving work in Jesus Christ: "He has rescued us from the power of darkness and transferred us into the kingdom of his beloved Son, in whom we have redemption, the forgiveness of sins" (Col. 1:13-14). Having sounded that astounding good news, Paul felt it wise to tell us who this Son really is, into whose kingdom we have been brought.

> *Paul called Christ's presence within each believer the great mystery of the Christian faith.*

He is the image of the invisible God, the firstborn of all creation; for in him all things in heaven and on earth were created, things visible and invisible, whether thrones or dominions or rulers or powers—all things have been created through him and for him. He himself is before all things, and in him all things hold together. He is the head of the body, the church; he is the beginning, the firstborn from the dead, so that he might come to have first place in everything. For in him all the fullness of God was pleased to dwell, and through him God was pleased to reconcile to himself all things, whether on earth or in heaven, by making peace through the blood of his cross. (Colossians 1:15-20)

So, in proclaiming this gospel, Paul underscores the importance of the Incarnation. Christ is the mystery of God and the kingdom now revealed. He is our salvation.

The second truth is the underscoring of Christ's ongoing presence in the life of the believer. Paul said it this way: "For this I toil and struggle with all the energy that he powerfully inspires within me" (v. 29).

The presence of a new power (Christ's energy) within is what enables us to break away from our old life. We turn from the old through repentance and are released to the new through forgiveness.

The third truth is the goal of the gospel's work in our life: that we might be presented "mature in Christ" (NRSV). So Christ is an immediate but also an ongoing, transforming power over our character. In the kingdom of God's dear Son, we have superhuman power over the evils of this present age. A careful reading of scripture and the writings of the saints make it clear: The presence of God in Jesus Christ is not to be experienced only on occasion; rather, the indwelling Christ is to become *the* shaping power of our lives.

New Testament scholar B. F. Westcott once pointed out that "the believer lives two lives in two different spheres, the eternal life in Christ, the temporal life in the world" (quoted in *Salvation Army Daily Scripture Devotional Guide*, Sunday, April 1, 2000). When Jesus uses words like "in me you may have peace" (John 16:33), the "in me" language is probably connected with his metaphor of the vine and the branches. So it is not a matter of an experience of Christ now and then, but the indwelling Christ as an ongoing reality, that becomes the shaping power of our lives.

An e-mail from a friend gave witness to this shaping power of Christ. He is in his mid-fifties and says he can't remember when he became a Christian. He does remember and talks glowingly about an eight-week study of *The Workbook on Becoming Alive in Christ*, which he and his wife shared with four other couples. In his words, "Christ came alive in me." The study took place over ten years ago. His e-mail shared the good news of a Chinese man who had that day professed his faith in Christ.

Bill and his wife had "adopted" this man, a student at a local university, simply to show hospitality and, of course, in the hopes of sharing a Christian witness. The fellow was not open to Christianity; in fact, he was hostile to it. But after a year of friendship with Bill and Sue, he not only became open to the gospel, he embraced it and claimed its saving power. In Bill's words, "It was Christ in us and through us, shaping our lives in love and concern for the stranger in our midst, that won this person."

REFLECTING AND RECORDING

Spend a few minutes pondering this claim: The presence of God in Jesus Christ is not to be experienced only on occasion; rather, the indwelling Christ is to become the shaping power of our lives. Do you believe this is true? How does it happen?

To what degree and in what ways does the indwelling Christ shape your life? Write your answer here.

Paul said the indwelling Christ "powerfully works in me" (Col. 1:29, NIV). Name two or three persons you know in whom Christ is working powerfully.

_____

_____

_____

DURING THE DAY

Continue to use John 6:35 as an act of spiritual recollection and the prayer "Lord, give me the grace to be wholly yours" as an ejaculatory prayer.

DAY
5

The Working Power of Christ
Brought into the Present

I give you a new commandment, that you love one another. Just as I have loved you, you also should love one another. By this everyone will know that you are my disciples, if you have love for one another." (John 13:34-35)

Yesterday we concentrated on the *mystery*: Christ in us. We considered a claim that grows out of the mystery: Christians are not supposed to experience the *presence* of God in Jesus Christ only occasionally; rather, the indwelling Christ is to become *the* shaping power of our lives. As we grow in being alive in Christ, every part of our life becomes connected to him. We learn to say yes to Christ every day. I doubt that a time will come in any of our lives when we will not need to change, when some aspect of our being, newly discovered, will not need Christ's transforming power. I doubt if the time will ever come—though I pray for it for myself—when we can say with all confidence and certainty, "I'm yours, Lord. Everything about me, and of me, is yours." For even as we pray that prayer, revelation comes, and a hidden area or concern emerges to awareness, and we have to make another commitment, and yield ourselves to transforming love.

God's immeasurable power in Christ is available now to:
- *redeem us from sin*
- *energize our wills*
- *heal the sick*
- *drive out demons*
- *renew our spirits*
- *reconcile our relationships*

A second claim that grows out of the mystery of Christ within is that the working power of Christ in the past must be brought into the present. The saints were clear about this. Thérèse of Lisieux made the point in reference to Jesus' command that we love one another as he has loved us; thus, his power is made real.

Jesus, you never ask what is impossible. You know better than I do how frail and imperfect I am. You know I shall never love others as you have loved them, unless you love them yourself within me. It is because you desire to grant me this grace, that you give a new commandment. I cherish it dearly, since it proves to me that it is your will to love in me all those you tell me to love.

When I show love towards others, I know that it is Jesus who is acting within me. The more closely I am united to him, the more dearly I love others. Should I wish to increase this love, and am put off by the defects of another person, I immediately try to look for that person's virtues and good motives. I call to mind that though I may have seen one fall, many victories over self may have been gained but have been concealed through humility. It can also be that what appears to be a fault may be an act of virtue, since it was prompted by an act of virtue. (*The Joy of the Saints*, 334)

In his book *Mortal Lessons*, surgeon Richard Selzer tells a poignant story about a young woman who has just experienced a profound change:

I stand by the bed where a young woman lies, her face post-operative, her mouth twisted in palsy, clownish. A tiny twig of the facial nerve, the one to the muscles of her mouth, has been severed. She will be thus from now on.

The surgeon had followed with religious fervor the curve of her flesh; I promise you that. Nevertheless, to remove the tumor in her cheek, I had cut the little nerve.

Her young husband is in the room. He stands on the opposite side of the bed, and together they seem to dwell in the evening lamplight, isolated from me, private. Who are they, I ask myself, he and this wry-mouth I have made, who gaze at and touch each other so generously, greedily? The young woman speaks.

"Will my mouth always be like this?" she asks.

"Yes," I say, "it will. It is because the nerve was cut."

She nods, and is silent. But the young husband smiles.

"I like it," he says. "It is kind of cute."

All at once I know who he is. I understand, and I lower my gaze. One is not bold in an encounter with a god. Unmindful, he bends to kiss her crooked mouth, and I so close I can see how he twists his own lips to accommodate hers, to show her that their kiss still works. (*Mortal Lessons*, 45–46)

What do you think about that? If Jesus' ultimate ministry was love, then love must prevail so that his working power in the past can be brought into the present. The young husband in the above scenario dramatically expressed such love. No change of circumstance thwarts love. A change in physical appearance and condition may alter how we express love, but it does not diminish love's meaning.

It is mind-boggling to consider that the working power of Christ in the past can be brought into the present. Paul breaks into singing prayer when he thinks of the benefits and privileges belonging to Christians:

I ask—ask the God of our Master, Jesus Christ, the God of glory—to make you intelligent and discerning in knowing him personally, your eyes focused and clear, so that you can see exactly what it is he is calling you to do, grasp the immensity of this glorious way of life he has for Christians, oh, the utter extravagance of his work in us who trust him—endless energy, boundless strength! (Ephesians 1:17-19, THE MESSAGE)

What Paul is saying is that the working power of God in the past can be brought into the present. This is the paramount miracle—that God's immeasurable power in Christ is available now to redeem us from sin, to energize our wills, to heal the sick, to drive out demons, to renew our spirits, to reconcile our relationships.

Is this our vision of reality? Or have we reduced the Christian faith to an intellectual concept, a set of dogmas, a religious system to which we give assent and which we practice by rote with no impact in power on our daily lives? The same power that raised Jesus from the dead is available to us. Those who claim that power receive it, and their lives are transformed.

REFLECTING AND RECORDING

Spend a few minutes reflecting on these two sentences from Thérèse:

"I cherish it [the new commandment of love] dearly, since it proves to me that it is your will to love in me all those you tell me to love."

"When I show love towards others, I know that it is Jesus who is acting within me."

Describe here your most recent experience of Christ's power working in your life.

Spend a few minutes thinking about this question: Why don't I experience more of Christ's power in my life?

DURING THE DAY

Be attentive today to the possibilities of Christ's power at work—especially in your life.

DAY

6

The Spirit of God's Son in Our Hearts

Millions of Christians worldwide revere John Wesley as the founder (or as one of the founders) of their denomination. Varieties of Methodists and Wesleyans, Nazarenes, and several holiness churches all claim John Wesley. But Wesley himself had no intention of founding so much as one denomination. His purpose was to lead a movement that would revive the Church of England by setting up a network of societies that would complement a believer's regular church attendance. He stated that his goal was to "reform the nation, especially the church—and to spread scriptural holiness through the land."

Because Christians are children of God, God has sent the spirit of Christ to dwell in our hearts.

Not an innovator, Wesley's strength was being able to adapt good ideas wherever he found them and using them to accomplish his purpose. He divided people into small groups called bands or classes so that they could nurture each other; he preached in the fields because churches were closed to him; he used lay preachers; he met with preachers in annual conference meetings. These were all good ideas, but they were not original with him. Though Wesley called himself a man of one book, he read widely in ancient as well as contemporary authors, but was always steeped in scripture. He used experience to test theological ideas, always seeking practical applications and results.

When the Methodist movement gained momentum, the questions became persistent: What is this renewal all about? Who are these "Methodists"? What do they believe? In 1739, Wesley published a tract entitled *The Character of a Methodist*. It was his explanation of what a Methodist seeks to do. A portion of it says:

Methodists are those who had *God's love poured into their hearts through the Holy Spirit that has been given to them, who love the Lord their God with all their hearts, and with all their souls, and with all their minds, and with all their strength.* God is the joy of their hearts, and the desire of their souls; which constantly cry out, *Whom have I in heaven but you? And there is nothing on earth that I desire other than you! My God and my all! You are the strength of my heart, and my portion for ever!*

They are therefore happy in God, yea, always happy, as having in them a spring of water gushing up to eternal life, and overflowing their souls with peace and joy. Perfect love having now cast out fear, they rejoice in the Lord always, even in God their Savior. Having found redemption through his blood, the forgiveness of their trespasses, they cannot but rejoice, whenever they look back on the horrible pit out of which they are delivered. They cannot but rejoice, whenever they look on the state wherein they now are; justified by God's grace as a gift, and having peace with God through our Lord Jesus Christ. For those who believe have the testimony of this in their hearts, being now the children of God by faith. Because they are children, God has sent the Spirit of his Son into their hearts, crying, "Abba, Father!" And that very Spirit bears witness with their spirits, that they are children of God. They rejoice also, whenever they look forward, in hope of the glory that shall be revealed. All their bones cry out, *"Blessed be the God and Father of our Lord Jesus Christ! By his great mercy he has given us a new birth into a living hope . . . into an inheritance that is imperishable, undefiled, and unfading, kept in heaven for [us!]"* (*A Longing for Holiness*, 39–40)

In this passage, the editor has italicized the scripture quotations and paraphrases. You can see that Wesley's writings were packed with scriptural quotations, allusions, paraphrases, and images. The passage succinctly expresses the core of the Christian faith. Like the apostle Paul, Wesley often contrasted the old and the new. Here he does it in a powerful way. He talks about the past—"the horrible pit out of which they are delivered"—and the present—they can now rejoice because they are "justified by God's grace as a gift, and having peace with God through our Lord Jesus Christ." He also talks about the future—"they rejoice also, whenever they look forward, in hope of the glory that shall be revealed."

A key for Wesley is his claim that we are now children of God, and God has sent the Spirit of Christ into our hearts. Again, he is using the language of Paul:

My point is this: heirs, as long as they are minors, are no better than slaves, though they are the owners of all the property; but they remain under guardians and trustees until the date set by the father. So with us; while we were minors, we were enslaved to the elemental spirits of the world. But when the fullness of time had come, God sent his Son, born of a woman, born under the law, in order to redeem those who were under the law, so that we might receive adoption as children. And because you are children, God has sent the Spirit of his Son into our hearts, crying, "Abba! Father!" So you are no longer a slave but a child, and if a child then also an heir, through God. (Galatians 4:1-7)

Our identity as Christians is that God has made us his children by sending "the Spirit of his Son into our hearts." With all the saints, Wesley sounded this note over and over again. Jesus was alive in his experience. One result of this, as Wesley defined the character of a Methodist, was that they *prayed without ceasing*:

Not that they are always in the house of prayer; though they neglect no opportunity of being there. Neither are they always on their knees, although they often are, or on their face, before the Lord their God. Nor yet are they always crying aloud to God, for many times the Spirit intercedes with sighs too deep for words. Their heart is ever lifted up to God, at all times and in all places. In this they are never hindered, much less interrupted, by any person or thing. In retirement or company, in leisure, business, or conversation, God is in all their thoughts; they walk with God continually, having the loving eye of their minds still fixed upon him, and everywhere seeing him that is invisible. (*A Longing for Holiness*, 40–41)

This life of unceasing prayer translates into acts of Christ through us as "the loving eye of [our] minds [is] still fixed upon him." Sometimes the way Christ acts through us is almost unbelievable. The following story shows how he acted through one person.

At age sixteen, Debbie Morris was kidnapped, raped, tortured, and almost murdered. Years passed before Debbie learned to forgive two men whose actions changed her life forever.

One peaceful night in Madisonville, Louisiana, sixteen-year-old Debbie Morris and her boyfriend Mark Brewster, parked their car at the Tchefuncte River and sipped milk shakes. A pickup truck pulled up beside them on the isolated riverfront, and before they knew what was happening, someone thrust a revolver through the driver's window and pointed it at Mark's head. A hand jerked Debbie's head back, and the barrel of a sawed-off shotgun pressed against her cheek. She has never forgotten the chilling words: "Don't do anything stupid! We've killed before, and we'll kill again."

The two men, Robert Willie and Joseph Vaccaro, were murderers and escapees from Angola Prison. They were high on drugs. The nightmare for Debbie and Mark began. The men shot Mark and left him for dead in an isolated wooded area. Though he is still alive, it will require a lifetime of therapy for him to perform even life's simplest tasks.

Willie and Vaccaro raped Debbie three times over the next seventy-two hours. She was certain that the men would kill her too, but mysteriously and miraculously, they released her near her home.

For months, Debbie worked with the police in their search for Willie and Vaccaro. They were successful. Joseph Vaccaro was imprisoned, and Robert Willie died in the electric chair. Denise George tells the rest of the story:

> In spite of her belief in Jesus Christ, the support of her family and her church family, Debbie's life began to deteriorate. She quit high school. She moved around the country, working odd jobs to meet living expenses. And she developed such a serious drinking problem that she experienced alcoholic blackouts.
>
> After Willie's execution, Debbie felt numb. "It's over at last," she told herself. But she felt spiritually confused. "As a kid and as a young teenager I believed in God," she said. "I trusted Him. And then He let me down. Okay, maybe He saved me and gave me another chance at life. But what about all the pain and unhappiness I've gone through—where was the Almighty in all that? If He really, truly loved me as the Bible claims, why would He let me go through all the heartache and suffering?" Debbie claims she was angry, and she was angry with God.
>
> Debbie also realized that "no punishment—not even the ultimate punishment (Willie's execution), the ultimate justice—could ever heal all the wounds."
>
> Debbie's mother finally convinced Debbie to get professional help. She checked herself into a thirty-day treatment program at a Baton Rouge hospital. And Debbie's messed-up life began to change.
>
> For a long time, Debbie walked the hard road of forgiveness. After Willie's execution, she asked God to forgive her for her attitude and mistakes. "As I came to know and feel God's forgiveness, it was suddenly easy to forgive myself," she said. "And what a new and incredible sense of freedom I felt!"
>
> Debbie returned to church. She renewed her relationship with God and her family. She forgave the evil men who kidnapped and violated her—the men who had shot her boyfriend.
>
> Some time later, Sister Helen Prejean wrote a book describing how she, a nun, had ministered to Robert Willie before his execution for the murder of Faith Hathaway. The book became the popular movie *Dead Man Walking*.
>
> Before he died, Robert Willie showed no sign of remorse for his crimes. "So many people ask me, 'How can you forgive someone like Robert Willie?'" Debbie said.
>
> "I couldn't begin to articulate it at the time," Debbie remembers, "but I knew I *had* to forgive him—not for his sake, but for mine. Until I did, there was no escaping the hold his evil had on my life. Until I forgave him, real healing couldn't begin."

REFLECTING AND RECORDING

Think of three or four persons you know who especially need something Christ offers, such as love, forgiveness, acceptance, healing, or freedom from some shameful habit or addiction. Write their names in the space below.

Is there one or two of these persons for whom you might be Christ—the channel through which Christ's ministry comes to them? Make some notes about how you might do that.

Pray for the persons you named—and for guidance and power to minister to them.

DURING THE DAY

Today, boldly seek to be Christ to and/or to receive Christ from every person you meet.

DAY
7

Dance for Joy in Heaven

At a time of particular trial, when Margery Kempe considered her own death, she heard God saying to her:

"You do not need to be afraid of dying in pain, for I will be with you and your mind will be fixed on me."

"I promise that you will have no more distress, for I have tested you for many years with doubts and fears in your thoughts and dreams."

"I will take your soul into my own hands which were nailed to the cross and offer it to my Father with incense and music, and you will see him."

"I shall take you by the hand and we will dance for joy in heaven with all the saints and angels who will rejoice at your coming." (Quoted from Margery Kempe, *The Joy of the Saints*, 39)

On Day 2 of this week, I told about an experience with my mother. I vividly remember her death. My wife and I were there, along with my two sisters and my father. We knew she was dying. We gathered around her bed, sang hymns, prayed, and quoted scripture. We loved her and worshiped with her as she made that journey through death into her eternal resting place, about one o'clock in the morning.

Earlier in the day, my father had been at my mother's bedside. Married for sixty-nine years, they both knew the end was near. My mother, in a moment of lucidity and love, squeezed my father's hand, and said, "I'll see you later." My father, not much of a talker, simply responded, "I'll be there."

The saints never ceased to give witness to the fact that death cannot separate us from Christ's love.

My father has since died. He and Momma are buried side by side in the cemetery behind the little Baptist church about three hundred yards from their home. On my mother's tombstone, we carved those words, "I'll see you later," and on my father's tombstone, his reply, "I'll be there."

What an inspiring witness—in keeping with the words of Margery Kempe: "I shall take you by the hand and we will dance for joy in heaven with all the saints and angels who will rejoice at your coming."

My wife and I often share the memory of the exchange between my mother and father at her death. And often we will spontaneously begin to sing what we can remember of a lovely old bluegrass song about death and the reuniting of loved ones on the "Far-Side Banks of Jordan."

Jesus often spoke of eternal life. To Nicodemus he said, "For God so loved the world that he gave his only Son, so that everyone who believes in him may not perish but may have eternal life" (John 3:16).

When the woman at the well questioned Jesus about the living water he had just told her about, he said, "Everyone who drinks of this water will be thirsty again, but those who drink of the water that I will give them will never be thirsty. The water that I will give will become in them a spring of water gushing up to eternal life" (John 4:13-14).

When the Jews threatened him for healing on the sabbath and for calling God "his own Father," Jesus rejoined:

Very truly, I tell you, the Son can do nothing on his own, but only what he sees the Father doing; for whatever the Father does, the Son does likewise. The Father loves the Son and shows him all that he himself is doing; and he will show him greater works than these, so that you will be astonished. Indeed, just as the Father raises the dead and gives them life, so also the Son gives life to whomever he wishes. The Father judges no one but has given all judgment to the Son, so that all may honor the Son just as they honor the Father. Anyone who does not honor the Son does not honor the Father who sent him. Very truly, I tell you, anyone who hears my word and believes him who sent me has eternal life, and does not come under judgment, but has passed from death to life.

Very truly, I tell you, the hour is coming, and is now here, when the dead will hear the voice of the Son of God, and those who hear will live. For just as the Father has life in himself, so he has granted the Son also to have life in himself; and he has given him authority to execute judgment, because he is the Son of Man. (John 5:19-27)

When the Jews confronted him, saying, "How long will you keep us in suspense? If you are the Messiah, tell us plainly," Jesus gave a stunning reply.

When Christ is alive in our experience, "death has been swallowed up in victory" (1 Cor. 15:54). The sting of death has been removed, and we know that nothing, not even death, can separate us from Christ's love (see Rom. 8:31-39). The saints never ceased to give witness to the fact that death cannot separate us from Christ and his love. Martin Luther said:

O death, where is thy sting? O grave, where is thy victory? This is so true that even Satan cannot deny it. Christ's resurrection and victory over sin, death and hell is greater than all heaven and earth. You can never imagine his resurrection and victory so great but that in actuality it is far, far greater. For as his person is mighty, eternal, without limit, incomprehensible, so also is his resurrection, victory and triumph mighty, eternal, without limit, incomprehensible. Were hell a thousand times more, and death ten thousand times more, it would all be but a spark, a mere drop, compared with Christ's resurrection, victory and triumph. But, his resurrection, victory and triumph gives Christ to all who believe in him. Since we have been baptized in his name, and believe in him, it follows that even if you and I underwent sin, death and hell a hundred thousandfold, it would amount to nothing; for Christ's resurrection, victory and triumph, which have been given me in the baptism and in the word by faith, and therefore are my own, are infinitely greater. If this is true, and I most certainly believe it to be true, then let sin, death and hell dog my steps and growl at me. What will they do to us? What can they do? What? (*The Joy of the Saints*, 124)

REFLECTING AND RECORDING

Spend a few minutes reflecting on death. How do you feel about it? How often do you think about it? When you think about it, what questions arise? Are you fearful?

Ponder Luther's claim: Jesus' "resurrection, victory and triumph gives Christ to all who believe in him."

How confident are you in the truth of Margery Kempe's word from God: "You do not need to be afraid of dying . . . for I shall take you by the hand and we will dance for joy in heaven with all the saints and angels who will rejoice at your coming"?

DURING THE DAY

Continue seeking to be Christ to and/or to receive Christ from every person you meet.

Group Meeting for Week 3

Leader: You will need a chalkboard or newsprint for this session.

INTRODUCTION

Two essential ingredients for a Christian fellowship are *feedback* and *follow-up*. Feedback keeps the group dynamic working positively for all participants. Follow-up expresses Christian concern and ministry.

The leader is the one primarily responsible for feedback in the group, but encourage all members to share their feelings about how the group is functioning. Listening is crucial. Listening to one another, as much as any other action, is a means of affirming others. When we listen to another, we are saying, "You are important; I value you." Being sure we understand the meaning of what others say is critical too. We often mishear. "Are you saying _____?" is a good question to check what we heard. If a couple of persons in a group listen and give feedback in this fashion, they can set the mood for the whole group.

Follow-up is a function for everyone. If we listen to what others are saying, we will discover needs and concerns beneath the surface, situations that deserve special prayer and attention. Make notes of these as the group shares. Follow up during the week with a telephone call, a written note of caring and encouragement, maybe a visit. What distinguishes Christian fellowship is caring in action. Ideally, our caring should be so evident that others notice and remark, "My, how those Christians love one another!"

Saint Augustine said, "All our good and all our evil certainly lies in the character of our actions. As they are, so are we; for we are the tree, and they the fruit, and, therefore, they prove what each one is" (*A Year with the Saints*, 227). So follow up each week with others in the group.

SHARING TOGETHER

By this time you are getting to know each other pretty well; persons are beginning to feel safe in the group and perhaps more willing to share. Still there is no place for pressure. The leader, however, can be especially sensitive to those slow to share. Seek to coax them out gently. Every person is a gift to the group. The gift is fully revealed by sharing.

1. Begin your time together by singing a chorus or stanza from a hymn everyone knows, such as "Amazing Grace."
2. Spend eight to ten minutes letting each participant talk about "how I'm doing" with this workbook. What is positive? negative? Are there special meanings? joys? difficulties? Encourage one another.

3. On Day 1 you were asked to recall and record your most vivid experience of feeling and knowing the presence of Christ. Invite a couple of persons to share their experiences.

4. Spend a few minutes discussing Luther's claim, "There is no other way to heaven than taking up the cross of Christ." What does Luther mean? Do you believe him? What does this mean to you? In terms of the "crosses" you may feel you are bearing, what is the difference between them and the cross of Christ? How do your "crosses" connect with his cross?

5. Paul connects being in the faith with the indwelling Christ Jesus. On Day 2, you were asked to list six characteristics of a person who is in the faith, in whom Christ is present. Let group members share their lists. Write them on newsprint or chalkboard. What are the five or six characteristics on which all agree?

6. Invite a couple of persons to share the experience they recorded on Day 3, when they would have collapsed under pressure—been defeated—if they had not had the support of their Christian faith, noting the role the indwelling Christ played in the experience.

7. Spend eight to ten minutes discussing this claim: The presence of God in Jesus Christ is not to be experienced only on occasion; the indwelling Christ is to become the shaping power of our lives. Press each other to talk about how this happens and how Christ is actually shaping your lives.

8. Invite a couple of persons to share the experience they described in their Reflecting and Recording on Day 5—their most recent experience of the working power of Christ brought into the present.

9. Discuss: Why don't we experience the working power of Christ in our lives more often?

10. Spend what time you have left talking about death. How often you think about it? Are you fearful? Do you have a witness to share? Discuss group members' responses to the last question under Reflecting and Recording on page 88.

PRAYING TOGETHER

William Law said the following about spiritual disciplines:

> Reading is good, Hearing is good, Conversation and Meditation are good; but then they are only good at Times and Occasions. . . .But the *Spirit of Prayer* is for all Times, and all Occasions; It is a Lamp that is to be always burning, a Light to be ever shining; every Thing calls for it, every Thing is to be done in it, and governed by it; because it is, and means, and wills nothing else, but the whole Totality of the Soul, not doing this or that, but wholly, incessantly given up to God, to be *where*, and *what*, and *how* he pleases. (*The Works of the Reverend William Law*, vol. 9, 183)

Leader: Read aloud the above excerpt as you begin your prayer time.

1. Invite the group to share special prayer concerns. They may want to refer to the Reflecting and Recording time in Day 6, when they thought about persons for whom they might be Christ. After each concern, ask a volunteer to offer a brief prayer.

2. Invite each member of the group to spend two minutes in quiet prayer for the person whose picture he or she selected in Week 1's group meeting. Ask the person praying to focus on concerns the individual has shared in this meeting.

3. Invite as many as will to offer brief prayers on behalf of persons who have shared special needs in this session.

4. Leader, close this time of prayer by reading the following words of poet Richard C. Trench:

> Lord, what a change within us one short hour
> Spent in Thy presence will avail to make!
> What heavy burdens from our bosoms take!
> What parched grounds refresh us with a shower!
> We kneel, and all around us seems to lower;
> We rise, and all, the distant and the near,
> Stands forth in sunny outline, brave and clear;
> We kneel, how weak! we rise, how full of power! . . .
> (Kepler, *A Journey with the Saints*, 81)

Offer a two- or three-sentence benediction.

WEEK 4

THEY BELIEVED THAT OBEDIENCE WAS ESSENTIAL

DAY
1

The Compass of Our Will

Many Religious [persons who have taken monastic vows] and others have been saints without meditation, but without obedience no one." All the saints would affirm this dogmatic assertion of Francis de Sales. Many things other than meditation might be named as disciplines we may do without, but all would insist that obedience is absolutely essential for spiritual life and growth. The saints took their cue from Jesus.

> *Beware of false prophets, who come to you in sheep's clothing but inwardly are ravenous wolves. You will know them by their fruits. Are grapes gathered from thorns, or figs from thistles? In the same way, every good tree bears good fruit, but the bad tree bears bad fruit. A good tree cannot bear bad fruit, nor can a bad tree bear good fruit. Every tree that does not bear good fruit is cut down and thrown into the fire. Thus you will know them by their fruits.*
>
> *Not everyone who says to me, "Lord, Lord," will enter the kingdom of heaven, but only the one who does the will of my Father in heaven. On that day many will say to me, "Lord, Lord, did we not prophesy in your name, and cast out demons in your name, and do many deeds of power in your name?" Then I will declare to them, "I never knew you; go away from me, you evildoers." (Matthew 7:15-23)*

We do have a right to ask, to seek, and to know the will of God, but once we know it, nothing but obedience will do. The saints sought to arrive at the place in their relationship to Christ that their one longing was to live and walk in a way that would please God and bring glory to God's name. De Sales insisted that attaining this goal is possible.

> *Obedience fits us to receive instruction and guidance about God's will for us.*

> It is a great error of certain souls otherwise good and pious that they believe they cannot retain interior repose in the midst of business and perplexities. Surely there is no commotion greater than that of a vessel in the midst of the sea; yet those on board do not give up the thought of resting and sleeping, and the compass remains always in its place, turning towards the pole. Here is the point: we must be careful to keep the compass of our will in order, that it may never turn elsewhere than to the pole of the divine pleasure. (*A Year with the Saints*, 249)

But how do we know God's will? How do we keep the compass of our will in order? The first and primary condition is complete surrender to obedience, which fits us to receive instruction and guidance about God's will for us. There are three seeds which, when planted in the soil of obedience, produce the fruit of God's will in our lives: (1) scripture study, (2) conferencing—deliberately and honestly sharing with godly persons for edification and discernment of God's will and guidance, and (3) divine conviction wrought by the Holy Spirit. Let's look at these.

God has a general will for all of God's people, which we can, to a marked degree, learn from the Bible. The apostle Paul makes it clear in his Second Letter to Timothy: "All scripture is inspired by God and is useful for teaching, for reproof, for correction, and for training in righteousness, so that everyone who belongs to God may be proficient, equipped for every good work" (2 Tim. 3:16-17).

The New International Version translates verse 16 as, "All Scripture is God-breathed." Christians believe the Bible is God's Word. The Bible contains everything we need for salvation; for growth and discipleship; for teaching, correction, and training in righteousness. Scripture has everything we need to be equipped for every good work.

In the divine school of obedience, there is only one textbook. Jesus is our model. Though he communicated directly with the Father, he still depended on scripture. He used it to teach and to convince others. He also needed it and used it for his own spiritual life and guidance. Throughout his public life, Jesus lived by the Word of God. He conquered Satan with the sword of the Spirit, saying, "It is written." The consciousness with which Jesus opened his public preaching of the gospel was shaped by scripture: "The Spirit of the Lord is upon me . . . that the scripture might be fulfilled" (Luke 4:18; John 19:36); this understanding was the light in which Christ accepted his suffering and gave himself to the cross. When he met with his disciples after his death and resurrection, he taught them "the things about himself in all the scriptures." In scripture Jesus found God's plan. He gave himself to fulfill it, and he used God's Word for his continual teaching.

Andrew Murray reminds us that

> By this we know the disposition in which we are to come to the Bible—with the simple desire to find there God's will concerning us and to do it. Scripture was not written to increase our knowledge but to guide our conduct—"that the man of God may be perfect, thoroughly furnished *unto all good works.*" "If any man will *do,* he shall know." Learn from Christ to consider all there is in Scripture of the revelation of God. His love and His counsel, as simply auxiliary to God's great end: that the man of God may be fitted to do His will as it is done in heaven, and that man may be restored to that perfect obedience on which God's heart is set, where alone lies blessedness. (*The Believer's Secret of Obedience,* 37)

The second resource for knowing God's will is *Christian conferencing.* Jesus promised that where two or three are gathered in his name, he will be present (Matt. 18:20). Conferencing with other godly persons who love Jesus, who want God's will for their lives and for us, is a trustful and dependable way to seek God's will.

I based one of the most dramatic moves in my life on accepting God's will as a result of Christian conferencing. My primary calling is clear: to be a pastor/preacher. I was exercising this vocation with great joy, fruitful response, deep meaning, and continual spiritual growth as senior minister of a large congregation. People were being converted, healed, and coming to maturity in Christ. Our church's outreach ministries to the "least of these" and to non-Christians were expanding. My wife and I could not have been happier. We had served that congregation for twelve years and intended to stay until retirement.

Then came the call to the presidency of Asbury Theological Seminary. For months I would not even consider the possibility, refusing even to talk with the search committee. The Holy Spirit impressed upon my wife the notion that I should at least consider what seemed to be a clear call through the committee. So we did—but without clarity on my part. In desperation, really, I began a conferencing process with godly persons I loved and trusted, some with whom I had shared my Christian walk for twenty-five years. I knew they loved God. I was certain they loved me and wanted God's best for me.

Through them I discerned God's will. Since making the decision to accept the seminary presidency seven years ago, I've had little doubt (and that has lasted only for brief periods) that I was in the center of God's will. Over and over again my calling to this ministry has been confirmed.

As stated earlier, God has a general will for all believers that we can, to a large degree, learn from the Bible. There is, however, a special individual application of God's will concerning each of us personally. This comes to us only through the Holy Spirit. On these occasions, the Holy Spirit plants solidly in our being certain convictions about God's will. We dare not quench the Spirit. Yet, it is altogether in keeping with God's direction that we test these convictions with scripture and Christian conferencing. Again, however, once we know God's will, nothing but obedience will do.

REFLECTING AND RECORDING

Recall and record here your clearest recollection of knowing and obeying God's will.

Spend some time reflecting on three common ways to discern God's will: through scripture, Christian conferencing, and the direct intervention of the Holy Spirit. How have you used these resources?

If you were wrestling with a decision, confused about direction, uncertain about God's leading, name the three or four people you would trust most for conferencing with you, seeking to discern God's will.

DURING THE DAY

Call or write one or two of the persons named above, telling them about your workbook venture, this exercise, and the fact you would feel comfortable turning to them for guidance in seeking God's will.

In Week 3 I introduced a form of praying called *ejaculatory prayer*. It is a brief sentence prayer used frequently throughout the day as an act of reminder and connection—punctuating our daily rounds with a conscious acknowledgment of God.

Use this commitment throughout this week as an ejaculatory prayer:

God's will: nothing more, nothing less, nothing else.

DAY
2

Obedience As Abandonment

As indicated yesterday, most of the saints concluded that obedience is a summary of perfection and of the entire Christian life. They were convinced that obedience was essential for their life and growth. The cultivation of virtue depended upon obedience.

Obedience means abandoning oneself to God. Jean-Pierre de Caussade wrote to someone who depended upon his spiritual guidance that abandonment to God "is, of all practices, the most divine."

> Your way of acting in times of trouble and distress gives me great pleasure. To be submissive, to abandon yourself entirely without reserve, to be content with being discontented for as long as God wills or permits, will make you advance more in one day than you would in a hundred days spent in sweetness and consolation.

Your total abandonment to God, practised in a spirit of confidence, and of union with Jesus Christ doing always the will of his Father, is, of all practices, the most divine. (*The Joy of the Saints*, 101)

What a simple yet profound expression of abandonment: "to be content with being discontented for as long as God wills or permits." A friend of mind, Norman Neaves, is pastor of The Church of the Servant in Oklahoma City. He tells about a member of his congregation who wrote him a letter, enclosing with the letter a reflection she had written at 2:47 A.M. The woman was upset and troubled and couldn't sleep, so she poured out her feelings in writing. Here is what she wrote:

> Which state of grief is this? Or is it grief at all? Just when I experience a little consistency in my new life alone, the next rug I step on is pulled out from under me. Is this all a part of adjusting, or am I being humbled for some greater purpose? My faith is not strong enough to stand on. But my instinct to survive this lonely stretch of my life is so compelling that I am able to leave the security of my past and go on. Why do my thoughts wake me up in the night, screaming out for paper and pen? There are so few answers, I've found. It would be nice to have the comfort back, but not at the expense of my very own soul. So what can I do? Well, I think I will continue to feel my way back through the dark, feeding my faith, until someday the lights come on again. ("Living Down in the Valley," sermon preached December 2, 1990)

Do this woman's words remind you of the apostle Paul?

> *Rejoice in the Lord always; again I will say, Rejoice. Let your gentleness be known to everyone. The Lord is near. Do not worry about anything, but in everything by prayer and supplication with thanksgiving let your requests be made known to God. And the peace of God, which surpasses all understanding, will guard your hearts and your minds in Christ Jesus. . . .*
>
> *I rejoice in the Lord greatly that now at last you have revived your concern for me; indeed, you were concerned for me, but had no opportunity to show it. Not that I am referring to being in need; for I have learned to be content with whatever I have. I know what it is to have little, and I know what it is to have plenty. In any and all circumstances I have learned the secret of being well-fed and of going hungry, of having plenty and of being in need. I can do all things through him who strengthens me. (Philippians 4:4-7, 10-13)*

Our spiritual formation is a dynamic process, a growing willingness, or even a willingness to be made willing, to say yes to God each day in every way possible—no matter what the circumstances. The more we pay attention to God, the more aware we will become of the yet-to-be redeemed areas of our life—and the more we will need to abandon ourselves to the transforming power of the indwelling Christ.

Jesus made clear how essential abandonment is when he taught us to pray, "Your will be done" (Matt. 6:10). There are two common ways we pray this prayer: (1) Sometimes we wrestle against God. We receive intimations of something God wants us to do, some call—and we wrestle against God because we are not sure we want to respond. (2) Or, we come face-to-face with an issue of God's justice and holiness—and we resist. We don't want to do it.

We pray "Your will be done" as a declaration of submission in which we confess that we do not know what is best.

But we also experience another kind of wrestling. It is not wrestling against God; it's a matter of wrestling with God against that which opposes God's will. It really becomes a matter of spiritual warfare. We sense that there are forces within our world that oppose God's will: sickness, hate, meanness, narrowness of spirit, fear, lethargy, prejudice, and ill will. I speak of our warfare against the forces of darkness—we wrestle against Satan himself. We set ourselves against all such forces and to them we cry, "God's will be done on earth as it is in heaven."

Then there is another way we pray "Your will be done." We abandon ourselves completely to God's will. We pray "Your will be done" as a declaration of submission in which we confess that we do not know what is best, but we want God's will. We struggle; we wrestle; we stay in God's presence until our hearts are made tender and we're ready to trust God and surrender our will to the Divine.

My favorite story about Lourdes, the famous place of healing in France, concerns an old priest who was asked one time by a newspaper reporter to describe the most impressive miracle he'd ever seen there. The reporter expected him to talk about the amazing recovery of someone who had come to Lourdes ill and walked away well. "Not at all," the old priest said, "if you want to know the greatest miracle that I have ever seen at Lourdes, it is the look of radiant resignation on the face of those who turn away unhealed!" Abandonment is declaring "Your will be done" in an attitude of submission, confessing that all we want is God's will—because we know that it is best for us.

REFLECTING AND RECORDING

Recall an experience from the past six months when either you wrestled against God, or you wrestled with the Almighty against something that opposed God's will. Record that experience here.

Write your prayer of abandonment, your expression of submission—"Your will be done."

DURING THE DAY

Continue to use the ejaculatory prayer, "God's will: nothing more, nothing less, nothing else."

DAY
3

Obedience and Trust

An indisputable connection exists between loving God and obeying God. The Gospel of John expresses it clearly:

> *"If you love me, you will keep my commandments. And I will ask the Father, and he will give you another Advocate, to be with you forever. This is the Spirit of truth, whom the world cannot receive, because it neither sees him nor knows him. You know him, because he abides with you, and he will be in you.*
>
> *I will not leave you orphaned; I am coming to you. In a little while the world will no longer see me, but you will see me; because I live, you also will live. On that day you will know that I am in my Father, and you in me, and I in you. They who have my commandments and keep them are those who love me; and those who love me will be loved by my Father, and I will love them and reveal myself to them." (John 14:15-21)*

What a simple yet powerful word, and what a gracious place Jesus gives to obedience. Obedience is possible only to a loving heart, yet it makes possible what God wants to give us—God's indwelling through Jesus Christ and the Holy Spirit—God's amazing love.

In the next chapter of his Gospel, following this promise of the Holy Spirit, John records Jesus' teaching metaphor of the vine and the branches. Most Christians know that passage very well, but how often do we ask *how* we are to abide continually in Christ? We seem to think that more Bible study would make that possible, or more prayer, or more regular attendance at worship or receiving Communion, or greater faith. To be sure, all of that is a part of abiding, but haven't we overlooked the simple truth that Jesus is teaching? "If you keep my commandments, you will abide in my love." He confirms the truth out of his own life, giving it divine sanction, "just as I have kept my Father's commandments and abide in his love." For Jesus, and for us, the only way to abide in God's love is to keep God's commandments.

When we trust God, we can depend on divine support and empowerment to be able to do God's will.

Just as there is a permanent connection between loving God and obeying God, likewise there is a connection between loving and obeying God and trusting him. In his book *The Prayer of Jabez*, Bruce Wilkinson tells a beautiful story about trust—a child trusting his father.

> One day when our kids were preschoolers, Darlene and I found ourselves with them at a large city park in southern California. It was the kind of park that makes a grown man wish he were a kid again. It had swings, monkey bars, and seesaws, but what was most enticing were the slides—not just one slide, but three—from small, to medium, to enormous. David, who was five at the time, took off like a shot for the small slide.
>
> "Why don't you go down with him?" Darlene suggested.
>
> But I had another idea. "Let's wait and see what happens," I said. So we relaxed on a nearby bench and watched. David clambered happily to the top of the smallest slide. He waved over at us with a big smile, then whizzed down.
>
> Without hesitation he moved over to the medium-sized slide. He had climbed halfway up the ladder when he turned and looked at me. I looked away. He pondered his options for a moment, then carefully backed down one step at a time.
>
> "Honey, you ought to go help him out," my wife said.
>
> "Not yet," I replied, hoping the twinkle in my eye would reassure her that I wasn't just being careless.
>
> David spent a few minutes at the bottom of the middle slide watching other kids climb up, whiz down, and run around to do it again. Finally his little mind was made up. He could do it. He climbed up . . . and slid down. Three times, in fact, without even looking at us.
>
> Then we watched him turn and head toward the highest slide. Now Darlene was getting anxious. "Bruce, I don't think he should do that by himself. Do you?"
>
> "No," I replied as calmly as possible. "But I don't think he will. Let's see what he does."
>
> When David reached the bottom of the giant slide, he turned and called out, "Daddy!" But I glanced away again, pretending I couldn't hear him.
>
> He peered up the ladder. In his young imagination, it must have reached to the clouds. He watched a teenage boy go hurtling down the slide. Then, against all odds, he decided to try. Step-by-step, hand over hand, he inched up the ladder. He hadn't reached a third of the way when he froze.
>
> By this time, the teenager was coming up behind him and yelled at him to get going. But David couldn't. He couldn't go up or down. He had reached the point of certain failure.

I rushed over. "Are you okay, son?" I asked from the bottom of the ladder. He looked down at me, shaken but clinging to that ladder with steely determination. And I could tell he had a question ready.

"Dad, will you come down the slide with me?" he asked. The teenager was losing patience, but I wasn't about to let the moment go.

"Why, son?" I asked, peering up into his little face.

"I can't do it without you, Dad," he said, trembling. "It's too big for me!"

I stretched as high as I could to reach him and lifted him into my arms. Then we climbed that long ladder up to the clouds together. At the top, I put my son between my legs and wrapped my arms around him. Then we went zipping down the slide together, laughing all the way. (*The Prayer of Jabez,* 49–52)

This story illustrates what loving and obeying God is like. When we trust God, we can abandon ourselves to God and depend on divine support and empowerment to be able to do God's will—whatever it may be. Francis de Sales makes a clear argument for abandonment:

> Some torment themselves in seeking means to discover the art of loving God, and do not know—poor creatures—that there is no art or means of loving Him but to love Him—that is, to begin to practice those things which are pleasing to Him. (*A Year with the Saints,* 312)

De Sales tells a story about one he calls Saint Elizabeth, the daughter of Alexander II, king of Hungary during the early thirteenth century. The story gives evidence of her abandonment to God.

> When the news of her husband's death in the war was brought to St. Elizabeth, she instantly raised her heart to God and said: "O Lord, Thou knowest well that I preferred his presence to all the delights of the world! But since it has pleased Thee to take him from me, I assent so fully to Thy holy will, that if I could bring him back by plucking out a single hair from my head, I would not do it, except at Thy will!" (*A Year with the Saints,* 343)

The lessons from the saints are clear:

1. Obedience means loving God enough to practice those attitudes and actions that you know will please God.

2. Obedience means trusting God enough to submit yourself to God's will even in what is most repugnant to you.

Reflecting and Recording

In the space beside the quotation, put de Sales's guidance in your own words.

Can you recall an occasion when God led you to do something that, on the surface and in the beginning, was repugnant? Make some notes here.

Anticipate the next twenty-four hours. Make a list of possible actions or ways of relating to persons around you that you know will please God.

DURING THE DAY

Practice doing those things you know will please God. Continue using the following as an ejaculatory prayer:

God's will: nothing more, nothing less, nothing else.

DAY
4

Doing God's Will Begets
Knowing More of God's Will

On Day 1 of this week we considered ways to discover God's will: through scripture, Christian conferencing, and conviction by the Holy Spirit. Today we consider another truth: Doing God's will begets knowing more of God's will.

Obedience requires that we do God's will as far we know it, but it also involves a commitment to do what the Holy Spirit reveals. The more we practice doing God's will, the more easily we discover God's will.

Doing is a condition for knowing. As this is true with every scholar in the discipline she studies, every apprentice with his trade, every artist and every athlete, so it is true in the spiritual realm. If our hearts are set on obedience, if we are surrendered to doing God's will, then we will know God's will; we will know more and more what God has to teach us.

This obedience is expressed in a practical pattern we can cultivate.

1. We must acknowledge our ignorance, our inability to know and do God's will by our own efforts. Scripture promises, "He leads the humble in what is right, / and teaches the humble his way" (Ps. 25:9). To be meek or humble means to have a teachable spirit.

2. We must cultivate our faith that God will give us wisdom of the heart. Head knowledge, until it becomes heart knowledge, has no power. God works in our hearts to give us life and light deeper than all our thoughts. Only heart knowledge makes joyful obedience possible. Paul says that heart obedience leads to righteousness.

   What then? Should we sin because we are not under law but under grace? By no means! Do you not know that if you present yourselves to anyone as obedient slaves, you are slaves of the one whom you obey, either of sin, which leads to death, or of obedience, which leads to righteousness? But thanks be to God that you, having once been slaves of sin, have become obedient from the heart to the form of teaching to which you were entrusted, and that you, having been set free from sin, have become slaves of righteousness. (Romans 6:15-18)

   We must count on God to make known what God wants us to do, and we must expect it with certainty.

3. Our ongoing prayer must be for God to give us the convincing light of the Holy Spirit. This is connected with what we discussed about divine conviction in Day 1 of

this week. We must bring everything into the light of God's Word and allow the Holy Spirit to explain and apply, to let us know that what we are doing pleases God.

Fénelon talks about how faithfulness and obedience lead to freedom and joy.

It appears to me that true fidelity consists in obeying God in everything, and following the light that points out our duty, and His spirit that prompts us to do it; with the desire of pleasing Him, without debating about great or little sins, about imperfections or unfaithfulness; for though there may be a difference in fact, to the soul that is determined to do *all* His will there is none. It is in this sense that the Apostle says that the law is not for the upright; the law constrains, menaces, if I may so speak, tyrannizes over us, enslaves us. But there is a superior law that raises us above all this and introduces us into the true liberty of the children of God. This ever desires to do all that it can to please its Father in heaven, according to the excellent instructions of St. Augustine. Love God and then do all you can. To this sincere desire to do the will of God we must add a cheerful spirit that is not overcome when it has failed, but begins again and again to do better, hoping always to the very end to be able to do it; bearing with its own involuntary weakness, as God bears with it; waiting with patience for the moment when it shall be delivered from it; going straight on in singleness of heart, according to the strength that it can command; losing no time by looking back, nor making useless reflections upon its falls, which can only embarrass and retard its progress. The first sight of our little failures should humble us, but then we must press on, not judging ourselves with a Judaical rigor, not regarding God as a spy who watches for our least offence, or as an enemy who places snares in our path, but as a father who loves and wishes to save us; trusting in His goodness, invoking His blessing, and doubting all other support; this is true liberty. (*Selections from the Writings of François Fénelon*, 27–28)

Fénelon gives guidance for continuing in God's will.

- True fidelity consists in obeying God in everything.

- To this sincere desire to do the will of God, we must add a cheerful spirit that is not overcome when it has failed.

- [Go] straight on in singleness of heart, according to the strength that it can command.

- Regard God . . . as a Father who loves and wishes to save us, trusting in His goodness, invoking His blessing.

REFLECTING AND RECORDING

Examine your own pattern of daily living in light of Fénelon's guidance. In the space beside his four instructions, record your reflections. You may note your failure in a particular area or register a commitment you want to make.

DURING THE DAY

As you go through this day, remember Fénelon's advice about not making "useless reflections" about your failures. Remember to press on, trusting in God's guidance and invoking God's blessing. Keep a cheerful spirit, and try again!

Continue praying:

God's will: nothing more, nothing less, nothing else.

DAY
5

Obedience in Little Things

My child, do not forget my teaching,
but let your heart keep my commandments;
for length of days and years of life
and abundant welfare they will give you.

Do not let loyalty and faithfulness forsake you;
bind them around your neck,
write them on the tablet of your heart.
So you will find favor and good repute
in the sight of God and of people.

Trust in the Lord with all your heart,
and do not rely on your own insight.
In all your ways acknowledge him,
and he will make straight your paths. (Proverbs 3:1-6)

I don't believe I have read the writings of any saint who didn't argue that the secret of spiritual growth is obedience to God in little things. Fénelon talked a great deal about faithfulness in little things being an indication of our love for God. In one passage he contrasted this with our inclination to think of great sacrifices as the heart of Christian devotion.

> Great virtues are rare; the opportunities for exercising them occur but seldom. When they present themselves we have been prepared beforehand, and we are excited by the very sacrifices we are making; we are sustained either by the brilliance of our actions in the eyes of others, or by our own satisfaction in making so unusual an effort. But the opportunities for little sacrifices are unforeseen; they occur hourly; they constantly oblige us to struggle with our pride, with

our indolence, with our hastiness or our discontent. If we would be truly faithful, nature can have no breathing time; she must die to all her own desires. People would far rather offer to God certain great sacrifices, however painful, provided they might still, in all lesser matters, follow their own tastes and inclinations. Nevertheless, it is by faithfulness in little things that the spirit of love and holiness is proved, and by which it can be distinguished from mere natural impulses. (*Christian Counsels*, 37–38)

Francis de Sales contended that great works are not always possible, "but every moment we may do little ones excellently, that is, with great love."

I beg you to remark the saint who gives a cup of water for God's sake to a poor thirsty traveller; he seems to do a small thing; but the intention, the sweetness, the love with which he animates his action, is so excellent that it turns this simple water into the water of life, and of eternal life. Bees gather honey from the lily, the iris, and the rose; but they get as much booty from the little minute rosemary flowers and thyme; they not only draw more honey from these, but even better honey, because in these little vessels the honey being more closely locked up is much better preserved. Truly in small and insignificant exercises of devotion charity [love] is practiced not only more frequently, but also as a rule more humbly too, and consequently more holily and usefully. Those condescensions to the humours of others, that bearing with the troublesome actions and ways of our neighbour, those victories over our own tempers and passions; . . . all this is more profitable to our souls than we can conceive, if heavenly love only have the management of them. (Baillie, *A Diary of Readings*, 122)

De Sales also warned against being preoccupied with how we might perform great deeds or make big sacrifices in the future, thus avoiding the burden of present deeds and sacrifices.

There are souls that form great projects of doing excellent services for our Lord by eminent deeds and extraordinary sufferings, but deeds and sufferings of which there is no present opportunity, and perhaps never will be, and upon this imagine that they have done a great matter in love, in which they are very often deceived—in this way, that embracing in desire what seems to them great future crosses, they studiously avoid the burden of such as are present, which are less. Is it not a great temptation to be so valiant in imagination and so cowardly in execution? Ah, God keep us from these imaginary fervours which very often breed in the bottom of our hearts a vain and secret self-esteem! Great works do not always lie in our way, but every moment we may do little ones excellently, that is, with great love. (*A Diary of Readings*, 122)

Being obedient in little things turns us from our wrong to God's right. As we yield ourselves to God inch by inch, we become the persons God wants us to be.

Yesterday I referred to some verses from the sixth chapter of Romans, expressing the idea that heart obedience leads to righteousness. Romans 6 is a meaning-packed section of scripture, powerful in its description of the radical transformation of Christian conversion. We die to our old sin nature and come alive to God. It's not an easy chapter in the Bible to read and understand because Paul's image of slavery is so alien to our experience. The New Living Translation helps us.

So you should consider yourselves dead to sin and able to live for the glory of God through Christ Jesus.

Do not let sin control the way you live; do not give in to its lustful desires. Do not let any part of your body become a tool of wickedness, to be used for sinning. Instead, give yourselves completely to God since you have been given new life. And use your whole body as a tool to do what is right for the glory of God.

Sin is no longer your master, for you are no longer subject to the law, which enslaves you to sin. Instead, you are free by God's grace.

So since God's grace has set us free from the law, does this mean we can go on sinning? Of course not! Don't you realize that whatever you choose to obey becomes your master? You can choose sin, which leads to death, or you can choose to obey God and receive his approval. Thank God! Once you were slaves of sin, but now you have obeyed with all your heart the new teaching God has given you. Now you are free from sin, your old master, and you have become slaves to your new master, righteousness.

I speak this way, using the illustration of slaves and masters, because it is easy to understand. Before, you let yourselves be slaves of impurity and lawlessness. Now you must choose to be slaves of righteousness so that you will become holy.

In those days, when you were slaves of sin, you weren't concerned with doing what was right. And what was the result? It was not good, since now you are ashamed of the things you used to do, things that end in eternal doom. But now you are free from the power of sin and have become slaves of God. Now you do those things that lead to holiness and result in eternal life. For the wages of sin is death, but the free gift of God is eternal life through Christ Jesus our Lord. (Romans 6:11-23, NLT)

Paul was telling the Roman Christians that before they were Christians they were slaves to a master called sin. They had no choice, no other option. But now, because Christ paid the price to set them free, they have a completely new set of options for their behavior.

In every situation, no matter how frustrating, threatening, or painful, we can choose our response. Our new master—"righteousness through Christ"—doesn't hold us in any chains; rather, we are "bound by love." We are still free to choose which master we want to obey. How often has it happened: we go back to our old master—sin—and when we realize what we have done, we say, "I wasn't myself"? We are never so right. We are not the persons God knows we can be.

> *As we yield ourselves to God inch by inch, we become the persons God wants us to be.*

Learning to submit to Christ's rule in our lives is the process of being a Christian, and that's the reason daily obedience—obedience in little things—is so important. Christian sanctification—living out the Christian life—is a matter of making daily choices with the help of the Holy Spirit.

REFLECTING AND RECORDING

Fénelon reminds us that while the world judges by appearance, God looks much deeper. God desires pure intentions, true docility, and sincere self-renunciation. Look back over your relationships, attitudes, and actions during the past five or six days. Would God judge your intentions as pure?

Docility is not a word I commonly use. Seldom do we hear a person described as docile, and when we do, it is hardly a positive affirmation. Some would use *weak-kneed* as a synonym for *docile*. Not so with the saints. True docility, as Fénelon used the term, meant humility, meekness, or submissiveness. A contemporary meaning would be "easily taught, led, or managed."

Again, reflect on your relationships, attitudes, and actions of the past five or six days. To what degree could true docility describe your character?

Could anything in your life during the past five or six days be characterized as self-renunciation?

Read again the last sentence of the second de Sales passage on page 108.

The condition required for our obedience in little things to be "profitable to our souls" is "if heavenly love only have the management of them." Write a brief prayer, committing yourself to allow heavenly love to manage the daily routine of your life.

DURING THE DAY

See how many little things you can do excellently today, that is, with great love.

Continue paying attention to the slightest hint of God's presence, your desire to be with God, and your use of the ejaculatory prayer: "God's will: nothing more, nothing less, nothing else."

DAY
6

A Will to Do God's Will

In the days of his flesh, Jesus offered up prayers and supplications, with loud cries and tears, to the one who was able to save him from death, and he was heard because of his reverent submission. Although he was a Son, he learned obedience through what he suffered; and having been made perfect, he became the source of eternal salvation for all who obey him, having been designated by God a high priest according to the order of Melchizedek. (Hebrews 5:7-10)

Francis de Sales captures a world of truth in two sentences:

To lose ourselves in God is simply to give up our own will to Him. When a soul can say truly, "Lord, I have no other will than Thine," it is truly lost in God, and united to Him. (*A Year with the Saints*, 346)

Yesterday we considered the topic of being faithful and obedient in little things. We gave attention to Paul's imagery of our having been slaves, but now we are free from our old sinful nature. The dynamic of this war between our two natures is demonstrated in a Peanuts cartoon. Lucy draws a picture of a heart, half-black and half-white. She tells Linus that this is a picture of the human heart, "One side is filled with hate and the other side is filled with love. These are the two forces which are constantly at war with each other," she explains. We know exactly how Linus feels as he grabs his middle and gulps, "I think I know just what you mean—I can feel them fighting!" (Ridenour, *I'm a Good Man, But . . .*, 36).

The struggle within us may not be a struggle between love and hate, but there is a struggle— a struggle between our will and God's will, a struggle of obedience. Sometimes the best we can do is to *will to do God's will.*

The choices are not clear, the path is uncertain.

The issues are confused.

Relationships are muddled.

Our actions may cause others pain.

The short-term gain seems clear, but the long-term implications could be destructive.

Not being clear and certain, we retain a solid resolution: We will to do God's will. This resolution is given perspective and empowered, according to Francis de Sales, by our loving God's will. He outlines a scale of that love.

To love God's will when all goes well is to love aright, as long as we really do love his will and not the comfortable effects of it. Nevertheless, it is a love that knows no opposition, no reluctance, no effort: surely anyone would love a will so deserving of love, so actively portrayed. To love God's will in his commandments, counsels, inspirations, is a stage higher, much more perfect. This leads us to give up and forgo our own wills, our own desires, so that we deprive ourselves of pleasure up to a point. To love suffering and distress out of love for God is charity's highest degree. There is nothing, then, to attract us but God's will; it goes very much against the grain of our nature; it leads to more than giving up pleasure—we actually choose toil and trouble. (De Sales, *The Love of God: A Treatise*, 360)

Why was it necessary for Christ, the perfect Son of God, to learn obedience? Hebrews 5:7-10 explains that he learned obedience by the things he suffered in order to become "the source of eternal salvation for all who obey him." In *The Believer's Secret of Obedience*, Andrew Murray writes a clear commentary on this Hebrews passage.

Suffering is unnatural to us, and therefore calls for the surrender of our will. Christ needed suffering to learn to obey through it and give up His will to the Father at any cost. He needed to learn obedience so that as our great High Priest He might be made perfect. He learned obedience. He became obedient unto death that He might become the author of our salvation. He became the author of salvation *through obedience* that He might save those *"who obey Him."* As obedience was with Him absolutely necessary to procure salvation, so with us it is absolutely necessary to inherit it. The very essence of salvation is obedience to God. Christ as the obedient One saves us as His obedient ones. Whether in His suffering on earth or in His glory in heaven, whether in himself or in us, obedience is what the heart of Christ is set upon. (*The Believer's Secret of Obedience*, 33–34)

So we return to our theme: Sometimes the best we can do is to will to do God's will. When we will to do God's will, we are given perspective and empowered by loving God's will. Though it was a radical concept for his time, Jesus taught that obedience is learned through suffering. It is no wonder, then, that De Sales and other saints insist that loving suffering and/or afflictions is the ultimate expression of loving God's will.

REFLECTING AND RECORDING

De Sales says that loving God's will in God's commandments, counsel, and inspiration is a second stage of God's love—it is higher than loving God's will when all goes well, but not on the level of loving and finding God's will in suffering. Reread the de Sales excerpt above.

Recall an occasion in the past three or four months when you were obedient to God—to God's commandments, counsels, and inspirations—a time you forsook your own desires and will. Record that experience in the following space:

Recall an experience when you accepted suffering and found in it God's presence and guidance. Record that incident here.

DURING THE DAY

On the previous days of this week, you were asked to use an ejaculatory prayer. On Days 4 and 5 you were asked to pay attention to and respond to the notion that "the moment you long for inward prayer is enough to bring you into God's presence." Putting those dynamics together throughout this day, use this ejaculatory prayer:

Lord, I have no other will than thine.

DAY
7

Kiss the Crosses

Therefore, since we are surrounded by so great a cloud of witnesses, let us also lay aside every weight and the sin that clings so closely, and let us run with perseverance the race that is set before us, looking to Jesus the pioneer and perfecter of our faith, who for the sake of the joy that was set before him endured the cross, disregarding its shame, and has taken his seat at the right hand of the throne of God.

Consider him who endured such hostility against himself from sinners, so that you may not grow weary or lose heart. In your struggle against sin you have not yet resisted to the point of shedding your blood. And you have forgotten the exhortation that addresses you as children—

"My child, do not regard lightly the discipline
of the Lord,
or lose heart when you are punished by him;
for the Lord disciplines those whom he loves,
and chastises every child whom he accepts."

Endure trials for the sake of discipline. God is treating you as children; for what child is there whom a parent does not discipline? If you do not have that discipline in which all children share, then you are illegitimate and not his children. Moreover, we had human parents to discipline us, and we respected them. Should we not be even more willing to be subject to the Father of spirits and live? For they disciplined us for a short time as seemed best to them, but he disciplines us for our good, in order that we may share his holiness. Now, discipline always seems painful rather than pleasant at the time, but later it yields the peaceful fruit of righteousness to those who have been trained by it. (Hebrews 12:1-11)

The secret of obedience is a close personal relationship with God. Without abiding fellowship with the Almighty, all our attempts at obedience will fail. The psalmist reiterated this truth throughout Psalm 119:

Happy are those who keep his decrees, / who seek him with their whole heart (v. 2).
With my whole heart I seek you; / do not let me stray from your commandments (v. 10).
I run the way of your commandments, for you enlarge my understanding (v. 32).
I shall walk at liberty, / for I have sought your precepts (v. 45).
I remember your name in the night, O Lord, / and keep your law (v. 55).
The Lord is my portion; / I promise to keep your words (v. 57).
You are good and do good; / teach me your statutes (v. 68).
Let your mercy come to me, that I may live; / for your law is my delight (v. 77).
If your law had not been my delight, / I would have perished in my misery (v. 92).
Your word is a lamp to my feet / and a light to my path (v. 105).
Your promise is well tried, / and your servant loves it (v. 140).

Great peace have those who love your law; / nothing can make them stumble (v. 165).
Let me live that I may praise you, / and let your ordinances help me (v. 175).

Since the time of the psalmist, we have Jesus Christ's abiding presence, which enables us to obey God.

Yesterday, we connected loving and obeying God with suffering. Jesus made the connection clear. The Book of Hebrews urges us to look to Jesus, "the pioneer and perfecter of our faith, who for the sake of the joy that was set before him endured the cross, disregarding its shame, and has taken his seat at the right hand of the throne of God" (12:2).

> *Kiss frequently the crosses which the Lord sends you.*
>
> —*Francis de Sales*

The Book of Hebrews uses the model of Jesus and the way he endured the cross to call us to view and experience hardship as discipline, concluding that "Now, discipline always seems painful rather than pleasant at the time, but later it yields the peaceful fruit of righteousness to those who have been trained by it" (12:11).

Francis de Sales might have been remembering this passage when he wrote:

Kiss frequently the crosses which the Lord sends you, and with all your heart, without regarding of what sort they may be; for the more vile and mean they are, the more they deserve their name. The merit of crosses does not consist in their weight, but in the manner in which they are borne. It may show much greater virtue to bear a cross of straw than a very hard and heavy one, because the light ones are also the most hidden and condemned, and therefore least comfortable to our inclination, which always seeks what is showy. (*A Year with the Saints*, 115)

What kind of image is that—"Kiss frequently the crosses which the Lord sends you"? Can you get beyond the strangeness of the notion and really hear what de Sales is teaching? We are to welcome the suffering that comes into our lives as an invitation to love and trust God more.

And what a great truth this statement contains: "The merit of crosses does not consist in their weight, but in the manner in which they are borne." François Fénelon also speaks to this truth about enduring difficult situations:

God has all sorts of circumstances to bring you the cross, and they all accomplish His purpose. He may even join physical weakness to your emotional and spiritual suffering. Of course the world may not see you dealing with the cross—they think you are just touchy or prone to fits of nervous exhaustion. So while you are bent double under the hidden work of the cross, onlookers often envy your apparent good fortune.

What do you say to God when you are under the work of the cross? You need not say a lot to Him, or even think of Him much. He sees your suffering, and your willingness to submit. With people you love you do not need to continually say, "I love you with all my heart." Even if you do not think about how much you love Him, you still love God every bit as much. True love is deep down in the spirit—simple, peaceful, and silent.

How do you bear suffering? Silently before God. Do not disturb yourself by trying to manufacture an artificial sense of God's presence. Slowly you will learn that all the troubles in your life—your job, your health, and your inward failings—are really cures to the poison of your old nature. Learn to bear these sufferings in patience and meekness. (*The Seeking Heart*, 23)

We have a student at our seminary who is a paraplegic. He has little use of his hands and arms and no use of his legs. He is brilliant. He has cultivated his memory, knowledge, use of language, and imagination and has become a powerful communicator. In a recent Thanksgiving service we had a love feast, a celebration of God's love and goodness through testimony and the sharing of bread and water. I wish you could have heard his testimony. No reference to his disability. No hint of self-pity. Just an eloquent expression of gratitude for the hospitality of our students, a Thanksgiving meal he had eaten with a student couple, and the fact that they had served him mashed potatoes and gravy.

The mashed potatoes and gravy were important to his testimony. His mother always made that dish a part of any special meal she fixed for him. She had been dead now for two years, and he missed her desperately. The warmth and hospitality of that student couple, and now their serving him mashed potatoes and gravy, symbolized for Sam the love and goodness of God in his life. The manner in which Sam bears his "cross" challenges our community. His patient endurance is an expression of Sam's obedience and has made him a deeply spiritual person with a sensitive soul.

REFLECTING AND RECORDING

Are you bearing some cross that you need to kiss? Name that cross, and write a prayer offering your response to it.

Think of two or three persons who are bearing crosses. Write their names on the lines below:

_____   _____   _____

Now make some notes about these people and their crosses. How do they bear them? Quietly? Do they talk about them? Do they try to attract attention or gain pity from others? Do they reflect love and obedience? Have their crosses made them better? empathetic? calloused? tender?

Have you or someone you know allowed a cross to cure "the poison of your old nature"? Make some notes here.

DURING THE DAY

Continue using the ejaculatory prayer "Lord, I have no other will than thine."

Group Meeting for Week 4

INTRODUCTION

Paul advised the Philippians, "Let your conversation be as it becometh the gospel of Christ" (Phil. 1:27, KJV). Most of us may not have yet seen the dynamic potential of the kind of conversation to which Paul calls the Philippians. Life is found in communion with God and also in conversation with others.

Speaking and listening with the sort of deep meaning that energizes us is not easy. All of us have experiences that are not easy to talk about. Therefore, listening and responding to what we hear is important. To really listen to another person, and to reflect back to him/her what you thought he/she said, helps that person to think clearly and gain perspective. Listening, then, is an act of love. When we listen to someone, we say nonverbally, "I value you. You are important." When we listen in a way that makes a difference, we surrender ourselves to the other person, saying, "I will hear what you have to say and will receive you as I receive your words." When we speak in a way that makes a difference, we speak for the sake of others; thus we are contributing to their understanding and wholeness.

SHARING TOGETHER

1. Ask the group if anyone would like to share something special that has happened during the past week or two, connected with using this workbook.

2. Spend a few minutes talking about how different persons are using the During the Day suggestions and what kind of difference it is making.

3. Invite two or three persons to share their clearest recollection of knowing and obeying God's will (Reflecting and Recording, Day 1).

4. Examine these testimonies by reflecting on how God's will was discerned. Talk about it. Was it through scripture, Christian conferencing, or the direct intervention of the Holy Spirit?

5. Spend ten to twelve minutes discussing a part of what we considered on Day 2 of this week—the two common ways we pray "Your will be done": (1) wrestling *against* God and surrendering, and (2) wrestling *with* God. Was this a new insight? What sort of attitude have you had as you prayed "Your will be done"?

6. Invite one person to share a recent experience of wrestling against God's will, and ask someone else to share an experience of wrestling with God against something that opposed God's will.

7. Invite a volunteer to read his or her paraphrase of Francis de Sales on Day 3 of this week.

8. Spend six to eight minutes discussing the two dimensions of obedience considered on Day 3: (1) Obedience is loving God enough to practice those attitudes and actions that you know are pleasing to God; and (2) Obedience is trusting God enough to submit yourself to God's will, even in what is most repugnant to you.

9. Invite someone to share the experience he or she recalled on Day 3: when he/she was led by God to do something that on the surface and in the beginning was repugnant. How did the person conclude this was God's will? What was the outcome?

10. Spend six to eight minutes discussing the following statements: (1) The more we practice doing God's will, the more easily we discover God's will; and (2) Doing is a condition for knowing God's will.

11. On Day 6, readers were asked to recall an occasion during the past three or four months when they forsook their own desires and will to obey God. Invite one or two persons to share that experience.

12. Spend what time you have left discussing de Sales's statement, "The merit of crosses does not consist in their weight, but in the manner in which they are borne." Encourage group members to talk about the crosses they and others may be bearing. How are they bearing their crosses? Quietly? With self-pity? Resentfully? Boastfully? Obediently? Have their crosses made them better? More empathetic? More calloused or more tender?

PRAYING TOGETHER

1. Leader, begin the prayer time by reading the following verses from Psalm 37:

    Trust in the LORD, and do good;
    Dwell in the land, and feed on His faithfulness.
    Delight yourself also in the LORD,
    And He shall give you the desires of your heart.

    Commit your way to the LORD,
    Trust also in Him,
    And He shall bring it to pass.
    He shall bring forth your righteousness as the light,
    And your justice as the noonday.
    (Psalm 37:3-6, NKJV)

    Sharing the prayers of our hearts with others not only confirms our prayerful desires and claims, but also it inspires the prayers of others and adds the "two-or-three-agreeing" condition for answered prayer (Matt. 18:20).

2. Invite a volunteer to share the prayer of abandonment and submission he or she wrote in the Reflecting and Recording period of Day 2.

3. Now, ask another volunteer to share the prayer of "allowing *heavenly love* to have the management over the daily routine of your life," prayed on Day 5.

4. Corporate prayer is one of the great blessings of Christian community. I invite you to go deeper now, experimenting with the possibilities of corporate prayer by sharing in the fashion described here.

   • Bow in silence and in prayerful concern. The leader calls the name of a person in the group, and someone else in the group offers a brief prayer for the individual named.

   • The leader calls another name and that person is prayed for.

   • The prayers may be brief—two or three sentences—or longer. Think of the person whose name is called. What concern or need has been shared tonight or in the past weeks that could be mentioned in prayer? You may want to express gratitude for the person's life and witness, the role he or she plays in the group, or that person's ministry in the community. Someone may be seeking direction or may need to make a crucial decision. Let someone pray for each individual in a particular way.

WEEK 5

THEY DID NOT SEEK ECSTASY BUT SURRENDER TO GOD

DAY
1

"Mould As Thou Wilt"

In her strange and beautiful book that is part memoir and part meditation, *The Cloister Walk*, Kathleen Norris describes how she became a Benedictine oblate. She said she knew two things: (1) She didn't feel ready to become an oblate, but she had to act, to take the plunge; and (2) She had no idea where doing so would lead.

An oblation is an abbreviated yet powerful profession of monastic vows. The oblate attaches himself/herself to a particular monastery by signing a document on the altar during Mass. The oblate promises to follow the Rule of Saint Benedict insofar as his/her situation will allow. Norris confessed,

> The fact that I'd been raised a thorough Protestant, with little knowledge of religious orders, and no sense of monasticism as a living tradition, was less an obstacle to my becoming an oblate than the many doubts about the Christian religion that had been with me since my teens. Still, although I had little sense of where I'd been, I knew that standing before the altar in a monastery chapel was a remarkable place for me to be, and making an oblation was a remarkable, if not incomprehensible, thing for me to be doing.
>
> The word "oblate" is from the Latin for "to offer," and Jesus himself is often referred to as an "oblation" in the literature of the early church. Many people now translate "oblate" as "associate," and while that may seem to describe the relationship modern oblates have with monastic communities, it does not adequately convey the religious dimension of being an oblate. Substituting the word "associate" for "oblation" in reference to Jesus demonstrates this all too well; no longer an offering, Jesus becomes a junior partner in a law firm. The ancient word "oblate" proved instructive for me. Having no idea what it meant, I appreciated its rich history when I first looked it up in the dictionary. But I also felt it presumptuous to claim to be an "offering" and was extremely reluctant to apply to myself a word that had so often been applied to Jesus Christ. (*The Cloister Walk*, xi–xii)

After making that confession, Norris told about the monk who was to be her oblate director—that is, the one who guided her studies of the Rule (a period that was supposed to last a year but rambled on for nearly three years). She spoke appreciatively of this spiritual guide who waited patiently for her to sort out her muddle. Finally she said to him, "I can't imagine why God would want me, of

Only when we can imagine what God wants with us or might do with us can we put ourselves in the position for the Holy Spirit to work within us.

all people, as an offering. But if God is foolish enough to take me as I am, I guess I'd better do it." The monk smiled broadly and said, "You're ready."

That kind of submission is the topic of this week's readings. The saints did not seek ecstasy, but surrender to God. They knew that in the Bible, *submission* is a love word, not a control word. It means letting another love, teach, influence, and shape you. On the human level, the degree to which we submit to others is the degree to which we will experience their love. Regardless of how much love another person has for us, we cannot appropriate that love unless we are open, vulnerable, and submissive.

The saints experienced the same thing in relation to God. They knew that it is only when we can imagine what God wants with us, or what God might do with us—and certainly when we are humble enough to know that anything God does for us or with us is all grace—that only then can we put ourselves in the position for the Holy Spirit to work within us.

Perhaps the most representative teaching about this topic in the New Testament is the story of Nicodemus, recorded in John's Gospel.

> *Now there was a Pharisee named Nicodemus, a leader of the Jews. He came to Jesus by night and said to him, "Rabbi, we know that you are a teacher who has come from God; for no one can do these signs that you do apart from the presence of God." Jesus answered him, "Very truly, I tell you, no one can see the kingdom of God without being born from above." Nicodemus said to him, "How can anyone be born after having grown old? Can one enter a second time into the mother's womb and be born?" Jesus answered, "Very truly, I tell you, no one can enter the kingdom of God without being born of water and Spirit. What is born of the flesh is flesh, and what is born of the Spirit is spirit. Do not be astonished that I said to you, 'You must be born from above.'" (John 3:1-7)*

John Wesley might have been thinking of this story when he wrote:

Many years ago, when one was describing the glorious privilege of a believer, I cried out, "If this be so, I have no faith." He replied, . . . "You have faith, but it is weak." The very same thing I say to you, my dear friend. You have faith, but it is only as a grain of mustard-seed. Hold fast what you have, and ask for what you want. There is an irreconcilable variability in the operations of the Holy Spirit on the souls of men; more especially as to the manner of justification. Many find Him rushing upon them like a torrent, while they experience

> The o'er whelming power of saving grace.

This has been the experience of many. . . . But in others, He works in a very different way:

> He deigns his influence to infuse,
> Sweet, refreshing, as the violet dews.

It has pleased Him to work the latter way in you, from the beginning; and it is not improbable He will continue (as He has begun) to work in a gentle and almost imperceptible manner. Let Him take His own way: He is wiser than you; He will do all things well. Do not reason against Him; but let the prayer of your heart be,—

> "Mould as Thou wilt Thy passive clay!"

> (*The Works of John Wesley*, vol. 13, 95)

REFLECTING AND RECORDING

Consider the occasion or process of your becoming a professing Christian. Would you describe your conversion time as a time of the Holy Spirit's "rushing upon [you] like a torrent," as you experienced "the o'erwhelming power of saving grace"? Or would your experience more aptly be described, "He deigns His influence to infuse, / Sweet, refreshing, as the violet dews"? Seek to get in touch with that experience. Make some notes describing your thoughts, feelings, struggles, joys. How much ecstasy did you experience? Did you think in terms of surrender?

Kathleen Norris says, "I can't imagine why God would want me, of all people, as an offering. But if God is foolish enough to take me as I am, I guess I'd better do it." Her spiritual director smiled broadly and said, "You're ready."

As you continue to reflect on your experience of becoming a professing Christian, was there anything about it that compares to Norris's experience of becoming an oblate?

DURING THE DAY

John Wesley said,

> Let Him take His own way:
> He is wiser than you;
>   He will do all things well.
>   Do not reason against Him;
>   but let the prayer of your heart be,—
> "Mould as Thou wilt Thy passive clay!"

On page 243 is the hymn version of Wesley's suggested prayer:

Mold me and make me after thy will,
while I am waiting, yielded and still.

Cut out the prayer and put it in a place where you will see it often. Make it your personal prayer.

DAY
2
Flame and Fire

Francis of Assisi is one of the most well-known saints and probably the favorite saint of many people. After he had established the Franciscan Order, Clare, a noblewoman influenced by Francis's preaching, gave up all her riches and established the Second Order of the Franciscans, the Poor Clares. When Francis stayed in Assisi, he often visited Clare and gave her spiritual advice. She wanted very much to eat a meal with him and asked him several times to grant her that wish, but for some reason he refused.

Love and disciplined attention to God (devotion) differ no more from each other than does the flame from the fire.

Some of Francis's brother friars heard about Clare's wish to eat with Francis, and they approached him about it. They said, "Father, it seems to us that this strictness is not according to divine charity—that you do not grant the request of Sister Clare . . . in such a little thing as eating with you, especially considering that she gave up the riches and pomp of the world as a result of your preaching. So you should not only let her eat a meal with you once, but if she were to ask an even greater favor of you, you should grant it to your little spiritual plant."

Finally they persuaded Francis to eat with Clare. He arranged for Clare and a sister nun to meet with him at the church of Saint Mary of the Angels, where Clare had taken her holy vows. A book about Saint Francis tells the story:

. . . St. Francis had the table prepared on the bare ground, as was his custom.

And when it was time to eat, St. Francis and St. Clare sat down together, and one of his companions with St. Clare's companion, and all his other companions were grouped around that humble table. But at the first course St. Francis began to speak about God in such a sweet and holy and profound and divine and marvelous way that he himself and St. Clare and her companion and all the others who were at that poor little table were rapt in God by the overabundance of divine grace that descended upon them.

And while they were sitting there in a rapture, . . . it seemed to the men of Assisi and Bettona and the entire district that the Church of St. Mary of the Angels and the whole Place and the forest which was at that time around the Place were all aflame and that an immense fire was burning over all of them. Consequently the men of Assisi ran down there in great haste to save the Place and put out the fire, as they firmly believed that everything was burning up.

But when they had reached the Place, they saw that nothing was on fire. Entering the Place, they found St. Francis with St. Clare and all the companions sitting around that very humble table, rapt in God by contemplation and invested with power from on high. Then they knew for sure that it had been a heavenly and not material fire that God had miraculously shown them to symbolize the fire of divine love which was burning in the souls of those holy friars and nuns. So they withdrew, with great consolation in their hearts and with holy edification. (*The Little Flowers of St. Francis,* 72–73)

The Holy Spirit's striking power was often demonstrated in the lives and work of the saints. Most of them had ecstatic experiences. Yet, it is clear, as you keep company with these women and men of God, that they did not seek ecstasy; instead, their deepest desire was surrendering themselves to God.

The blaze that the villagers saw, which symbolized the fire of divine love burning in the souls of Saint Francis and his companions, calls to mind this word of Francis de Sales:

Devotion is simply that spiritual agility and vivacity by which charity works in us or by aid of which we work quickly and lovingly. Just as it is the function of charity to enable us to observe all God's commandments in general and without exception, so it is the part of devotion to enable us to observe them more quickly and diligently. Hence a man who does not observe all God's commandments cannot be held to be either good or devout. To be good he must have charity, and to be devout, in addition to charity he must have great ardor and readiness in performing charitable actions.

Since devotion consists in a certain degree of eminent charity, it not only makes us prompt, active, and faithful in observance of God's commands, but in addition it arouses us to do quickly and lovingly as many good works as possible, both those commanded and those merely counselled or inspired.

. . . charity and devotion differ no more from one another than does flame from the fire. Charity is spiritual fire and when it bursts into flames, it is called devotion. Hence devotion adds nothing to the fire of charity except the flame that makes charity prompt, active, and diligent not only to observe God's commandments but also to fulfill his heavenly counsels and inspirations. (*Introduction to the Devout Life,* 40–41)

Notice how de Sales distinguished *love* (charity) from *devotion*. He said that love enables us to obey all God's commandments, while devotion enables us to obey God's commandments more quickly and diligently. Devotion is our disciplined attention to God. Sometimes this attention can result in different levels or degrees of ecstasy. But whenever devotion and love are disconnected, the expression of Christian faith and life is skewed, distorted—sometimes to our and others' harm.

Paul gave concrete expression to the connection between love and devotion. In First Corinthians 12, he discusses spiritual gifts.

> *Now there are varieties of gifts, but the same Spirit; and there are varieties of services, but the same Lord; and there are varieties of activities, but it is the same God who activates all of them in everyone. To each is given the manifestation of the Spirit for the common good. To one is given through the Spirit the utterance of wisdom, and to another the utterance of knowledge according to the same Spirit, to another faith by the same Spirit, to another gifts of healing by the one Spirit, to another the working of miracles, to another prophecy, to another the discernment of spirits, to another various kinds of tongues, to another the interpretation of tongues. All these are activated by one and the same Spirit, who allots to each one individually just as the Spirit chooses. (1 Corinthians 12:4-11)*

Then he elaborates on his descriptive image of the Christian community as a body, "the body of Christ." He closes that discussion of spiritual gifts (some of them ecstatic such as "tongues") and how these gifts are to operate in the "body," with these words: "But strive for the greater gifts. And I will show you a still more excellent way" (1 Cor. 12:31). That more excellent way is love.

Paul's incomparable "Hymn of Love" follows in First Corinthians 13. Then he summarizes again in the first verse of chapter 14: "Follow the way of love and eagerly desire spiritual gifts" (NIV). Paul would agree with Francis de Sales that love and disciplined attention to God "differ no more from one another than does flame from the fire." When we give love free reign in our lives, it becomes a spiritual fire, breaking out into a flame of devotion. And reciprocally our devotion, our disciplined attention to God, adds a flame to the fire of love, activating and energizing love for doing God's will and work.

REFLECTING AND RECORDING

In the space provided on the previous page, translate de Sales's words into your own, using *love* for *charity* and *disciplined attention to God* for *devotion*.

Spend a few minutes reflecting on your life as a Christian. To what degree have you known ecstasy, a mystical, perhaps unusual sensation of God's presence—maybe even to the point of having an out-of-body experience? Have you longed for more emotional experiences, more ecstasy? Have you questioned, even scorned the ecstatic experiences of others? Make some notes here.

In your own life and in others', what connection have you observed between ecstasy and surrender? Between personal "spiritual" experience and a life of Christian service?

During the Day

Continue the prayer of surrender given yesterday.

> Mold me and make me after thy will,
> While I am waiting, yielded and still.

DAY
3

The Heaven of Heavens

All the saints I have studied would join Wesley in affirming that "love is the highest gift of God; humble, gentle, patient love; . . . the heaven of heavens is love." Paul made this absolutely clear in his Love Chapter.

If I speak in the tongues of mortals and of angels, but do not have love, I am a noisy gong or a clanging cymbal. And if I have prophetic powers, and understand all mysteries and all knowledge, and if I have all faith, so as to remove mountains, but do not have love, I am nothing. If I give away all my possessions, and if I hand over my body so that I may boast, but do not have love, I gain nothing.

Love is patient; love is kind; love is not envious or boastful or arrogant or rude. It does not insist on its own way; it is not irritable or resentful; it does not rejoice in wrongdoing, but rejoices in the truth. It bears all things, believes all things, hopes all things, endures all things.

Love never ends. But as for prophecies, they will come to an end; as for tongues, they will cease; as for knowledge, it will come to an end. For we know only in part, and we prophesy only in part; but when the complete comes, the partial will come to an end. When I was a child, I spoke like a child, I thought like a child, I reasoned like a child; when I became an adult, I put an end to childish ways. For now we see in a mirror, dimly, but then we will see face to face. Now I know only in part; then I will know fully, even as I have been fully known. And now faith, hope, and love abide, these three; and the greatest of these is love. (1 Corinthians 13)

As indicated yesterday, this "Hymn of Love" is positioned in the context of Paul's discussions of gifts and service in the life of the church—the body of Christ. Chapter 12 closes with Paul's reminding the Corinthians that within the body, some are apostles, some prophets, some teachers, some workers of miracles and healing, some with the practical gift of administration, and some gifted for "speaking in various kinds of tongues." With all these diverse gifts within the body, all believers are encouraged to eagerly desire the greater gift, which Paul describes as "a more excellent way." In revealing and challenging words Paul paints a picture of love, "the heaven of heavens," in chapter 13.

> *Love is the highest gift of God . . . all visions, revelations, manifestations, whatever, are little things compared to love.*
>
> *—John Wesley*

Again, note the positioning. The "hymn" is bracketed on one side with the naming of gifts in chapter 12, and on the other with a warning about misusing gifts, and making sure gifts are seen in the perspective of the servant ministry of the church, in chapter 14.

Paul is no stranger to ecstasy. In his Second Letter to the Corinthians, he lays bare his heart and becomes vulnerable, sharing at one time his glory and his pain.

It is necessary to boast; nothing is to be gained by it, but I will go on to visions and revelations of the Lord. I know a person in Christ who fourteen years ago was caught up to the third heaven—whether in the body or out of the body I do not know; God knows. And I know that such a person—whether in the body or out of the body I do not know; God knows—was caught up into Paradise and heard things that are not to be told, that no mortal is permitted to repeat. On behalf of such a one I will boast, but on my own behalf I will not boast, except of my weaknesses. But if I wish to boast, I will not be a fool, for I will be speaking the truth. But I refrain from it, so that no one may think better of me than what is seen in me or heard from me, even considering the exceptional character of the revelations. Therefore, to keep me from being too elated, a thorn was given me in the flesh, a messenger of Satan to torment me, to keep me from being too elated. Three times I appealed to the Lord about this, that it would leave me, but he said to me, "My grace is sufficient for you, for power is made perfect in weakness." So, I will boast all the more gladly of my weaknesses, so that the power of Christ may dwell in me. Therefore I am content with weaknesses, insults, hardships, persecutions, and calamities for the sake of Christ; for whenever I am weak, then I am strong. (2 Corinthians 12:1-10)

In a strange way, Paul stands outside himself when he says, "I know a person." The person he is referring to is himself, but he tells the story of this amazing experience with wondrous detachment and amazement that it had happened to him. We can only wonder ourselves at what happened. There is no value in trying to probe for meaning in the details he shares. What is clear is that Paul's spirit rose in ecstasy; he experienced a nearness to God that is beyond surpassing.

Note that after the ecstasy came his witness of pain, which Paul described as a messenger of Satan sent to torment him. There was no deliverance from the "thorn in the flesh." Rather, the thorn became an ongoing reminder of the sufficiency of God's grace, as well as Paul's need to be humble and to find strength in his weakness.

So Paul was no stranger to ecstasy, but he kept ecstasy in perspective. Return to Day 2's discussion of gifts and Paul's "Hymn of Love." He made this claim: "I thank God that I speak in tongues more than all of you" (1 Cor. 14:18) only after he had sounded a warning.

> *For those who speak in a tongue do not speak to other people but to God; for nobody understands them, since they are speaking mysteries in the Spirit. On the other hand, those who prophesy speak to other people for their upbuilding and encouragement and consolation. Those who speak in a tongue build up themselves, but those who prophesy build up the church. Now I would like all of you to speak in tongues, but even more to prophesy. One who prophesies is greater than one who speaks in tongues, unless someone interprets, so that the church may be built up. (1 Corinthians 14:2-5)*

Though they were open to and at home with the extraordinary working of the Holy Spirit, which often defied rational explanation, the saints and Paul did not seek ecstasy but rather surrender to God. They knew they were working, as Wesley said, "to aim at nothing more, but more of that love described in the thirteenth [chapter] of [First] Corinthians."

> Love is the highest gift of God; humble, gentle, patient love; . . . all visions, revelations, manifestations whatever, are little things compared to love. . . .
>
> It were well you should be thoroughly sensible of this, "the heaven of heavens is love." There is nothing higher in religion; there is, in effect, nothing else; if you look for anything but more love, you are looking wide of the mark, you are getting out of the royal way. And when you are asking others, "Have you received this or that blessing?" if you mean anything but more love, you mean wrong; you are leading them out of the way, and putting them upon a false scent. Settle it then in your heart, that from the moment God has saved you from all sin, you are to aim at nothing more, but more of that love described in the thirteenth [chapter] of [First] Corinthians. You can go no higher than this, till you are carried into Abraham's bosom. (*The Works of John Wesley*, vol. 11, 430)

Reflecting and Recording

Call to mind and describe here an experience that might be labeled ecstasy, such as a vision, dream, healing, feeling Christ's presence so powerfully that you knew he was there, knowing with certainty that God has spoken to you, praying in tongues, discerning a specific direction for your life, being clearly led to call or visit someone—any experience that you would have difficulty explaining rationally. Be honest and record your experience without feeling you have to explain it.

Spend a few minutes reflecting on the experience you have described. Make some notes about the effect the experience has had on your Christian life and growth.

Spend the balance of your time with these questions: Why haven't I had more of this kind of experience? Would having more of such experiences enhance my Christian growth, witness, and discipleship?

DURING THE DAY

Wesley said, "If you look for anything but more love, you are looking wide of the mark." Look for ways to expand and express your love throughout the day. Continue your prayer of surrender.

DAY
4

Ecstasy and Surrender

The apostle Paul had a one-track mind. He wrote to the Corinthians, "I decided to know nothing among you except Jesus Christ, and him crucified" (1 Cor. 2:2). Galatians 2:19-20 is his one-sentence autobiography: "I have been crucified with Christ, and it is no longer I who live, but it is Christ who lives in me." Paul's commitment to Christ shaped every decision he made and determined every step he took. No one can doubt his high intelligence quotient or question his capacity for rational debate. At the same time, his intelligent, objective reasoning never supplanted his subjective openness to the Holy Spirit's working in his life in many miraculous, rational-defying ways. He had an amazing balance between a rational, objective apprehension of the gospel and a subjective grasping of the power of the Spirit. As indicated in Day 3, Paul would boldly declare, "I thank God that I speak in tongues more than all of you" (1 Cor. 14:18) after confessing, "If I speak in the tongues of mortals and of angels, but do not have love, I am a noisy gong or a clanging cymbal" (1 Cor. 13:1).

While we are not to seek ecstasy but surrender, Paul weds the two in a remarkable way. Here is one example of how he unites ecstasy and surrender:

> *When we open ourselves to the Holy Spirit and cease trusting in our own wisdom and power, our actions and accomplishments will far exceed our normal potential and capacity.*

> *They went through the region of Phrygia and Galatia, having been forbidden by the Holy Spirit to speak the word in Asia. When they had come opposite Mysia, they attempted to go into Bithynia, but the Spirit of Jesus did not allow them; so, passing by Mysia, they went down to Troas. During the night Paul had a vision: there stood a man of Macedonia pleading with him and saying, "Come over to Macedonia and help us." When he had seen the vision, we immediately tried to cross over to Macedonia, being convinced that God had called us to proclaim the good news to them. (Acts 16:6-10)*

Paul was not seeking an ecstatic experience, but he was open and responsive to the Spirit's working in his life. He followed what some would certainly label ecstatic—a vision of a man begging, "Come over to Macedonia and help us." Paul interpreted this vision as God's call to go to Macedonia and preach the gospel.

He went specifically to Philippi, the major city in the Macedonian region, a port city that was easily accessible. Miraculous things happened there. Lydia, a Gentile businesswoman, was converted, and the Philippian church was established in her house. A slave girl was delivered of "a spirit of divination," which led to Paul and Silas's being beaten and thrown into jail. There in jail the third miracle took place. While Paul and Silas were praying and praising God at midnight, God honored their trust and faithfulness by throwing open the prison doors and freeing them. This miracle led to the conversion of the jailer and all of his family.

> *About midnight Paul and Silas were praying and singing hymns to God, and the prisoners were listening to them. Suddenly there was an earthquake, so violent that the foundations of the prison were shaken; and immediately all the doors were opened and everyone's chains were unfastened. When the jailer woke up and saw the prison doors wide open, he drew his sword and was about to kill himself, since he supposed that the prisoners had escaped. But Paul shouted in a loud voice, "Do not harm yourself, for we are all here." The jailer called for lights, and rushing in, he fell down trembling before Paul and Silas. Then he brought them outside and said, "Sirs, what must I do to be saved?" They answered, "Believe on the Lord Jesus, and you will be saved, you and your household." They spoke the word of the Lord to him and to all who were in his house. At the same hour of the night he took them and washed their wounds; then he and his entire family were baptized without delay. (Acts 16:25-33)*

The conversion of a Gentile businesswoman and a jailer, along with the healing of a demon-possessed slave girl—all resulted from Paul's surrender to an ecstatic vision. The lesson is clear: When we open ourselves to the Holy Spirit and cease trusting in our own wisdom and power, our actions and accomplishments will far exceed our normal potential and capacity. Jean-Pierre de Caussade addressed the issue of surrender in this fashion:

> Those who have gauged the depths of their own nothingness can no longer retain any kind of confidence in themselves, nor trust in any way to their works in which they can discover nothing but misery, self-love and corruption.
>
> This absolute distrust and complete disregard of self is the source from which alone flow those delightful consolations of souls wholly abandoned to God, and form their unalterable peace, holy joy and immovable confidence in God only. (*The Joy of the Saints,* 249)

We need to keep balance: We must never trust in our own resources alone, but at the same time never doubt that the Spirit will use us, often in remarkable, even miraculous, ways. Again, the key is not to seek ecstasy but surrender and openness to the Spirit's working.

REFLECTING AND RECORDING

In the space provided beside the quotation above, paraphrase de Caussade's words into your own.

Spend a few minutes examining your life. Do you usually trust in your own resources?

How open are you to the Spirit's working through you?

What kind of "miracles" have you experienced?

What is the difference between seeking ecstasy and being open to the Spirit's working?

DURING THE DAY

Continue as suggested yesterday, looking for an expansion of your love and ways to express your love throughout the day. Seek to sense the Spirit's leading in your life, and follow that leading.

DAY
5

Keeping Our Feelings in Perspective

Not only did the saints not seek ecstasy, but they also urged us to keep our feelings in perspective. Francis de Sales warned about two mistakes related to our feelings, which he found "common among spiritual persons."

> One is that they ordinarily measure their devotion by the consolations and satisfactions which they experience in the way of God, so that if these happen to be wanting, they think they have lost all devotion. No, this is no more than a sensible devotion. True and substantial devotion does not consist in these things, but in having a will resolute, active, ready, and constant not to offend God, and to perform all that belongs to His service. The other mistake is that if it ever happens to them to do anything with repugnance and weariness, they believe they have no merit in it. On the other hand, there is then far greater merit; so that a single ounce of good done thus by a sheer spiritual effort, amidst darkness and dullness and without interest, is worth more than a hundred pounds done with great facility and sweetness, since the former requires a stronger and purer love. And how great soever may be the aridities and repugnance of the sensible part of our soul, we ought never to lose courage, but pursue our way as travelers treat the barking of dogs. (*A Year with the Saints*, 15)

The depth of our faith and how it works in our lives does not depend upon how we feel. Devotion and emotion are not always connected. A year ago, I went through a three-month "dry spell" in my devotional life. Though I set aside time each morning for scripture and devotional reading, meditation, and prayer, I did not come to this time expectantly or joyfully. I had no real sense of God's presence when I prayed. During that period, however, Jerry, my wife, and I became burdened to pray for a particular person connected with our family. She had been in and out of our lives for at least fifteen years, and we knew she needed a personal relationship with Christ. Yet, faithfully praying for her had not been a priority for us. Now it was. Even during this dry spell, I remained disciplined in my praying and intercession for our friend.

> *The depth of our faith and how it works in our lives does not depend on how we feel.*

A miraculous transformation occurred. Our friend entered an intimate relationship with Christ and was delivered from powerful, negative, destructive spirits. I have seen few more dramatic changes. Now, I do not credit this transformation altogether to our prayers, but I do believe our intercession had something to do with it. And for me, the intercession occurred during a dry spell, a time of forced praying when I didn't sense God's presence.

We need to learn from the saints. We must not measure our "devotion by the consolations and satisfactions which [we] experience," and if positive feelings are not present, we must not discount our devotion or question whether God is present.

De Sales identified another common mistake related to feelings to which we need to give attention. How often are we tempted to discount the "merit" of our good acts when we must force ourselves to perform them? De Sales is rather dogmatic: "A single ounce of good done thus by a sheer spiritual effort, amidst darkness and dullness . . . is worth more than a hundred pounds done with great facility and sweetness, since the former requires a stronger and purer love."

We are not supposed to do good only when we feel good any more than we are to pray only when we tangibly sense God's presence. Paul integrated a word about not becoming "weary in doing what is right" into his teaching about the inevitable connection between sowing and reaping.

> *Do not be deceived; God is not mocked, for you reap whatever you sow. If you sow to your own flesh, you will reap corruption from the flesh; but if you sow to the Spirit, you will reap eternal life from the Spirit. So let us not grow weary in doing what is right, for we will reap at harvest time, if we do not give up. So then, whenever we have an opportunity, let us work for the good of all, and especially for those of the family of faith. (Galatians 6:7-10)*

There is still another issue related to keeping our feelings in perspective. It is the fact that rarely are we as keenly aware and sensitive to God's favor and forgiveness as we are conscious of our ongoing sin and failure. In his commentary on the Book of Galatians, Martin Luther expressed it this way:

> Brother, you would like to feel God's favor as you feel your sin. But you are asking too much. Your righteousness rests on something much better than feelings. Wait and hope until it will be revealed to you in the Lord's own time. Don't go by your feelings, but go by the doctrine of faith, which pledges Christ to you. (*Commentary on the Epistle to the Galatians*, 6)

While retaining a sensitivity to sin is normal, we must guard against allowing this sensitivity to make us doubt our salvation. Luther said it well:

> For my righteousness is not yet perfect, it cannot yet be felt; yet I do not despair; for faith showeth unto me Christ in whom I trust; and when I have laid hold of Him by faith, I wrestle against the fiery darts of the devil, and I take good heart through hope against the feeling of sin, assuring myself that I have a perfect righteousness prepared for me in heaven. (Baillie, *A Diary of Readings*, 340)

REFLECTING AND RECORDING

De Sales named two mistakes "common among spiritual persons." Examine yourself in relation to these.

1. They ordinarily measure their devotion by the consolations and satisfactions which they experience . . . if these happen to be wanting, they think they have lost all devotion.

2. If they do "anything with repugnance or weariness, they believe they have no merit in it."

De Sales identified another common mistake—discounting the merit of our good acts when we have to force ourselves to perform them. Examine your attitude in relation to this mistake.

Martin Luther identified another problem in keeping our feelings in perspective. Hardly ever are we as keenly aware and sensitive to God's favor and forgiveness, he said, as we are of our ongoing sin and failure. Spend the balance of your time thinking about how preoccupied you may be with your sin and failure, compared with how unaware and/or insensitive you may be to God's favor and forgiveness.

DURING THE DAY

Continue to look for ways to expand and express your love throughout the day. Seek the Spirit's guidance in your life circumstances, and follow that leading.

DAY
6

The Habitual Conviction
of the Presence of God

Yesterday we focused on keeping our feelings in perspective. To that discussion we must add the fact that we should never discount our feelings. To reduce the Christian faith to rational explanation, or to think of salvation only in terms affirming certain propositions or accepting well-defined, rationally stated doctrine, is to miss the richness of God's desired relationship with us, God's children. Salvation is not merely a belief transaction; it is relationship. Charles de Foucauld, whose spiritual influence in the twentieth century has been compared to that of Thomas Merton and Mother Teresa, described the Christian life as relationship: "He [Christ] gives me his hand so that we can go through life together, hand in hand" (Lepetit, *Two Dancers in the Desert*, 114).

We need to cultivate our conviction of the habitual presence of God.

According to the foreword of de Foucald's biography, the author used the image of "an invisible dance of two main characters on the road of life" to grasp de Foucald's essential mystery. The characters "are man and God, two partners who are always in search of one another" (*Two Dancers in the Desert*, v). In his foreword, Carlo Carretto described de Foucauld like this:

> Charles de Foucauld was precisely that kind of dancer—a bit out of place because he was so out of the ordinary. God was his obvious and wholly attentive partner, helping him to take the right steps and guiding him so that he stayed on life's strange dance-floor; teaching him to aim for the ultimate reaches of love; looking ahead and secretly intervening to obviate any really bad slip-ups or absolute disasters.
>
> What an amazing partnership! In the end it was the very same relationship that we all have with God, but one that was especially meaningful for someone like Charles de Foucauld; for someone who was always liable to wheel about suddenly, and therefore needed the unfailingly sensitive response of his divine partner if he was to keep his balance.
>
> De Foucauld was an aristocrat and yet he had to learn to humble himself infinitely. He was a man of action who had to discover how to be still. He was impetuous and intense, and had to learn the meaning of caution and patience. (*Two Dancers in the Desert*, vi)

Though unique, the image of dancing with God is a good description of how God relates to us as feeling beings; also, it illuminates salvation as relationship. So, to keep ecstasy and any levels of feelings in perspective, the habitual conviction of the presence of God is necessary.

I get this phrase, "*the habitual conviction of the presence of God*," from Fénelon. He says that this conviction is the sovereign remedy for dealing with temptation.

> There are two things that we can do against temptations. The first is to be faithful to the light within us, in avoiding all exposure to temptation which we are at liberty to avoid. I say, all that we are at liberty to avoid, because it does not always depend upon ourselves whether we shall escape occasions of sin. Those that belong to the situation in life in which Providence has placed us are not under our control. The other is to turn our eyes to God in the moment of temptation, to throw ourselves immediately upon the protection of heaven, as a child when in danger flies to the arms of its parent.
>
> The habitual conviction of the presence of God is the sovereign remedy; it supports, it consoles, it calms us. We must not be surprised that we are tempted. We are placed here to be proved by temptations. Everything is temptation to us. Crosses irritate our pride and prosperity flatters it; our life is a continual warfare, but Jesus Christ combats with us. We must let temptations, like a tempest, beat upon our heads, and still move on; like a traveller surprised on the way by a storm, who wraps his cloak about him, and goes on his journey in spite of the opposing elements.
>
> In a certain sense, there is little to do in doing the will of God. Still it is true that it is a great work, because it must be without any reserve. His Spirit enters the secret folding of our hearts, and even the most upright affections and the most necessary attachments must be regulated by His will; but it is not the multitude of hard duties, it is not the constraint and contention, that advances us on our course. *On the contrary it is the yielding of our wills without restriction to tread cheerfully every day in the path in which Providence leads us*; to seek nothing, to be discouraged by nothing, to see our duty in the present moment, to trust all else without reserve to the will and power of God. (Baillie, *A Diary of Readings*, 123, italics mine)

It should be obvious that we need to cultivate the conviction of the presence of God—not only in handling temptation but also in keeping ecstasy and all our feelings in perspective. While the spiritual life is a gift of the Holy Spirit, it also requires human effort. Jesus made that abundantly clear.

> *As he was setting out on a journey, a man ran up and knelt before him, and asked him, "Good Teacher, what must I do to inherit eternal life?" Jesus said to him, "Why do you call me good? No one is good but God alone. You know the commandments: 'You shall not murder; You shall not commit adultery; You shall not steal; You shall not bear false witness; You shall not defraud; Honor your father and mother.'" He said to him, "Teacher, I have kept all these since my youth." Jesus, looking at him, loved him and said, "You lack one thing; go, sell what you own, and give the money to the poor, and you will have treasure in heaven; then come, follow me." When he heard this, he was shocked and went away grieving, for he had many possessions.*
>
> *Then Jesus looked around and said to his disciples, "How hard it will be for those who have wealth to enter the kingdom of God!" And the disciples were perplexed at these words. But Jesus said to them again,*

"Children, how hard it is to enter the kingdom of God! It is easier for a camel to go through the eye of a needle than for someone who is rich to enter the kingdom of God." They were greatly astounded and said to one another, "Then who can be saved?" Jesus looked at them and said, "For mortals it is impossible, but not for God; for God all things are possible."

Peter began to say to him, "Look, we have left everything and followed you." Jesus said, "Truly I tell you, there is no one who has left house or brothers or sisters or mother or father or children or fields, for my sake and for the sake of the good news, who will not receive a hundredfold now in this age—houses, brothers and sisters, mothers and children, and fields, with persecutions—and in the age to come eternal life. But many who are first will be last, and the last will be first." (Mark 10:17-31)

In his insightful book *Making All Things New*, Henri Nouwen argues that Jesus was concerned with only one thing: doing the will of the Father.

Nothing in the Gospels is as impressive as Jesus' single-minded obedience to his Father. From his first recorded words in the Temple, "Did you not know that I must be busy with my Father's affairs?" (Luke 2:49), to his last words on the cross, "Father, into your hands I commit my spirit" (Luke 23:46), Jesus' only concern was to do the will of his Father. He says, "The Son can do nothing by himself; he can do only what he sees the Father doing" (John 5:19). The works Jesus did are the works the Father sent him to do, and the words he spoke are the words the Father gave him. He leaves no doubt about this: "If I am not doing my Father's work, there is no need to believe me ..." (John 10:37); "My word is not my own; it is the word of the one who sent me" (John 14:24). (*Making All Things New*, 46)

This Jesus who is single-mindedly obedient to the Father calls us to a habitual conviction of God's presence by shifting the point of gravity

to relocate the center of our attention, to change our priorities. Jesus wants us to move from the "many things" to the "one necessary thing." It is important for us to realize that Jesus in no way wants us to leave our many-faceted world. Rather, he wants us to live in it, but firmly rooted in the center of all things. Jesus does not speak about a change of activities, a change in contacts, or even a change of pace. He speaks about a change of heart. This change of heart makes everything different, even while everything appears to remain the same. This is the meaning of "Set your hearts on his kingdom first ... and all these other things will be given you as well." *What counts is where our hearts are.* (Nouwen, *Making All Things New*, 42, italics mine)

REFLECTING AND RECORDING

Think back on the past three months. Name two temptations you have had to deal with.

1.

2.

Examine the way you dealt with those temptations. To what degree did you practice Fénelon's suggestions for two things we can do against temptation? Here are the actions he said we can take:

- "To be faithful to the light within us, in avoiding all exposure to temptation which we are at liberty to avoid."
- "To turn our eyes to God in the moment of temptation, to throw ourselves immediately upon the protection of heaven."

What counts is where our hearts are.

Fénelon acknowledges that it is not within our power to escape occasions for sin. Have you found this to be true? Reflect on how you deal with this reality.

Spend a few minutes reflecting on Fénelon's following assertions:

We must not be surprised that we are tempted. We are placed here to be proved by temptations.

Crosses irritate our pride and prosperity flatters it.

In the space provided beside the quotation on page 139, translate Fénelon's last paragraph into your own words.

DURING THE DAY

As you move through the day, deliberately acknowledge and cultivate a "habitual conviction of the presence of God."

DAY
7

We Cannot Control the Spirit

All the saints I have studied give witness to the vivid presence of the Holy Spirit. As I indicated on Day 2, the Spirit's power was often demonstrated strikingly in their lives, and most of them had ecstatic experiences. We always need to remember that the important issue is the presence of God, not how God makes that presence known.

Jean-Pierre de Caussade spoke of how one must forget everything else and think only of God. Sometimes as this happens, a person may pass entire days without thinking of anything else, "as though one had become quite stupid." Then, said de Caussade,

> It often happens that God even places certain souls in this state, which is called the emptiness of the spirit and of the understanding, or the state of nothingness.
>
> The annihilation of one's own spirit wonderfully prepares the soul for the reception of that of Jesus Christ.
>
> This is the mystical death to the working of one's own activity, and renders the soul capable of undergoing the divine operation. (*The Joy of the Saints*, 69)

This "mystical death" is what Jesus was talking about when he called us to deny ourselves (Matt. 16:24). It is the rhythm of the Christian life: dying and rising with Christ (Col. 3:3-4).

Richard Foster identified a charismatic tradition in the history of Christian faith and practice that is relevant to de Caussade's claim. The tradition gives special attention to the work of the Holy Spirit and abounds with charismatic, ecstatic experience. Foster identified Saint Francis of Assisi, his life and ministry, as a historical paradigm for the charismatic tradition. You read about an ecstatic experience connected with Saint Francis on Day 2 of this week.

Foster identified the Azusa Street Revival in the early 1900s as a contemporary paradigm of the charismatic tradition. Many of the present-day charismatic/Pentecostal movements grew out of that revival. C. H. Mason, founder of the African-American Church of God in Christ, was one of many Pentecostal leaders whose defining experience of the Holy Spirit was in the Azusa Street Mission. He testified of that experience:

> The Spirit came upon the saints and upon me. . . . Then I gave up for the Lord to have His way within me. So there came a wave of Glory into me and all of my being was filled with the Glory of the Lord. So when He had gotten me straight on my feet, there came a light which enveloped my entire being above the brightness of the sun. When I opened my mouth to say "Glory," a flame touched my tongue which ran down to me. My language changed and no

word could I speak in my own tongue. Oh! I was filled with the Glory of the Lord. My soul was then satisfied. (Foster, *Streams of Living Water*, 133)

Doesn't that sound like Isaiah's witness?

In the year that King Uzziah died, I saw the Lord sitting on a throne, high and lofty; and the hem of his robe filled the temple. Seraphs were in attendance above him; each had six wings: with two they covered their faces, and with two they covered their feet, and with two they flew. And one called to another and said:

"Holy, holy, holy is the LORD of hosts;
the whole earth is full of his glory."

The pivots on the thresholds shook at the voices of those who called, and the house filled with smoke. And I said: "Woe is me! I am lost, for I am a man of unclean lips, and I live among a people of unclean lips; yet my eyes have seen the King, the LORD of hosts!"

Then one of the seraphs flew to me, holding a live coal that had been taken from the altar with a pair of tongs. The seraph touched my mouth with it and said: "Now that this has touched your lips, your guilt has departed and your sin is blotted out." (Isaiah 6:1-7)

And can't you hear in C. H. Mason's testimony the sounds of Pentecost?

When the day of Pentecost had come, they were all together in one place. And suddenly from heaven there came a sound like the rush of a violent wind, and it filled the entire house where they were sitting. Divided tongues, as of fire, appeared among them, and a tongue rested on each of them. All of them were filled with the Holy Spirit and began to speak in other languages, as the Spirit gave them ability. (Acts 2:1-4)

Again, remember: The presence of God, not how God makes that presence known, is what is important. De Caussade spoke of "the mystical death to the working of one's own activity." That means giving up control, surrendering to God. C. H. Mason used different language to express the same truth: "Then I gave up for the Lord to have His way within me."

The point is, we cannot control the Spirit's working. Nor should we try.

It is presumptuous, to say the least, and madness, to label it correctly, for us to seek to direct or limit the work of the Spirit. Yet, that is a perennial tendency. We want to domesticate God. But the Spirit blows where it wills (John 3:8), so there is no way to institutionalize the working of the Spirit.

I remember visiting a worship service held on the back porch of a restaurant at the beach. We were on vacation, and a friend invited us to go to church with her. I was hesitant about going. I knew that this church was outside my faith tradition, but my wife and I felt that attending worship with our friend would show our support for her.

Honestly, I got very little out of the experience. It was not a style of worship I appreciated, and the worship was not well planned or well executed. Yet, the worship of that small church and the sense of community our friend found there, as well as an expression of the gospel in language she understood, completely transformed her life.

So who am I to say that this church's worship was not valid? We need to thank God that all our attempts to control or manage the Holy Spirit ultimately fail. Why can't we accept that and joyfully surrender to the Spirit's leading, moving from day to day, open and expectant that God will surprise us with an outbreaking of the Spirit as we have not yet imagined?

REFLECTING AND RECORDING

How do you respond to de Caussade's phrase, "the annihilation of one's own spirit"? Live with this question for a minute.

Were you turned off by that phrase? Did de Caussade's next words register for you as his explanation of "the annihilation of one's own spirit"—the "mystical death to the working of one's own activity"? Write a brief prayer expressing your desire and willingness to die to the working of your own activity in order for the Holy Spirit to work in your life.

DURING THE DAY

Continue seeking to deliberately acknowledge or cultivate a habitual conviction of God's presence.

Group Meeting for Week 5

INTRODUCTION

The disciplines needed for prayerful living—praying without ceasing, or living in a continual state of prayer—are *intention* and *attention*. These disciplines are also necessary for meaningful group sharing. We cannot be lazy and dull. We must pay attention to what is going on around us.

In group settings the easy route is to be lazy. The temptation for individual group members is to "play it safe" and not risk being honest and vulnerable.

Energy is another issue. Listening and speaking demand physical as well as emotional energy. So the temptation is to hold back, to be only half-present, not to invest the attention and focus essential for full participation.

I urge you to withstand these temptations. These sharing sessions are important. Don't underestimate the value of each person's contribution. Stay sensitive to the possibility of slinking into laziness.

SHARING TOGETHER

1. Begin your time together with prayer by the group leader or someone else (consulted ahead of time). Then sing a chorus or a couple of stanzas of a hymn everyone knows.

2. Ask each person to share the most challenging and meaningful insight or experience gained during this week.

3. Invite someone to read aloud the paragraph on page 124, beginning with the sentence "That kind of submission is the topic . . ." and the next paragraph, concluding with ". . . only then can we put ourselves in the position for the Holy Spirit to work within us."

4. Discuss this from the perspectives of the claims that in the Bible *submission* is a love word, not a control word; and our relationship to God is not unlike our relationship to another person. In healthy relationships the degree to which we submit to others most likely is the degree to which we will experience their love. Spend eight to ten minutes in this discussion.

5. Ask for a volunteer to read his/her paraphrase of the Francis de Sales quotation on page 127.

6. Invite a couple of persons to share an experience that might be labeled ecstasy, which they recorded in their reflection on Day 3 of this week.

7. Spend six to eight minutes talking about the meaning and value of ecstatic experiences, why we don't have more such experiences, and whether such experiences would enhance our Christian growth, witness, and discipleship.

8. Invite persons to name "miracles" they have experienced—then discuss the difference between seeking ecstasy and being open to the Spirit's working.

9. On Day 5 we focused on keeping our feelings in perspective. Ask someone to read de Sales's words on that day, then take five to seven minutes discussing the two mistakes related to our feelings that he identifies.

10. Now spend a few minutes allowing the group to respond to this statement: The presence of God, not how God makes that presence known, is what matters most deeply. Is this true? What is the distinction, and why is the statement important? Has anyone been confused or questioned how God seems to make divine presence known to others?

11. Spend what time you have left discussing the difference between ecstasy and surrender and why the saints sought surrender rather than ecstasy.

PRAYING TOGETHER

Teresa of Avila said, "God is well pleased to see a soul humbly taking His Son as Mediator, and yet loving Him so much that . . . it realizes its unworthiness" (*The Complete Works of Saint Teresa of Jesus*, vol. 1, 141). And William Law said, "Praying is not speaking forth eloquently, but simply, the true Desire of the Heart" (*The Works of the Reverend William Law*, vol. 7, 132). Remember this as you pray together now in a conversational style. Spontaneous, conversational prayer is a creative and guiding source in our corporate life. You may want to offer some of the ejaculatory prayers you have prayed in past weeks. One or two persons may want to share the prayer they wrote during their Reflecting and Recording period today. Close your time together by inviting as many as will to offer brief prayers growing out of tonight's sharing. Before you begin this, ask if anyone in the group has specific prayer requests, especially about areas where he or she or others need guidance. When as many as wish to have prayed, close by inviting everyone to pray together the Lord's Prayer.

THEY THIRSTED FOR HOLINESS

DAY

1

Imitation of Christ

If the differences between a Christian and a non-Christian are not obvious, something is wrong—seriously wrong. Paul made a pointed distinction between those who belong to the day and those who belong to the night.

> *But you, beloved, are not in darkness, for that day to surprise you like a thief; for you are all children of light and children of the day; we are not of the night or of darkness. So then let us not fall asleep as others do, but let us keep awake and be sober; for those who sleep sleep at night, and those who are drunk get drunk at night. But since we belong to the day, let us be sober, and put on the breastplate of faith and love, and for a helmet the hope of salvation. For God has destined us not for wrath but for obtaining salvation through our Lord Jesus Christ, who died for us, so that whether we are awake or asleep we may live with him. Therefore encourage one another and build up each other, as indeed you are doing. (1 Thessalonians 5:4-11)*

Do you see the sharp distinction between "children of light" and "children of darkness"? As Karl Heim wrote, "What Jesus wants is not admirers, but disciples—those who will conform their lives to his." Meister Eckhart, a thirteenth-century Dominican mystic, reiterated this idea when he said, "There are many who are willing to follow our Lord half way—but not the other half" (Steere in Introduction to *The Imitation of Christ,* 8).

Let us run with perseverance the race that is set before us, looking to Jesus the pioneer and perfecter of our faith.

—Hebrews 12:1

Continuing to write about Thomas à Kempis's spiritual classic, Douglas Steere says:

> The *Imitation* not only recruits disciples from those who have been admirers. It would train and draw these disciples along until they were willing to enter "the other half," the half where the easy charts and pocket maps vanish and where there are no return tickets available. It, too, would launch them out upon the 70,000 fathoms of water where the foot can no longer touch bottom, where there is no longer any trusting God and keeping your powder dry, but where one must now trust God and take what comes a day at a time. (*The Imitation of Christ,* 8–9)

All the saints acknowledged this truth. They thirsted for holiness and sought to conform their lives wholly to Christ. In *The Imitation,* Thomas à Kempis gives the call.

"He that followeth me walketh not in darkness," saith the Lord. These are the words of Christ, by which we are taught to imitate his life and manners, if we would be truly enlightened, and be delivered from all blindness of heart. Let therefore our chief endeavor be to meditate upon the life of Christ. . . . Whosoever would fully and feelingly understand the words of Christ must endeavor to conform his life wholly to the life of Christ. . . . Surely great words do not make a man holy and just; but a virtuous life maketh him dear to God.

"Some have me in their mouths, but little in their hearts."

Thou hast good cause to be ashamed in looking upon the life of Jesus Christ, seeing thou hast not as yet endeavored to conform thyself more unto him, though thou hast been a long time in the way of God.

For a small income a long journey is undertaken; for ever-lasting life many will scarce once lift a foot from the ground.

If thou wilt reign with me, bear the cross with me. For only the servants of the cross can find the way of blessedness and of true light. (*The Imitation of Christ*, 13)

The saints believed the witness of scripture—that salvation from Jesus Christ is not limited to the forgiveness of sin; it also has the power to break sin's control over lives. As we considered on Day 5 of Week 4, we are to count ourselves "dead to sin" (Rom. 6:11), therefore we "do not let sin exercise dominion" (Rom. 6:12). We can "be conformed to the image" of Christ (Rom. 8:29).

John Wesley described this transformation—being conformed to the likeness of Christ—as a process that continues throughout the Christian's life, leading to *perfection in love*: loving God with all of our heart, soul, mind, and strength, and loving our neighbor as ourselves. Wesley's most important contribution to theology and understanding the Christian life was maintaining the dynamic between God's work of grace in our life and our own efforts to live in response to this grace. In his *Plain Account of Christian Perfection*, Wesley warned,

It is scarcely conceivable how narrow the way is wherein God leads those who follow him and how dependent on him we must be unless we are wanting in our faithfulness to him. (*A Longing for Holiness*, 68)

Elaborating on this warning, he wrote:

We ought to be in the church as the saints are in heaven, and in the house as the holiest people are in the church: doing our work in the house as we pray in the church, worshiping God from the ground of the heart.

We should be continually laboring to cut off all the useless things that surround us. God usually removes the excesses of our souls in the same proportion as we do those of our bodies.

The best means of resisting the devil is to destroy whatever of the world remains in us in order to raise for God, upon its ruins, a building all of love. Then shall we begin, in this fleeting life, to love God as we shall love him in eternity. . . .

If, after having renounced all, we do not watch incessantly and beseech God to accompany our vigilance with his, we shall be again entangled and overcome.

As the most dangerous winds may enter at little openings, so the devil never enters more dangerously than by little unobserved incidents, which seem to be nothing, yet insensibly open the heart to great temptations.

It is good to renew ourselves from time to time by closely examining the state of our souls, as if we had never done it before. For nothing tends more to the full assurance of faith than to keep ourselves by this means in humility and the exercise of all good works.

To continual watchfulness and prayer ought to be added continual employment. For grace flies a vacuum as well as nature, and the devil fills whatever God does not fill. (*A Longing for Holiness*, 68–69)

REFLECTING AND RECORDING

In the space provided on page 150, paraphrase à Kempis's words into your own.

List some differences that should be obvious between a Christian and a non-Christian.

What is the "other half" that Meister Eckhart was talking about when he said, "There are many who are willing to follow our Lord half way—but not the other half"? Reflect and make some notes.

Spend the balance of your time reflecting on this word from the *Imitation*: "If thou wilt reign with me, *bear the cross with me*" (italics mine).

DURING THE DAY

Be sensitive to occasions today when you might deliberately choose to bear the cross with Jesus.

DAY

2

The Holiness Stream

In his landmark work *Streams of Living Water*, Richard Foster examines six dimensions of faith and practice that define Christian tradition. He calls these streams, or traditions. He identifies the following traditions: the contemplative tradition, the holiness tradition, the charismatic tradition, the social justice tradition, the evangelical tradition, and the incarnational tradition.

These traditions span Christian history. They overlap in time but have specific periods of flowering. Many of the saints we have covered in our study would belong to more than one of these traditions.

Foster says that the contemplative tradition, or the prayer-filled life, "forms the foundation for holy living. . . . The Holiness Stream of Christian life and faith focuses upon the inward reformation of the heart and the development of 'holy habits.' We can rely upon these deeply ingrained habits of virtue to make our lives function appropriately and to bring forth substantial character formation" (*Streams of Living Water*, 61).

The holiness tradition holds before us the ultimate goal of the Christian life:

an ever deeper formation of the inner personality so as to reflect the glory and goodness of God; an ever more radiant conformity to the life and faith and desires and habits of Jesus; an utter transformation of our creatureliness into whole and perfect sons and daughters of God. (*Streams of Living Water*, 85)

Foster pointed to Phoebe Palmer as an inspiring and defining example of this holiness stream. Charles Edward White said Palmer might well be "the most influential female theologian the Church has yet produced" (*Wesleyan Theological Journal*, Spring-Fall 1988, 208).

Phoebe Palmer was an extraordinary teacher, passionate in her concern for humanity, and a powerful preacher of the holiness way. She was born in 1807 and lived until 1874. Her father was a young convert of John Wesley, so "the history and teachings of prominent Methodist leaders dominated the family's religious life"(Foster, *Streams of Living Water,* 62).

Palmer married a physician, and they had six children. The third child, Eliza, died in an especially tragic accident—the family's maid dropped a burning oil lamp on the gauze curtain covering the baby's crib, burning her to death. That loss was a life-changing point for Phoebe. She turned to the Bible and to God.

> While pacing the room, crying to God, amid the tumult of grief, my mind was arrested by a gentle whisper, saying, "Your Heavenly Father loves you. He would not permit such a great trial, without intending that some great good proportionate in magnitude and weight should result." . . .
>
> In the agony of my soul I had exclaimed, "O, what shall I do!" And the answer now came,—"Be still, and know that I am God." I took up the precious WORD, and cried, "O teach me the lesson of this trial," and the first lines to catch my eye on opening the Bible, were these, "O, the depth of the riches, both of the wisdom and knowledge of God! How unsearchable are his judgments and his ways past finding out!"
>
> . . . The tumult of feeling was hushed. . . . "What thou knowest not now, thou shalt know hereafter," was assuringly whispered. Wholly subdued before the Lord, my chastened spirit nestled in quietness under the wing of the Holy Comforter.
>
> . . . And now I have resolved, that . . . the time I would have devoted to her, shall be spent in work for Jesus. And if diligent and self-sacrificing in carrying out my resolve, the death of this child may result in the spiritual life of many. (*Phoebe Palmer: Selected Writings*, 99–100)

This dramatic, ecstatic event gave Phoebe an unquenchable zeal for the work of Christ. However it was another experience, what she called her "Valley of Decision," that shaped her life and made her a leader in the holiness tradition of spirituality, identifying her with the saints with their unquenchable thirst for holiness.

John Wesley, who markedly impacted Phoebe's life, was profoundly shaped by *Rules and Exercises of Holy Living and Dying* by Jeremy Taylor, *The Imitation of Christ* by Thomas à Kempis, and *A Serious Call to a Devout and Holy Life* by William Law. So Phoebe joined that holiness stream of Christian life and faith. We will consider her again on Day 5. For now, look at a passage from *The Imitation of Christ*.

The Holiness Stream of Christian life and faith focuses upon the inward re-formation of the heart and the development of "holy habits."

—Richard Foster

> So much inclined to outward things, so negligent in things inward and spiritual: So prone to laughter and unbridled mirth, so indisposed to tears and compunction: So prompt to ease and pleasures of the flesh, so dull to strictness of life and zeal: So curious to hear news and to see beautiful sights, so slack to embrace what is humble and low: So covetous of abundance, so [stingy] in giving, so fast in keeping: So inconsiderate in speech, so reluctant to keep silence: So uncomposed in manners, so fretful in action: So eager about food, so deaf to the word of God: In such a hurry to rest, so slow to labor: So wakeful in vain conversation, so drowsy at sacred services: So hasty to arrive at the end thereof, so inclined to be wandering and inattentive: So negligent in the prayers, so lukewarm in celebrating the holy eucharist, so dry and heartless in

receiving it: So quickly distracted, so seldom wholly gathered into thyself: So suddenly moved to anger, so apt to take displeasure against another: So ready to judge, so severe to reprove: So joyful in prosperity, so weak in adversity: Make thou a firm resolution always to be amending thy life, and to be endeavoring always after a farther progress in holiness. (*The Imitation of Christ*, 16–17)

The call was clear—and the saints thirsted for it: holiness—the conformity of our life, faith, and desires to Jesus.

REFLECTING AND RECORDING

Recall and record here an experience that had a life-changing impact for you.

Read again *The Imitation* passage on pages 153–154. Pay attention to the negative/positive contrasts. In the following space, note those things of which you are guilty—for instance, "So covetous of abundance, so [stingy] in giving."

Write a prayer confessing those things you have listed, repenting, and asking God's forgiveness.

DURING THE DAY

Continue the practice you began yesterday—to identify occasions when you might deliberately choose to bear the cross with Christ.

DAY
3

"Sweet Is the Burning"

Bernard of Clairvaux, a twelfth-century French saint, wrote a descriptive passage about the purifying fire of God, which burns within us to make us holy.

> It is sent by God to arouse you and make you realize what you are in yourself, so that you may afterwards taste more sweetly what you are soon to become by the power of God. But the Fire which God is consumes indeed, but without causing pain; sweet is the burning, blissful devastation that its flames effect. For it is truly a "hot burning coal" but it acts like fire on our faults, only in order that it may act as unction to the soul. (*Selections from the Writings of Bernard of Clairvaux*, 21)

What a challenging phrase: "sweet is the burning." The saints sought *purity of heart*, which is what holiness is about—the inward re-formation of the heart. It is from the heart that our actions spring. Most of us know that, sooner or later, what is on the inside of a person will express itself outwardly. This is what the Epistle of James is all about. Richard Foster reminds us,

> If the central core of who we are is "earthly, unspiritual, devilish," what flows out will be "disorder and wickedness of every kind." Conversely, if the central core of who we are is "pure, . . . peaceable, gentle, willing to yield, full of mercy and good fruits, without a trace of partiality or hypocrisy," then what flows out will be "a harvest of righteousness [which] is sown in peace for those who make peace" (James 3:15-18). (*Streams of Living Water*, 71)

James emphasizes purifying the source. See how he concludes his teaching on discipline and "taming the tongue."

> *Not many of you should become teachers, my brothers and sisters, for you know that we who teach will be judged with greater strictness. For all of us make many mistakes. Anyone who makes no mistakes in speaking is perfect, able to keep the whole body in check with a bridle. If we put bits into the mouths of horses to make them obey us, we guide their whole bodies. Or look at ships: though they are so large that it takes strong winds to drive them, yet they are guided by a very small rudder wherever the will of the pilot directs. So also the tongue is a small member, yet it boasts of great exploits.*

How great a forest is set ablaze by a small fire! And the tongue is a fire. The tongue is placed among our members as a world of iniquity; it stains the whole body, sets on fire the cycle of nature, and is itself set on fire by hell. For every species of beast and bird, of reptile and sea creature, can be tamed and has been tamed by the human species, but no one can tame the tongue—a restless evil, full of deadly poison. With it we bless the Lord and Father, and with it we curse those who are made in the likeness of God. From the same mouth come blessing and cursing. My brothers and sisters, this ought not to be so. (James 3:1–10)

The divinely transformed heart produces right actions. Thus, an identifiable expression of holiness is a person's character. As indicated in Day 2, God's command to God's people through Moses was, "Be holy, for I the Lord your God am holy" (Lev. 19:2). Peter repeats that command when he describes how Christians are to live:

Instead, as he who called you is holy, be holy yourselves in all your conduct; for it is written, "You shall be holy, for I am holy." (1 Peter 1:15)

In Exodus 19:5-6, God summarizes in an introductory word the characteristics the Divine One wants to see in his people:

"Now therefore, if you obey my voice and keep my covenant, you shall be my treasured possession out of all the peoples. Indeed, the whole earth is mine, but you shall be for me a priestly kingdom and a holy nation. These are the words that you shall speak to the Israelites." (Exodus 19:5-6)

The fire that burns within us is the presence of the Holy Spirit re-forming our hearts to obedience and love.

Then, in Exodus 20, Moses records God's Ten Commandments, spelling out in detail characteristics of a holy people. God is looking for a holy people who will express the divine character in righteousness and love. We are to respond to God's standard of righteousness with obedience and to God's love with love.

Martin Luther reminds us that the sins addressed in the Ten Commandments all deal with "nothing else but self-love."

In the sins instanced in the Ten Commandments we see nothing else but self-love, which seeks its own interest, takes from God what is his, from men what is theirs, and from all it is, has and does, gives nothing back to God or man. St Augustine well says, "The beginning of all sin is the love of one's own self . . ." Therefore, he lives best who lives not for himself, and he who lives for himself, lives worst. (*The Joy of the Saints*, 108)

Because of this fact, the fire of what burns within us, whose burning Bernard of Clairvaux described as sweet, is the presence of God's Holy Spirit re-forming our hearts to obedience and love. *The Imitation of Christ* gives expression to this nature and shape of this re-formation:

What harm can the words or injuries of any man do thee? He hurteth himself rather than thee, nor shall he be able to avoid the judgment of God, whosoever he be. Do thou have God before thine eyes, and contend not with peevish words.

Thou art not the more holy for being praised; nor the more worthless for being dispraised. What thou art, that thou art; neither by words canst thou be made greater than what thou art in the sight of God. If thou consider what thou art in thyself, thou wilt not care what men say of thee. Man looketh on the countenance, but God on the heart. Man considereth the deeds, but God weigheth the intentions.

He that seeketh no testimony on his behalf from without, doth show that he hath wholly committed himself unto God. (*The Imitation of Christ*, 29)

REFLECTING AND RECORDING

Martin Luther said that all the Ten Commandments deal with self-love. Here is a summary of those commandments, found in Exodus 20:3-17.

- You shall have no other gods before me.
- You shall not make for yourself an idol.
- You shall not make wrongful use of the name of the Lord your God.
- Remember the sabbath day, and keep it holy.
- Honor your father and your mother.
- You shall not murder.
- You shall not commit adultery.
- You shall not steal.
- You shall not bear false witness against your neighbor.
- You shall not covet.

Look at each one. How does it deal with self-love?

To be holy, we are to respond to God's standard of righteousness with obedience. What particular standards of righteousness as stated in the Ten Commandments are you most prone to violate? List those here.

To be holy, we must respond to God's love with love. Make some brief notes about your failure to respond to God's love with love.

Reread James 3:1-10 (on pages 155–156) and reflect on how your tongue—the way you speak—witnesses to the degree of your holiness.

DURING THE DAY

The following is a prayer for purification taken from *The Imitation of Christ.* Read it prayerfully:

> O thou everlasting Light, surpassing all created lights, dart the beams of thy brightness from above, to pierce all the most inward parts of my heart. Purify, rejoice, enlighten and enliven my spirit with all the powers thereof, that I may cleave unto thee with abundance of joy and triumph. Amen. (*The Imitation of Christ,* 38)

Translate the above prayer from *The Imitation* into your own words on a card or piece of paper you can carry with you for the next few days. Find opportunity to pray it four or five times each day.

DAY
4

Heart-Work

As yesterday's reading emphasized, the fire that burns within us ("sweet is the burning") is the presence of God's Holy Spirit reforming our hearts to obedience and love. The end toward which we move in our thirst for holiness is purity of heart. The Puritan spiritual writers and preachers labeled this *heart-work.* John Flavel, a seventeenth-century English Puritan, gave this perspective: "The greatest difficulty in conversion is to win the heart to God; and the greatest difficulty after conversion is to keep the heart with God . . . heart-work is hard work indeed" (*The Works of John Flavel*, vol. 5, 423, 428).

The crux of our heart-work toward holiness is fully surrendering our will to Christ so that all of us belongs to God. The apostle Paul expressed it autobiographically:

> But if, in our effort to be justified in Christ, we ourselves have been found to be sinners, is Christ then a servant of sin? Certainly not! But if I build up again the very things that I once tore down, then I demonstrate that I am a transgressor. For through the law I died to the law, so that I might live to God. I have been crucified with Christ; and it is no longer I who live, but it is Christ who lives in me. And the life I now live in the flesh I live by faith in the Son of God, who loved me and gave himself for me. I do not nullify the grace of God; for if justification comes through the law, then Christ died for nothing. (Galatians 2:17-21)

The saints talked about the heart-work required for holiness in many different ways. Fénelon centered on the uprooting of self-love.

> While we are so imperfect, we can understand only in part. The same self-love that causes our defects injuriously hides them from ourselves and from others. Self-love cannot bear the view of itself. It finds some hiding place; it places itself in some flattering light to soften its ugliness. Thus there is always some illusion in us while we are so imperfect and have so much love of ourselves.
>
> Self-love must be uprooted, and the love of God take its place in our hearts before we can see ourselves as we are. Then the same principle that enables us to see our imperfections will destroy them. When the light of truth has risen within us, then we see clearly what is there. Then we love ourselves without partiality, without flattery, as we love our neighbor. In the meantime, God spares us by revealing our weakness to us just in proportion as our strength to support the view of it increases. We discover our imperfections one by one as we are able to cure them. Without this merciful preparation that adapts our strength to the light within, we should be in despair. (*Selections from the Writings of François Fénelon*, 20)

Holiness requires fully surrendering our own will so that God can eradicate our self-orientation and self-love. I have a young friend named Tammy who lives this Jesus style dramatically. She was converted at the University of Georgia. She arrived at Asbury Seminary as a student about the same time I came as president. I didn't learn her story until a couple of years later. She came to school with only enough money to take her through the first semester. Hers is a modern faith miracle story. She worked as much as she could, but there was no way she could work enough to pay her tuition and living expenses. So she prayed. She never asked for money, but time and again when she had nothing, no money to continue, somehow the money she needed would come.

The crux of our heart-work toward holiness is fully surrendering our will to Christ.

The summer before her last year in seminary, she went to India on a short-term mission trip. As a result of a series of circumstances and following God's call, she returned to India a year later to establish Grace House, a home for street children. When I last heard from Tammy, there were sixty children under her care in two different facilities. The story is the same as it was during her years in seminary. She depends totally upon God. I have never known her to ask anyone for money, but miraculously she receives what she needs.

She sends e-mails to a number of her friends, telling the story of what is going on and the miracles that are taking place. Always she confesses her dependence upon God and her willingness to live sacrificially in order to fulfill God's call upon her life.

In an e-mail that came October 4, 2000, she wrote:

I encourage you to let God take you deeper in prayer and intimacy. I know these are the "Christian catch phrases" these days. But . . . well . . . it's the truth. I guess my prayer for you is that you would go deeper with Jesus, that you would let Him wash through you like a rushing river, cleansing, soothing, filling you in every good way. Intimacy . . . Just more of Jesus. That place where you utter a prayer and in an instant, you know it has been answered. That place where you are convicted of your self and sin and in the same moment, encouraged and refreshed. That place in your heart where man's words cannot reach, but one word from God, and you melt.

Tammy knows that we must be convicted of self and sin, that holiness requires fully surrendering our independent self-will in order that God can eradicate our self-orientation. As authors Allan Coppedge and William Ury say, "This is the negative side of this experience in the sense that something has to go before God's full presence can come" (*In His Image*, 108).

God's full presence through the Holy Spirit results in God's complete possession of an individual. Without a person's surrender of his or her will and self-interest, God's full controlling presence cannot take possession of that person's life.

REFLECTING AND RECORDING

The movement toward holiness is from purification from self-will, to full presence of the Holy Spirit, to full possession of our life. Reflect on how that movement operates in your life.

Fénelon said, "The same self-love that causes our defects . . . hides them from ourselves and from others." Probe yourself in this light. What defects is self-love causing in you? How does your self-love hide your defects from you and others?

Read again Fénelon's second paragraph on the previous page. Spend the balance of your time reflecting on the claim that "self-love must be uprooted, and the love of God take its place in our hearts before we can see ourselves as we are."

DURING THE DAY

Continue using the prayer from *The Imitation* that you translated into your own words yesterday.

DAY
5

"My All in All"

On Day 2 of this week, I introduced Phoebe Palmer, a powerful preacher of "the holiness way," and a moving example of the holiness stream of Christian life and faith. Her teaching and speaking ministry, which spread worldwide, began in a weekly meeting, initially for women, in her New York home. The weekly meeting became known as "the Tuesday Meeting for the Promotion of Holiness" and continued for nearly forty years.

We live in a state of holiness and sanctification as we continually give ourselves as a living sacrifice to Christ, our altar.

—Phoebe Palmer

Palmer's teaching responsibility and her willingness to wrestle with the questions and concerns of the Tuesday Meeting participants kept her struggling and growing. She longed for "entire sanctification." She wrestled mentally and emotionally with John Wesley's teaching that believers should not consider themselves sanctified "till there is added the testimony of the Spirit witnessing his entire sanctification as clearly as his justification" (*A Plain Account of Christian Perfection*, 52).

Her struggle and searching led to what she later called her "day of days." Almost exactly one year after the tragic death of her daughter, Eliza, Palmer totally consecrated her life to God and experienced sanctifying grace in such measure that it became the energizing factor and shaping influence of her life. The way she talked about it is still vibrant and alive:

> Between the hours of eight and nine [in the evening]—while pleading at the throne of grace for a present fulfillment of the exceeding great and precious promises; pleading also the fullness and freeness of the atonement, its unbounded efficacy, and making an entire surrender of body, soul, and spirit; time, talents, and influence; and also of the dearest ties of nature, my beloved husband and child; in a word, my earthly *all—I received the assurance that God the Father, through the atoning Lamb, accepted the sacrifice*; my heart was emptied of self, and cleansed of all idols, from all filthiness of the flesh and spirit, and I realized that I dwelt in God, and felt that he had become the portion of my soul, my *ALL IN ALL.*" (*Phoebe Palmer: Selected Writings*, 115)

Phoebe Palmer developed and taught the rest of her life what she called "altar theology." According to this theology, as Christians, our altar is Christ. Upon this altar we offer ourselves as sacrifices. Palmer taught that, "Since everything that touches the altar is holy, we are holy when we place everything we are upon the altar. We, therefore, live in a state of holiness and sanctification as we continually give ourselves as a living sacrifice to Christ, our altar" (Foster, *Streams of Living Water*, 65).

Phoebe Palmer often quoted the words of Jesus, "The altar . . . sanctifieth the gift" (Matt. 23:19, KJV), but her "altar theology" is best expressed by Paul:

> *I appeal to you therefore, brothers and sisters, by the mercies of God, to present your bodies as a living sacrifice, holy and acceptable to God, which is your spiritual worship. Do not be conformed to this world, but be transformed by the renewing of your minds, so that you may discern what is the will of God—what is good and acceptable and perfect. (Romans 12:1-2)*

Thomas à Kempis, along with Phoebe Palmer and many others, contended that there is no holiness apart from our being on the altar, "no holiness, if thou, O Lord, withdraw thine hand."

> Shall the clay boast against him that formed it? There is therefore no holiness, if thou, O Lord, withdraw thine hand. No wisdom availeth, if thou cease to guide. No courage helpeth, if thou leave off to defend. No chastity is secure, if thou do not protect it. No vigilance of our own availeth, if thy sacred watchfulness be not present with us. For, if we be left of thee, we sink and perish; but being visited of thee, we are raised up and live. Truly we are inconstant, but by thee we are established: we wax lukewarm, but by thee we are inflamed. (*The Imitation of Christ*, 17)

REFLECTING AND RECORDING

Has there been a "day of days" in your Christian pilgrimage—maybe not as dramatic as Phoebe Palmer's, but a time when you realized you "dwelt in God," and you felt God "had become [your] . . . *ALL IN ALL*"? Describe that experience.

Spend some time reflecting on Palmer's claims (paraphrased here):

- We are holy when we place everything we are upon the altar.

- We live in a state of holiness and sanctification when we continually give ourselves as living sacrifices to Christ.

Now spend some time seeking the meaning of à Kempis's words (paraphrased here) for your daily living.

- There is no holiness, Lord, if you withdraw your hand.

- Our wisdom is not adequate if you, Lord, cease to guide.

- If you do not defend us, our courage is inadequate.

- None of our own vigilance will save us; you, oh Lord, must be present with us.

DURING THE DAY

Many hymns employ Phoebe Palmer's "altar theology," especially gospel hymns written during the "holiness revival" of which Phoebe was a part. One of these was "I Surrender All."

> All to Jesus I surrender;
> all to him I freely give;
> I will ever love and trust him,
> in his presence daily live.
> I surrender all, I surrender all,
> all to thee, my blessed Savior,
> I surrender all.
>
> Words by J. W. Van Deventer, 1896.

These words are printed on page 243. Cut them out and carry them with you for the next few days. Read them as a prayer many times during the day, especially as your prayer to begin and close the day. If you know the hymn, sing it two or three times a day. Consider singing it for two or three days at a meal you share with family or friends.

DAY
6
Pruning Time

I cringed when I first read the following paragraph. It still stings sharply every time I read it.

> People do not drift toward holiness. Apart from grace-driven effort, people do not gravitate toward godliness, prayer, obedience to Scripture, faith, and delight in the Lord. We drift toward compromise and call it tolerance; we drift toward disobedience and call it freedom; we drift toward superstition and call it faith. We cherish the indiscipline of lost self-control and call it relaxation; we slouch toward prayerlessness and delude ourselves into thinking we have escaped legalism; we slide toward godlessness and convince ourselves we have been liberated. (D. A. Carson, *For the Love of God*, vol. 2, 23)

On Day 1 of this week we looked at a portion of First Thessalonians, which made the case that if there is no obvious difference between Christians and non-Christians, then something is seriously wrong. Paul designated Christians as children of light, and he said that for no reason should children of light be confused with children of darkness.

Even so, one of Paul's ongoing concerns—for himself and others—was the fact that the way back into the darkness is always open, and living in the light requires vigilance and discipline.

> *Do you not know that in a race all the runners run, but only one gets the prize? Run in such a way as to get the prize. Everyone who competes in the games goes into strict training. They do it to get a crown that will not last; but we do it to get a crown that will last forever. Therefore I do not run like a man running aimlessly; I do not fight like a man beating the air. No, I beat my body and make it my slave so that after I have preached to others, I myself will not be disqualified for the prize. (1 Corinthians 9:24-27, NIV)*

The Corinthians wanted to take the easy way, but Paul reminded them that no one can achieve anything of worth without the sternest self-discipline. In ancient Greece, the Isthmian Games, second only to the Olympic Games, took place in Corinth. The Corinthians could identify with Paul's fascination with the picture of the athlete. They knew the thrill of athletic contests. Paul reminded them of how intensely the athlete must train in order to compete and win. He also made the point that the athlete, for all his self-discipline and training, wins a crown of laurel leaves that withers within a few days, but the discipline of the Christian life results in a crown that lasts forever—eternal life.

Paul is dramatic: "I beat my body and make it my slave so that after I have preached to others, I myself will not be disqualified for the prize" (v. 27).

We considered earlier (Week 2, Days 2 and 5) the whole notion of mortification. In the history of Christianity, especially the monastic movement, many persons have taken mortification to extremes, starving themselves, beating themselves, treating their bodies as enemies of spirituality, confusing Paul's warning about "the flesh" with the physical body and senses. For this reason I have tried to make the case that *holiness is primarily heart-work*. Holiness re-forms and purifies the heart, bringing our wills in subjection to Christ's—conforming our life, faith, and desires to the desires of Jesus.

Where your soul is concerned, it is no good pruning only once; you must do it often, always if possible. If you are honest with yourself, there will always be something that needs cutting back.

—Bernard of Clairvaux

Even though mortification may have been distorted, even perverted, we must keep Paul's advice—to remain alert and self-controlled—predominant in our awareness. Many Christians have become casualties to casualness and carelessness. Our enemy, Satan, constantly seeks to penetrate our souls' defenses, which makes vigilance essential. Luther wrote a colorful passage about this need for vigilance over the heart:

> When I am assailed with heavy tribulations, I rush out among my pigs, rather than remain alone by myself. The human heart is like a millstone in a mill; when you put wheat under it, it turns and grinds and bruises the wheat to flour; if you put no wheat, it still grinds on, but then 'tis itself it grinds and wears away. So the human heart, unless it be occupied with some employment, leaves space for the devil, who wriggles himself in, and brings with him a whole host of evil thoughts, temptations, and tribulations, which grind out the heart. (*The Table Talk of Martin Luther*, 290–91)

But discipline and vigilance alone are not enough. The saints talked a lot about pruning. Bernard of Clairvaux wrote:

> Lord Jesus, how few souls there are who want to follow Thee! Everyone wants to reach Thee in the end, because they know that "at Thy right hand are pleasures forever more." They want the happiness that Thou canst give, but not to imitate Thee; they want to reign with Thee, but not to suffer. Even the carnal minded would like a holy death, although they cannot stand a holy life.
>
> He says moreover, "the time of pruning has come." . . . I would point out also that, where your soul is concerned, it is no good pruning only once; you must do it often always, if possible. For, if you are honest with yourself, there will always be something that needs cutting back; for whatever progress you may make while you are still in the body, you are mistaken if you think your faults are dead, rather than merely repressed. . . . In view of this great danger, I can only advise you to watch yourself most carefully and to cut away all offending growths as soon as they appear. For virtues and vices cannot grow together; if your virtues are to grow, your faults must be prevented from making any development at all.
>
> So it is always pruning time with us, brethren, because there is always need for it. (*Selections from the Writings of Bernard of Clairvaux*, 19–20)

Consider one other pruning challenge from Francis de Sales:

> "The flowers have appeared in our land; the time of pruning is come," says the Sacred Spouse. What other flowers do we have in our hearts . . . except good desires? As soon as they appear we must take a pruning knife in order to remove from our conscience all dead and worthless

works. . . . a soul that hopes for the honor of being made spouse of the Son of God must "put off the old man, and put on the new" by forsaking sin and removing and cutting away whatever obstructs union with God. For us the beginning of good health is to be purged of our sinful tendencies. . . .

The usual purgation and healing, whether of body or of soul, takes place only little by little and by passing from one advance to another with difficulty and patience. . . . The soul that rises from sin to devotion has been compared to the dawning day, which at its approach does not drive out the darkness instantaneously but only little by little. A slow cure, as the maxim says, is always surest. Diseases of the soul as well as those of the body come posting on horseback but leave slowly and on foot.

. . . we must have courage and patience. . . .

The work of purging the soul neither can nor should end except with our life itself. We must not be disturbed at our imperfections, since for us perfection consists in fighting against them. How can we fight against them unless we see them, or overcome them unless we face them? Our victory does not consist in being unconscious of them but in not consenting to them. (*Introduction to the Devout Life*, 48–49)

REFLECTING AND RECORDING

In Roman Catholic spiritual writing, the image of becoming a spouse of Christ is often employed, with wedding and marriage used as a metaphor for union with Christ. De Sales used the imagery of incision and circumcision to challenge us in our pruning.

> *Healing, whether of body or of soul, takes place only little by little and by passing from one advance to another with difficulty and patience.*
>
> —Francis de Sales

The greater part of Christians usually practice incision instead of circumcision. They will make a cut indeed in a diseased part; but as for employing the knife of circumcision, to take away whatever is superfluous from the heart, few go so far. (*A Year with the Saints*, 84)

Focusing on that image, how willing are you "to take away whatever is superfluous from the heart"? Make some notes about what needs to be taken away from your heart.

Write a prayer expressing your desire to do the heart-work essential for holiness and your willingness to allow the Holy Spirit to prune you so that you may bear fruit for God's kingdom.

DURING THE DAY

Continue to pray the words of "I Surrender All."

DAY
7

Growth in Grace

A feature newspaper article entitled "The Morning After" describes how it really feels to play pro football every Sunday. These were the first paragraphs:

Monday mornings are the toughest for Jerome Bettis.

Shortly after 9 o'clock, the Pittsburgh Steelers running back awakens and can barely move his neck. One of his ankles is purple and swollen. His left hip still hurts. His ribs sting at even the lightest touch. There is a piercing sensation in his lower back. His shoulders, he says, "feel like they are on fire."

He begins the laborious process of getting out of bed, shimmying to the mattress' edge and gingerly lowering his sore feet to the floor. He rests there for a few minutes, feeling his blood start to circulate.

Usually, he hoists himself upright and limps slowly to the bathroom. On the rough days, there is an additional challenge: the stairs from the second floor of his immaculate home to the first. At the edge of the first step, he sometimes has no choice but to have a seat, then either carefully slide himself down, one excruciating step at a time, or literally crawl until he has reached the ground level. (*USA Today*, 7 December 2000, 1)

Jarrett Bell, writer of the article, went on to describe Jerome Bettis's following week.

By midafternoon Monday, Bettis had received treatment, including electrical stimulation and ice. He rode his stationary bike for twenty minutes, then walked on a treadmill for another twenty. That was Monday. During the week Bettis would ride his bike each day for forty-five minutes. He had one-hour, full-body massages on Tuesdays and Thursdays. Daily team practices were complemented by weight-lifting sessions, and he was in the training room daily.

"Everybody sees us on Sundays," Bettis said, stretching his limbs on the floor of his spacious family room Monday afternoon. "But if people saw us on Monday through Saturday and got a sense of the toll this can take on your body, they would really understand that we love this game 10 times more than they imagined.

"You definitely need to stay motivated because it can be easy to be demoralized. Especially if your team's not doing well. It can be tough to get up on Mondays, thinking about getting yourself ready for the next week." (*USA Today*, 7 December 2000, 2A)

I read this story when I was concentrating on the saints' thirst for holiness. The saints would all agree on the following rule: No pain, no gain. Enabled by the Spirit, Christians are to "mortify the deeds of the body" of our evil nature (Rom. 8:13, KJV), or as another translation says, we are to "put to death the deeds of the body" (NRSV). While putting to death these deeds requires discipline, renunciation, and vigilance, a rigid adherence to rules and regulations—a consuming asceticism—leads to a dismal, joyless perfectionism. Rather, as we become more and more dead to sin, we are more and more alive to God. We go on from grace to grace.

Sanctifying grace, which leads to holiness, just like justifying grace, is utterly and completely a work of grace, undeserved and unearnable. John Wesley traced the process:

> At the same time that we are justified, yea, in that very moment, sanctification begins. In that instant we are born again, born from above, born of the Spirit: there is a *real* as well as *relative* change. We are inwardly renewed by the power of God.
>
> From the time of our being born again, the gradual work of sanctification takes place. We are enabled "by the Spirit" to "mortify the deeds of the body" of our evil nature; and as we are more and more dead to sin, we are more and more alive to God. We go on from grace to grace.
>
> It is thus that we wait for entire sanctification; for a full salvation from all our sins—from pride, self-will, anger, unbelief; or, as the apostle expressed it, "go on unto perfection."
>
> But what is perfection? The word has various senses. Here it means perfect love. It is love excluding sin; love filling the heart, taking up the whole capacity of the soul. It is love "rejoicing evermore, praying without ceasing, in everything giving thanks." (*The Joy of the Saints*, 344)

Wesley gives us three defining dimensions of perfection, or holiness, all of them aspects of love:

1. Love excluding sin

2. Love filling the heart

3. Love rejoicing evermore

The saints thirsted for this perfection/holiness and claimed that it could be theirs. This was no empty claim but solidly grounded in scripture. Paul, who closed his greeting to the Corinthians with this word, "Put things in order, listen to my appeal, agree with one another, live in peace" (2 Cor. 13:11), was only urging others to do what he practiced himself.

We must guard against the pitfall of connecting holiness with works/righteousness. We must allow God to re-form our hearts, shape our character, and empower us for kingdom living.

> *Yet whatever gains I had, these I have come to regard as loss because of Christ. More than that, I regard everything as loss because of the surpassing value of knowing Christ Jesus my Lord. For his sake I have suffered the loss of all things, and I regard them as rubbish, in order that I may gain Christ and be found in him, not having a righteousness of my own that comes from the law, but one that comes through faith in Christ, the righteousness from God based on faith. I want to know Christ and the power of his resurrection and the sharing of his sufferings by becoming like him in his death, if somehow I may attain the resurrection from the dead.*
>
> *Not that I have already obtained this or have already reached the goal; but I press on to make it my own, because Christ Jesus has made me his own. Beloved, I do not consider that I have made it my own; but this one thing I do; forgetting what lies behind and straining forward to what lies ahead, I press on toward the goal for the prize of the heavenly call of God in Christ Jesus. Let those of us then who are mature be of the same mind; and if you think differently about anything, this too God will reveal to you. Only let us hold fast to what we have attained.*
>
> *Brothers and sisters, join in imitating me, and observe those who live according to the example you have in us. (Philippians 3:7-17)*

As we press on toward holiness, we must guard against the pitfall of connecting holiness with works/righteousness. We strive "to enter in" as Jesus calls us, but our striving is not "works" that have to do with merit or something we earn. Effort—our striving—is kept connected to grace. We use all the classical disciplines—prayer, fasting, confession, silence, scripture meditation—not for merit or as virtue, but as a way to place and keep ourselves before God, allowing God to re-form our hearts, shape our character, and empower us for kingdom living.

REFLECTING AND RECORDING

God does not seek to improve us but to radically *transform* us. C. S. Lewis was adamant in his expression of this truth: "The goal towards which [God] is beginning to guide you is absolute perfection; and no power in the whole universe, except you yourself, can prevent Him from taking you to that goal" (*Mere Christianity*, 158).

Do you believe that? Reflect on your Christian pilgrimage—have you practiced the faith as though you believe in the possibility of perfection?

Wesley provided three defining dimensions of holiness—all of them aspects of love. Spend some time reflecting on each of these in turn.

1. Love excluding sin
2. Love filling the heart
3. Love rejoicing evermore

If you believe with C. S. Lewis that the goal toward which God is guiding you is perfection, and that only you can prevent God from taking you to that goal, write a prayer that expresses your conviction, desire, and willingness to yield to God; and allow the Almighty to accomplish the divine will for your holiness.

DURING THE DAY

Continue to use the "I Surrender All" prayer (page 163).

Group Meeting for Week 6

SHARING TOGETHER

You are approaching the end of this workbook venture. Only two more planned group meetings remain, so your group may want to discuss its future. Would the group like to stay together for a longer time? Are there resources (books, tapes, periodicals) that the group would like to use corporately? This workbook is a sequel to my previous one, *The Workbook on Keeping Company with the Saints*. If you have not already used that resource, you may want to consider doing so. If all group members attend the same church, think about ways to share this workbook study with others.

1. Invite someone to read his or her paraphrase of *The Imitation* passage on page 150 (Day 1 of this week), then spend twelve to fifteen minutes discussing with the group the statements under the crosses below and on page 172. As you consider each statement, answer the following questions:

    • Do you believe the statement is true?

    • What are its implications?

    • How have you experienced this statement as true or false in your life?

The saints believed the witness of scripture—that the salvation of Jesus Christ is not limited to the forgiveness of sin; it also has the power to break sin's control over our lives.

"There are many who are willing to follow our Lord half way, but not the other half" (Meister Eckhart).

Jesus does not want admirers but disciples.

"The best means of resisting the devil is to destroy whatever of the world remains in us in order to raise for God, upon its ruins, a building all of love." (John Wesley)

2. On Day 2, we considered the experience that had a profound, life-changing impact on Phoebe Palmer. Invite a couple of persons to tell about an experience that profoundly changed their lives.

3. Ask someone to read the Ten Commandments, printed on page 157 (Day 3, Reflecting and Recording); then discuss how each of the commandments, as Luther contended, deals with self-love. Which of the Ten Commandments do we most frequently break?

4. The movement toward holiness is from
   purification from self-will
                    to
   full presence of the Holy Spirit
                    to
   full possession of our life.

   Putting this together with Cassian's claim that "renunciation is nothing but the evidence of the cross" in our lives (Day 4), invite the group to talk about whether their lives show any evidence of the cross, what that evidence is, and how holiness is operating in their lives. Spend ten to fifteen minutes in this discussion.

5. Invite a couple of persons to share an experience like Phoebe Palmer described in our text for Day 5 and which they recorded in their reflection time on that day—a "day of days" when they felt God "had become their *ALL IN ALL*."

6. Spend eight to ten minutes discussing the meaning of the four sentences from à Kempis, recorded in the Reflecting and Recording section on page 162 (Week 6, Day 5).

7. Spend the remaining time discussing each of Wesley's three defining dimensions of holiness:

   a. love excluding sin

   b. love filling the heart

   c. love rejoicing evermore

PRAYING TOGETHER

1. As you begin your prayer time, invite someone to lead in singing a stanza or two of a familiar hymn or chorus. If possible, choose a song with the theme of longing for holiness, such as "Take Time to Be Holy."

2. Invite a volunteer to pray the prayer of confession and repentance he or she wrote on Day 2 of this week.

3. Now invite someone to pray the prayer found in Day 6 of this week, which expresses the desire to do the heart-work essential for holiness.

4. Invite another person to pray the prayer he or she wrote today, expressing a willingness to yield to God so that God's will for his or her holiness could be accomplished.

5. Invite the group to share any prayer concerns—personal, church, community, world— then ask a couple of people to pray in response to these needs.

6. Close with the Lord's Prayer.

WEEK 7

They Lived Not for Themselves but for Others

DAY
1

One Labor of Love

John Wesley was a genius at summarizing the expansive dimensions of Christian faith and life. He did it over and over again, expressing himself in different ways but always clear about the essentials. It is obvious from reading his *Sermons, Notes on Scripture*, and journals and letters that Wesley believed repetition and redundancy were effective teaching methods. He did not hesitate to communicate his understanding and convictions repeatedly through different means.

One of Wesley's common themes was the nature of Christian faith and life—what it means to be a child of God.

> What is it to be born of God? . . . it is, in the judgment of the Spirit of God, to be a son or a child of God: It is, so to *believe* in God, through Christ, as "not to commit sin," and to enjoy at all times, and in all places, that "peace of God which passeth all understanding." It is, so to *hope* in God through the Son of his love, as to have not only the "testimony of a good conscience," but also the Spirit of God "bearing witness with your spirits, that you are the children of God;" whence cannot but spring the rejoicing in Him, through whom "you have received the atonement." It is, so to love God, who hath thus loved you, as you never did love any creature: So that ye are constrained to love all men as yourselves; with a love not only ever burning in your hearts, but flaming out in all your actions and conversations, and making your whole life one "labour of love," one continued obedience to those commands, "Be ye merciful, as God is merciful:" "Be ye holy, as I the Lord am holy:" "Be ye perfect, as your Father which is in heaven is perfect." (*The Works of John Wesley*, vol. 5, 220–21)

In one way or another, Wesley always connects God's love for us and our love for God with our love for others. This was consistent with one of the characteristics of the saints: They lived not for themselves but for God and others. Our whole life is to be "one labour of love." This life-as-a-labor-of-love is the natural expression of God's unconditional love for us, expressed most dramatically in God's gift to us in Jesus Christ and his death on the cross.

On a plaque hanging in the Martin Luther King Jr. National Historical Site in Atlanta is one of King's most challenging words: "Each of us must decide whether [we] will walk in the light of creative altruism or in the darkness of the destructiveness of selfishness." Destructive selfishness comes naturally, while "creative

There is no way that we can love others as ourselves through our own strength. God's love, burning in our hearts, flames out in "actions and conversations" as love for others.

altruism" comes supernaturally. It is only when we love God and cease living solely for ourselves that we can live for the benefit of others.

Wesley connects our love for God with our love for others in a compelling way. He says that we are to love God "as you never did love any creature," so that we "are constrained to love all men as yourselves." This is a perspective-giving, power-providing insight. There is no way, within ourselves and our own strength, that we can love others as ourselves. It is God's love burning in our hearts, and our disciplined awareness of God's extravagant love for us, that flame out in "actions and conversations" as love for others. Such living is "one continued obedience" to the commands of God the Father, and Jesus his Son: Be holy, be merciful, be perfect.

The call to "be ye merciful, as God is merciful" comes at the close of Jesus' challenging teaching about love and generosity.

> *But I say to you that listen, Love your enemies, do good to those who hate you, bless those who curse you, pray for those who abuse you. If anyone strikes you on the cheek, offer the other also; and from anyone who takes away your coat do not withhold even your shirt. Give to everyone who begs from you; and if anyone takes away your goods, do not ask for them again. Do to others as you would have them do to you.*
>
> *If you love those who love you, what credit is that to you? For even sinners love those who love them. If you do good to those who do good to you, what credit is that to you? For even sinners do the same. If you lend to those from whom you hope to receive, what credit is that to you? Even sinners lend to sinners, to receive as much again. But love your enemies, do good, and lend, expecting nothing in return. Your reward will be great, and you will be children of the Most High; for he is kind to the ungrateful and the wicked. Be merciful, just as your Father is merciful. (Luke 6:27-36)*

Again, the connection is clear—just as God has loved us and expressed unbounded mercy to us, so we are to love and be merciful to others.

A pastor has the uncommon opportunity to see this teaching of Jesus lived out. Though pastors may preach this radical love for others, when we see one of our parishioners live it out, it seems incredible. I remember Ruth (not her real name). Her husband was unfaithful, walked all over her, used her, went his own perverted, selfish way—in one affair after another. But he kept coming back to Ruth, asking for forgiveness, wanting to be accepted and promising to be faithful. That same story repeated itself over and over again.

A caring group within our congregation sustained Ruth. She had confided in them, but even in spite of their sometimes urging her to break the relationship, she stayed faithful, gave herself sacrificially to the relationship, until finally the miracle happened. Her husband, unable to continue violating the love and mercy that he was receiving, repented and came into a deep relationship with Jesus Christ. Their marriage relationship was restored.

I received a letter from Ruth a couple of years ago telling me that her husband had died. She knew that I would remember the details of their relationship. In her letter, she said, "All the suffering that I endured was worth it for the happiness that we have known during the past fifteen years."

I believe John would have died long before if he and Ruth had divorced. Ruth's love, forgiveness, and faithfulness redeemed their relationship and restored meaning and joy.

REFLECTING AND RECORDING

Look back at your own experiences and relationships. Describe here an experience in which someone was merciful to you in a way that might be a response to Jesus' call, "Be merciful, just as your Father is merciful" (Luke 6:36, NRSV).

Now, record an experience or relationship in which you sought to be merciful to someone else "as your Father is merciful."

Reflecting on the ease or difficulty of recalling the experiences above, how would you assess the degree to which you are living not for yourself, but for God and others? Spend some time in self-examination.

DURING THE DAY

Look for ways to show mercy to the persons around you.

DAY
2

Jesus' Style—Ours

Let the same mind be in you that was in Christ Jesus,
  who, though he was in the form of God,
  did not regard equality with God as something to be exploited,
  but emptied himself,
  taking the form of a slave,
  being born in human likeness.
  And being found in human form,
  he humbled himself
  and became obedient to the point of death—
  even death on a cross.

Therefore God also highly exalted him
  and gave him the name that is above every name,
  so that at the name of Jesus
  every knee should bend,
  in heaven and on earth and under the earth,
  and every tongue should confess that Jesus Christ is Lord,
  to the glory of God the Father. (Philippians 2:5-11)

The *New American Standard Bible* translates verse 5 like this: "Have this attitude in yourselves which was also in Christ Jesus." The "mind of Christ" is an *attitude*, but it encompasses more than that. It is not something that we can take on or put off at will. The mind of Christ is the controlling dynamic of our life. The saints all knew that the mind of Christ in us is what enables us to live not for ourselves but for God and others. The apostle Paul urged the Romans, and us, to "accept one another . . . just as Christ accepted you."

Accept one another, then, just as Christ accepted you, in order to bring praise to God. For I tell you that Christ has become a servant of the Jews on behalf of God's truth, to confirm the promises made to the patriarchs so that the Gentiles may glorify God for his mercy, as it is written:

  "Therefore I will praise you among the Gentiles;
  I will sing hymns to your name."
Again, it says,
  "Rejoice, O Gentiles, with his people."

And again,
> *"Praise the Lord, all you Gentiles,*
> *and sing praises to him, all you peoples."*

And again, Isaiah says,
> *"The Root of Jesse will spring up,*
> *one who will arise to rule over the nations;*
> *the Gentiles will hope in him."*

May the God of hope fill you with all joy and peace as you trust in him, so that you may overflow with hope by the power of the Holy Spirit. (Romans 15:7-13, NIV)

Paul made one last appeal for the people of the church to be bound together as one—he called for those who are strong in the faith and those who are weak in the faith to be united in one body. Jews and Gentiles alike are to find a common fellowship in the family of the church.

Paul was giving special attention to Christ's work for Jews and Gentiles alike. Though Jesus was born a Jew, subject to Jewish law, and came into the world as a member of the Jewish race, He came not only for Jews, but also for Gentiles.

William Barclay reminds us that to prove this pivotal idea he was seeking to communicate, Paul cited four passages from the Old Testament:

> He quotes them from the Septuagint, the Greek version of the Old Testament, which is why they vary from the translation of the Old Testament as we know it. The passages are *Psalm 18:50; Deuteronomy 32:43; Psalm 117:1; Isaiah 11:10.* In all of them Paul finds ancient forecasts of the reception of the Gentiles into the faith. He is convinced that, just as Jesus Christ came into this world to save all men, so the Church must welcome all men, no matter what their differences may be. Christ was an inclusive Saviour, and therefore his Church must be an inclusive church. (Barclay, *The Letter to the Romans*, 198)

Other translations of Romans 15:7 say, "Welcome one another." And still another says, "Receive one another as Christ also received us." To me, *receive* seems stronger than *accept* or *welcome.* To receive means we identify with others, or take them to ourselves. In writing to a friend, Martin Luther quoted these words from Paul to the Romans and the Philippians, then added,

> *Let the same mind be in you that was in Christ Jesus.*
>
> *—Philippians 2:5*

> In like manner, if you think of yourself as on a higher level of spirituality than they, do not reckon this righteousness as booty to be snatched at, as if it were your own, but humble yourself, forget what you are, and, after the fashion of Christ, be as one of them so that you can help them.
>
> Pray for whatever you lack, kneeling before Christ. Christ will teach you all things. This one thing do: keep your eyes fixed on that which he has done for you and for all men so that you may learn what you should do for others. If Christ had sought to live only among nice people, and to die only for his friends, with whom would he have ever lived, for whom then would he have died? Go and do thou likewise, my dear friar, and continue to pray for me. The Lord be with you. (*The Joy of the Saints*, 73)

My young friend, Tammy, to whom I referred on Day 4 of last week, is living the Jesus style. In an e-mail that came October 4, 2000, she wrote:

> Well, God has been good to teach me a lot in the past months. It has been a tough year, but He has given me some awesome treasures. I don't think I would trade any of the tough stuff when

I taste the fruit of the trials. Doesn't it say somewhere in the Bible that trials produce fruit and all kinds of good stuff? Hey, maybe there is something to that…He has been teaching me about the difference between true love and compassion and self-driven love and pity. He has shown that the purest way to receive His heart comes through prayer and worship and undivided time with Him. He has also spoken some pretty freeing things to me on a personal level which I have been waiting my whole life to hear. I am grateful…His love for us is so rich and full and pure and I could go on and on. As I taste it, strength and grace flow in me in ways I have only dreamed about.

I doubt that Tammy has ever read Luther's words, which are quoted above, but isn't she saying some of the same things? Let's put some of her words beside those of Luther and look at them together:

Luther	**Tammy**
Pray for whatever you lack, kneeling before Christ. Christ will teach you all things. This one thing do: keep your eyes fixed on that which he has done for you and for all men so that you may learn what you should do for others.	It has been a tough year, but He has given me some awesome treasures . . . He has been teaching me . . . the difference between true love and compassion and self-driven love and pity. He has shown me that the purest way to receive his heart comes through prayer and worship and undivided time with him.

REFLECTING AND RECORDING

Read again both Luther's and Tammy's words, seeking to discover their message to you.

Record here two lessons Luther and Tammy teach us in their comparative words.

Spend a bit of time reflecting on these questions: What is the difference between true love and compassion? What is the difference between self-driven love and pity?

DURING THE DAY

Luther urged us to keep our eyes fixed on what Christ has done for us so that we may learn what we should do for others. A contemporary saint, Mother Teresa of Calcutta, once said, "Pray for me that I do not loosen my grip on the hands of Jesus even under the guise of ministering to the poor."

Take two or three opportunities today to specifically remember what Christ has done for you and all persons. Renew your grip on the hands of Christ, so that you may be responsive to occasions for serving others.

DAY
3

Instruments in the Hands of God

The saints would not be described as "activists" in the way we use that term today. But they acted. To be sure, the monastic life in which many participated was a life removed from the world. The vows many persons took included cloistered living. Amazingly, however, many of them were in touch with "real life" in an uncanny way.

One of my most meaningful relationships was with a person with whom I spent only one day. Simon was a Trappist monk who lived in a monastery in Oregon. Strangely and providentially, we met through the mail. (I told some of this story in my book *Alive in Christ*.)

When we met he was eighty-two. We corresponded for eight years until he died at age ninety. The only occasion we met face-to-face was a day we spent together at his monastery. Yet, we had a deep and personal relationship. He has been dead now for almost twenty years, and I still miss him. Now and then I pull out the folder of his letters that I kept; I read them and find joy in the memory of our relationship, and I still get counsel and direction from his writing.

Even in his late eighties and living in a monastery, Simon was in touch with life in an uncanny, unexplainable way. Whenever I wrote him about an issue, thoughts I was having, or problems I was facing, his response was exactly the word I needed to hear from God through him.

Many persons living a monastic lifestyle have counseled persons who are active in the world. Brother Simon was my counselor for eight years. Also, many monastic communities have active ministries, especially to the poor. The wisdom these communities provide us is not only that we must give ourselves to God and others, but also they teach us how we are to serve. We are to see ourselves as instruments of God, not preoccupied with our own needs, but serving others out of our love for Christ.

This service is not done in a driven, activist style; it does not rush from one good deed to another or become guilt-stricken if we fail to respond to a call no matter where it comes from. Rather, such service is intentional, always aware and responsive to need. But it is also unhurried, quiet, and dependent on God's leading and God's empowering. Jean-Pierre de Caussade expressed it well:

> When, in all our actions, we look upon ourselves as instruments in the hands of God to work out his hallowed designs, we shall act quietly, without anxiety, without hurry, without uneasiness about the future, without troubling about the past, giving ourselves up to the fatherly providence of God and relying more on him than on all possible human means. (*The Joy of the Saints*, 55)

The Book of Proverbs is full of wisdom about how God will direct our paths if we are willing, and how we should relate to God's purposes and to others' and thus be used by God. Here is a sample of that wisdom from Proverbs 16:

> *All one's ways may be pure in one's own eyes,*
>   *but the Lord weighs the spirit.*
> *Commit your work to the LORD,*
>   *and your plans will be established.*
> *The LORD has made everything for its purpose,*
>   *even the wicked for the day of trouble. (vv. 2-4)*
>
> *When the ways of people please the LORD,*
>   *he causes even their enemies to be at peace with them.*
> *Better is a little with righteousness than large income with injustice.*
>   *The human mind plans the way, but the LORD directs the steps. (vv. 7-9)*
>
> *How much better to get wisdom than gold!*
>   *To get understanding is to be chosen rather than silver.*
> *The highway of the upright avoids evil;*
>   *those who guard their way preserve their lives.*
> *Pride goes before destruction,*
>   *and a haughty spirit before a fall. (vv. 16-18)*
>
> *Gray hair is a crown of glory;*
>   *it is gained in a righteous life.*
> *One who is slow to anger is better than the mighty,*
>   *and one whose temper is controlled than one who captures a city.*
> *The lot is cast into the lap, but the decision is the Lord's alone. (vv. 31-33)*

We are to see ourselves as instruments of God, not preoccupied with our own needs but serving others out of our love for Christ.

To seek to fit into God's purposes is a mark of wisdom. The desire to be used as God's instrument will be rewarded.

Sometimes we are not even aware that we are instruments. A few years ago there was a wonderful movie titled *Mr. Holland's Opus*, the story of a dedicated music teacher named Glenn Holland. At the beginning of his career, Holland dreamed of becoming a famous composer, living in Hollywood, making lots of money, writing theme songs for movies. But he never realized those dreams.

After getting married, the realities of feeding his family and paying the mortgage led Holland to take a job as a band director at the local high school. He spent his entire career teaching the students there. Some of those students felt special as a result of how he treated them.

A redheaded girl with pigtails wanted desperately to play the clarinet, but she had a terrible time finding the right notes. No one believed in her or took time to help her, but Mr. Holland treated her with great tenderness.

An African-American student had to be a part of the band to keep his eligibility for the football team. He wanted to learn to play the drums but had a difficult time finding the beat. With great compassion, Mr. Holland poured himself into that young man.

With great patience, he worked with a streetwise, tough kid named Lenny. Lenny had a lousy attitude and was mad at the world, but Mr. Holland's positive attitude paid dividends. Student after student was affirmed and found direction through Mr. Holland.

As the movie closes, the school loses the funding for its music program and Holland is forced to retire. He tells his wife and son that he feels like a failure because he never accomplished his great dream—never went to Hollywood, never became a famous composer. In one of the final scenes he cleans out his classroom and heads out of the school, shoulders slumped—a picture of self-defeat and failure. Then it happens. He hears noises in the auditorium, and his family leads him there. He opens the door and finds the auditorium packed with his former students. As he walks in, they give him a long, thunderous standing ovation while chanting his name. Students from past years had returned from all over the nation to express their love and appreciation to this man who had dedicated his life to them.

The little girl with the red pigtails had grown up and was now the governor of the state. She went to the microphone. "Mr. Holland, we know that you never became the famous composer you dreamed of being. But don't you see it today? Your great composition is what you did with us, your students. Mr. Holland, look around you. *We* are your great opus! We are the music of your life."

Mr. Holland may not have seen himself as an instrument in the hands of God, but God uses all of us. How much more God can use persons who are willing and committed to the Almighty, who give themselves to providence, and rely on God more "than on all possible human means," as de Caussaude said.

All of us can name someone who has been for us an instrument of God, influencing and shaping our lives. Some of us can give witness to how God has used us as instruments to influence and shape the lives of others.

REFLECTING AND RECORDING

What two or three persons, other than your parents, have influenced you more than any others? Name them here.

How have those persons acted as instruments in the hands of God, shaping your life? Make some notes here about how God might have used them to change you.

Lay aside your false humility now, and name a person or persons for whom you may have been used or are presently being used by God for their sake.

Offer a prayer of gratitude for persons God used to shape your life and for the opportunity you have had to influence others.

Spend a bit of time reflecting on de Caussade's direction for being instruments in the hands of God:

- act quietly
- act without anxiety
- act without hurry
- act without uneasiness about the future
- act without troubling about the past

DURING THE DAY

If God used any of the persons you named above to shape your life, find a way to express your gratitude today.

As you did yesterday, take two or three occasions today to specifically remember what Christ has done for you and everyone, to renew your grip on the hands of Christ, so that you may be responsive to occasions for serving others.

DAY
4

Testing Our Love

Paul sets forth the dynamic style of the Christian life in one sentence: "The only thing that counts is faith working through love" (Gal. 5:6).

The Galatians had heard the gospel and had experienced its transforming power through Paul's ministry. But now Paul was gone—continuing his missionary/evangelism work in Asia Minor. Other teachers had come, distorting the gospel, demanding that these new Christians—not only converted Jews but also Gentiles—return to the laws and customs of Judaism, especially circumcision. These new teachers sought to establish rules as a means of becoming good. This has been the error of much religious teaching through the ages. The pursuit of goodness or holiness for its own sake never leads to that end. Christianity rests upon grace, not upon how good we are at obeying rules. When we experience the love of Christ, as we mature in his likeness, we are empowered to love others.

The Pharisees of Jesus' day, and no doubt these new teachers in Galatia were among them, attempted to make people slaves to their standards of measurement—"do not taste" and "do not touch" (Col. 2:21). They could not accept grace because they could not fathom a God who would be concerned with the undeserving, unclean, and unworthy.

So Paul wrote,

> *For freedom Christ has set us free. Stand firm, therefore, and do not submit again to a yoke of slavery.*
>
> *Listen! I, Paul, am telling you that if you let yourselves be circumcised, Christ will be of no benefit to you. Once again I testify to every man who lets himself be circumcised that he is obliged to obey the entire law. You who want to be justified by the law have cut yourselves off from Christ; you have fallen away from grace. For through the Spirit, by faith, we eagerly wait for the hope of righteousness. For in Christ Jesus neither circumcision nor uncircumcision counts for anything; the only thing that counts is faith working through love. (Galatians 5:1-6)*

The inward expression of our Christian life is faith in God. The outward expression of the Christian life is faith working in love toward others.

Yesterday we considered the style of our working and serving. Not only do we fall into the snare of frantic busyness, but too often we also seek to assess the quality of our deeds. We need to pay attention to what Martin Luther says about this.

> Paul sets forth the whole life of a Christian man in Galatians 5:6, namely, that inwardly it consists of faith towards God, and outwardly in charity and good works to our neighbour.
>
> In faith all works are equal, and any one work the same as any other. God does not consider how little, or how great the works are, but God looks on the heart, which performs in faith and obedience to God the demands of its calling.
>
> I cannot turn my neighbour away without turning God away: and that is to fall into unbelief.
>
> We are, if I may be allowed so to express it, Christs to our neighbour.
>
> God pays no heed to the insignificance of the work being done, but looks at the heart which is serving him in the work; and this is true of such mundane tasks as washing the dishes or milking the cows. (*The Joy of the Saints*, 38)

What a penetrating word of judgment: "I cannot turn my neighbour away without turning God away: and that is to fall into unbelief." As I have pondered this gloomy and painful appraisal, I recalled William C. Duckworth's modern parable of Jesus' judgment:

> For when I was hungry, you were obese. I was thirsty, and you were watering your lawn. I was a stranger, and you called the police and had me taken away. I was naked while you were saying, "I must buy some new clothes. I just don't have a thing to wear." I was ill, and you asked, "Is it contagious?" I was in prison and you said, "That's where your kind belongs." (quoted in William R. Bouknight, *The Authoritative Word*, 88)

Paul's claim in Galatians 5:6—"the only thing that counts is faith working through love"—contains both judgment and promise. Judgment comes as a result of our failure to let our faith work through love. As Jesus' parable of the Last Judgment (Matt. 24:31-46) makes clear, judgment is certain. Nobody gets away with anything. Judgment may be immediate, delayed, or waiting at the door of eternity, but it is certain.

We are . . . Christs to our neighbour.
—*Martin Luther*

Promise in that all we do is important. Luther said, "God pays no heed to the insignificance of the work." The promise and the judgment are that God looks at "the heart which is serving him in the work."

Coming from a different perspective and sounding the same warning as Luther but adding dimensions to it, Francis de Sales called for Christians to test their love.

> It is not enough to have love for our neighbor—we should notice of what sort it is, and whether it is true. If we love our neighbor because he does us good, that is, because he loves us, and brings us some advantage, honor, or pleasure, that is what we call a love of complacency, and is common to us with the animals. If we love him for any good that we see in him, that is, on account of beauty, style, amiability or attractiveness, this is love of friendship, which we share with the heathens. Therefore, neither

of these is a true love, and they are of no merit, because purely natural and of short duration, being founded upon motives which often cease to exist. In fact, if we love anyone because he is virtuous, or handsome, or our friend, what will become of this love if he should cease to be virtuous, or handsome, or to love us, or, still worse, if he should become our enemy? When the foundation upon which our love rested, sinks, how can it support itself? The true love which alone is meritorious and lasting is that which arises from the charity which leads us to love our neighbor in God and for God; that is, because it pleases God, or because he is dear to God, or because God dwells in him, or that it may be so. There is, however, no harm in loving him also for any honorable reason, provided that we love him more for God's sake than for any other cause. Yet the less mixture our love has of other motives, the purer and more perfect it will be. . . .

Love not according to the flesh, but according to the Holy Spirit. (*A Year with the Saints*, 331)

REFLECTING AND RECORDING

Identify in your memory an experience of turning a neighbor away. Call that experience vividly to awareness.

As you think of that experience, would you agree with Luther? Were you turning God away, and was it an act of unbelief?

Read de Sales's word carefully, and in the space provided, condense it and translate it into your own words.

Spend a bit of time reflecting on Luther's claim that "We are . . . Christs to our neighbours."

DURING THE DAY

Seek for opportunities to be Christ to someone today.

DAY

5

In the Shadows: Serving Incognito

On Days 2 and 3 of this week, we considered how Christians should serve. Yesterday we focused on the quality of our actions, with how we love being the determining factor. We considered Luther's radical admonition that we "cannot turn [our] neighbour away without turning God away: and that is to fall into unbelief." Expressing the same truth from a positive perspective, Luther said, "We are . . . Christs to our neighbour."

In our consideration of how we serve, we looked at Jesus' example of sacrificial giving, and also his lifestyle in terms of activity, considering de Caussade's admonition:

> When, in all our actions, we look upon ourselves as instruments in the hands of God to work out his hallowed designs, we shall act quietly, without anxiety, without hurry, without uneasiness about the future, without troubling about the past, giving ourselves up to the fatherly providence of God and relying more on him than on all possible human means. (*The Joy of the Saints*, 55)

As the saints lived not for themselves but for God and others, they demonstrated a humility that, paradoxically, resulted in power and influence. Thérèse of Lisieux provides a wonderful picture of such humility:

> Some time ago I was watching the flicker, almost imperceptible, of a tiny night-light. One of the sisters came up, and having lit her own candle in the dying flame, passed it round to light the candles of the others. And the thought came to me: "Who dares glory in their own good works? It needs but one faint spark to set the world on fire."
>
> We come in touch with burning and shining lights, set high on the candlestick of the Church, and we think we are receiving from them grace and light. But from where do they borrow their fire?
>
> Very possibly from the prayers of some devout and hidden soul whose inward shining is not apparent to human eyes—some soul of unrecognized virtue, and in her own sight of little worth: a dying flame!

What mysteries we shall one day see unveiled! I have often thought that perhaps I owe all the graces with which I am laden to some little soul whom I shall know only in heaven. (*The Joy of the Saints*, 259)

When we look at the people who have influenced our lives, we sometimes find "burning and shining lights, set high on the candlestick of the Church." But more often than not, the persons who most influence us have no recognized place in history.

I admire the way Paul closed most of his letters, by naming persons who joined him in sending greetings. Note the way he closes his Letter to the Colossians:

> *Tychicus will tell you all the news about me; he is a beloved brother, a faithful minister, and a fellow servant in the Lord. I have sent him to you for this very purpose, so that you may know how we are and that he may encourage your hearts; he is coming with Onesimus, the faithful and beloved brother, who is one of you. They will tell you about everything here.*
>
> *Aristarchus my fellow prisoner greets you, as does Mark the cousin of Barnabas, concerning whom you have received instructions—if he comes to you, welcome him. And Jesus who is called Justus greets you. These are the only ones of the circumcision among my co-workers for the kingdom of God, and they have been a comfort to me. Epaphras, who is one of you, a servant of Christ Jesus, greets you. He is always wrestling in his prayers on your behalf, so that you may stand mature and fully assured in everything that God wills. For I testify for him that he has worked hard for you and for those in Laodicea and in Hierapolis. Luke, the beloved physician, and Demas greet you. Give my greetings to the brothers and sisters in Laodicea, and to Nympha and the church in her house. (Colossians 4:7-15)*

Check the names in these verses. Mark, Barnabas, and Luke show up in other places in the New Testament, but the others do not. They are serving in the shadows. They are even nameless in many instances, such as in Paul's final greeting to the Philippians: "All the saints greet you, especially those of the emperor's household" (Phil. 4:22). Who could have believed it—devoted followers of Christ serving the emperor, who thought *he* was God! But we don't know their names.

It is true. There are "burning and shining lights, set high on the candlestick of the Church," but there are many, countless more, from whom these named and recognized ones borrow their fire.

More often than not, the persons who most influence us have no recognized place in history.

When I think of persons who influenced me most, I recall Olga Clifton, my English/literature teacher in high school. I grew up in poverty. Our family had no books. We didn't have the money to subscribe to magazines. In fact, during my growing-up years, we didn't read a weekly, much less a daily, newspaper. I don't remember reading a book before I was in high school.

Miss Clifton was unmarried, lived with and cared for her elderly mother, and poured her life into teaching. She introduced me to the strange "Olde English" of Chaucer and the poetry of Wordsworth, Coleridge, and Robert Burns. The first book I ever purchased in college, apart from textbooks, was a volume of Burns's poetry. Because of a memorization assignment from Miss Clifton, Burns's words are a part of the wisdom that has shaped my life.

Burns's words	**A modern paraphrase**
O wad some Pow'r the giftie gie us	Oh, that God would give us the very smallest of gifts:
To see oursels as others see us!	To be able to see ourselves as others see us!
It wad frae monie a blunder free us	It would save us from many mistakes
An' foolish notion:	and foolish thoughts.
What airs in dress an' gait was lea'e us,	We would change the way we look and gesture
And ev'n Devotion!	and to how and what we apply our time and attention.

(A Collection of English Poems 1660–1800, 1062)

But more important, Miss Clifton's affirmation of me and my gifts, and her cultivation of my appreciation for words, style of writing, and the power of expression, contributed immensely to my ministry of writing.

Another person who was not "set high on the candlestick of the Church" but touched my life was Clara Mae Sells. Clara Mae was a retired deaconess who became a member of the church I organized as my first appointment out of seminary. She had taught English grammar and literature in mission schools all across America—in some of the poorest urban and rural sections of the nation.

I wrote a weekly column for the daily newspaper in Gulfport, Mississippi, where I pastored this new congregation. After about three years, Clara Mae showed up at my office one day with a collection of articles I had written. She had organized them thematically and had come to insist that I seek to have them published as a book. We worked together on that project, and as a result, my first book was published.

Who (besides me and some of my peers) recognizes the names Olga Clifton and Clara Mae Sells? Though my name may be recognized because of my writing, behind my ministry of writing was the powerful influence and intervention of those two persons.

And who knows the name Wiley Grissom? He was the pastor of the little Eastside Baptist Church, located about two hundred yards up the road from my home. On any given Sunday, twenty or twenty-five people—sometimes as many as fifty—might be present in that congregation. It was Brother Grissom's preaching that brought me to my conversion, which not only set me on the road of Christian discipleship, but also resulted in my answering the call to preach.

All of us have persons like this, not "set high on the candlestick of the Church," but for us, they are burning and shining lights.

Thérèse reminds us that beyond even those unknown persons who impacted and shaped our lives, very possibly there are devout and hidden souls "whose inward shining is not apparent to human eyes," but to whom we "owe all the graces with which [we are] laden"—"little souls" we will know only in heaven. These persons prayed for us, and they prayed for the persons who have influenced us. Many of them, in their own sight, are of little worth, "a dying flame," but they have embodied the light and have passed it on. They have lived in the shadows, serving incognito, but they have joined the saints in thinking not of themselves, but of God and others.

REFLECTING AND RECORDING

Name two persons who have played a significant, shaping role in your life.

Make some notes describing how those two persons influenced you.

Was either of these persons a shining light, "set high on the candlestick of the Church"? Or did these persons stay in the shadows, serving, for the most part, incognito? Ponder their lifestyle and influence for a few minutes and thank God for them.

Recall Luther's word that we considered yesterday: "We are . . . Christs to our neighbour." Other than the persons you have identified, name in your heart some persons who have been Christ to you, and spend time praying for them, offering God your gratitude for these perhaps unknown but noble and great-souled persons.

DURING THE DAY

If anyone who has been Christ to you is still alive, call that person or write him/her a letter today, expressing your gratitude.

As you did yesterday, seek to be Christ to someone today.

DAY
6

Loving the Unlovely

I heard a wonderful story about Jimmy Carter when he was president of the United States. The time was early in his presidency. The setting was the memorial service for Hubert Humphrey, an icon of American politics during the last part of the twentieth century. People from all over the world came to honor and pay their respects to this great man.

One prominent person who attended the memorial service, though, was ignored by most of the people attending. They refused to speak to him and shunned him as though he had some horrible disease. That person was former President Richard Nixon, and this was his first visit back to Washington since the Watergate scandal. Nixon kept slipping over to the edge of the crowd, obviously nervous and ill at ease.

President Carter and his entourage came into the room and were about to be seated. Mr. Carter saw Mr. Nixon over in the corner of the room, left his entourage, and went directly to him. He disregarded Mr. Nixon's extended hand; instead he embraced him, saying, "Welcome home, Mr. President, welcome home."

Newsweek magazine, which recorded that story, said: "It was this event that started restoration. If there was a turning point in Nixon's long ordeal in the wilderness, it was that moment and that gesture of love and compassion." ("You've Got to Be Kidding!"—sermon preached by Barry P. Boulware on February 23, 1992)

In living not for themselves but for God and others, the saints knew they must love the unlovely and seek to serve them especially. It is easy to love and serve "beautiful" people, those we like because they are most like us. Most American Christians belong to churches whose membership is quite homogeneous. We feel comfortable and unthreatened because there is little diversity. We are "at ease," forgetting the prophet Amos's warning, "Alas for those who are at ease in Zion" (Amos 6:1).

Thérèse of Lisieux took note of how we tend to give our attention to people we like and love those who are "the holiest."

> I have noticed that it is the holiest who are most loved: everyone seeks their company and is on the watch to do them a service without waiting to be asked. Holy people who can bear to be treated with a want of respect and attention find themselves surrounded by an atmosphere of

> *It is easy to love and serve the "beautiful people." But in living for God, we must love the unlovely and seek to serve them especially.*

love. St. John of the Cross says: "All good things have come to me since I no longer seek them for myself." (*The Joy of the Saints*, 177)

It's easy and natural to seek the company of people who can bless us, in whose presence we are inspired and challenged. But Jesus taught that we are to seek other company—people who bless us in another way.

> *When he noticed how the guests chose the places of honor, he told them a parable. "When you are invited by someone to a wedding banquet, do not sit down at the place of honor, in case someone more distinguished than you has been invited by your host; and the host who invited both of you may come and say to you, 'Give this person your place,' and then in disgrace you would start to take the lowest place. But when you are invited, go and sit down at the lowest place, so that when your host comes, he may say to you, 'Friend, move up higher'; then you will be honored in the presence of all who sit at the table with you. For all who exalt themselves will be humbled, and those who humble themselves will be exalted."*
>
> *He said also to the one who had invited him, "When you give a luncheon or a dinner, do not invite your friends or your brothers or your relatives or rich neighbors, in case they may invite you in return, and you would be repaid. But when you give a banquet, invite the poor, the crippled, the lame, and the blind. And you will be blessed, because they cannot repay you, for you will be repaid at the resurrection of the righteous."*
>
> *One of the dinner guests, on hearing this, said to him, "Blessed is anyone who will eat bread in the kingdom of God!" (Luke 14:7-15)*

Thérèse continued her observation of how we treat others:

> Imperfect people, on the other hand, are left alone. They receive the measure of politeness, but their company is avoided for fear a word spoken will hurt their feelings. When I say imperfect people, I mean those who, being supersensitive or wanting in tact or refinement, make life unpleasant for others. Defects of this kind seem incurable. (*The Joy of the Saints*, 177)

Jesus lived what he preached. Recall the story of the leper. Chapter 1 of Mark's Gospel records a series of healings. Jesus' reputation as a healer spread after he healed a man with an unclean spirit and also healed Simon Peter and Andrew's mother. Mark 1:32-34*a* says: "That evening, at sundown, they brought to him all who were sick or possessed with demons. And the whole city was gathered around the door. And he cured many who were sick with various diseases. Jesus couldn't stay there in Capernaum; others needed his ministry of preaching and healing, so he went to villages throughout Galilee."

One of the first miracles Mark records in that chapter is the healing of the leper. It's a vivid picture. The leper comes to Jesus, flings himself at the Lord's feet, doesn't wait or question—instead, the leper interrupts what is going on and makes this piteous plea: "If you choose, you can make me clean" (v. 40). The scripture says that Jesus was filled with compassion and reached out, touched the man, and said, "I am willing. Be clean!" (v. 41, NIV).

It is hard for us to grasp the full meaning of this story. The leper knew he had no right to be there. Because of his repulsive disease, he was considered an outcast in society. But somehow the leper knew that despite his grotesque appearance, Jesus would see him. He was right. Jesus not only saw the leper, but he also listened to him, looked at him, and touched him. If we are to love the unlovely, those same acts of compassion are required of us.

The saints were convinced that how we relate to others is a measure of our growth in holiness. They also knew that others can provide impetus for self-examination, self-correction, and growth. Fénelon provides a clear teaching about this:

> Charity does not demand of us that we should not see the faults of others; we must, in that case, shut our eyes. But it commands us to avoid attending unnecessarily to them, and that we be not blind to the good, while we are so clear-sighted to the evil that exists. We must remember, too, God's continual kindness to the most worthless creature and think how many causes we have to think ill of ourselves; and finally we must consider that charity embraces the very lowest human being. It acknowledges that in the sight of God the contempt that we indulge for others has in its very nature a harshness and arrogance opposed to the spirit of Jesus Christ. The true Christian is not insensible to what is contemptible; but he bears with it.
>
> Because others are weak, should we be less careful to give them their due? You who complain so much of what others make you suffer, do you think that you cause others no pain? You who are so annoyed at your neighbor's defects, are you perfect?
>
> How astonished you would be if those whom you cavil at should make all the comments that they might upon you. But even if the whole world were to bear testimony in your favor, God, who knows all, who has seen all your faults, could confound you with a word; and does it never come into your mind to fear, lest he should demand of you why you had not exercised toward your brother a little of that mercy which He who is your Master so abundantly bestows on you? (*Letters and Reflections of François de Fénelon*, 135–36)

God planned for us to live in communities and environments of grace. We all need grace. All of us enter relationships with others with a mixed bag of strengths and weaknesses. Some folks engender immediate trust; others give us reason to disregard them and write them off. But God created us for community, meaning that we need to trust him and others.

In such a community and environment, we not only deliberately pay attention to and seek to care for others, but we also begin to trust people who are different from us. You can see this dynamic in action at any Alcoholics Anonymous meeting. In those settings you'll find different ethnic groups—Hispanics, African-Americans, Asians, Caucasians. There will be rich and poor folks, men and women, young and old. All have one thing in common: They're battling an addiction. The primary dynamic of the meeting is humility and trust, expressed in statements like, "Hi, I'm Tom, and I'm an alcoholic." That beginning point of humility and trust breaks the grip of alcoholism. If grace can happen in an arena like AA, it can certainly happen with the church.

REFLECTING AND RECORDING

In the space provided on page 196, translate the first paragraph of Fénelon into your own words.

Spend time reflecting on Fénelon's claim that the contempt we have for others, no matter how vile they may appear, opposes the spirit of Christ.

Consider the following thought for a few minutes: Any contempt or condemnation we have for another reflects at least some degree of arrogance on our part.

Read paragraphs two and three of Fénelon on the previous page and, in the space beside them, write a prayer of confession and a request for pardon for how you may have treated others, and the self-righteousness you may have expressed as you judged or condemned others.

DURING THE DAY

Designate in your mind now the "unloveliest" person in your circle of acquaintances. Do something today to express love for that person.

DAY
7

The Family—Our Neighbors

One of the most important persons in Vincent van Gogh's life was his brother Theo. Theo was faithful to Vincent throughout his tragic life. Perhaps Theo was the one who understood his brother best. He certainly remained Vincent's closest confidant and ally throughout their lives. Theo's was not an easy road—in fact, it was a very painful one. Vincent refused his brother's advice, spurned any counsel that Theo offered him, and refused to accept support.

Though a very religious man, Vincent could not trust God and others with himself, with the inevitable consequences being pain and loss. Against the counsel of his loving brother, Vincent gave up art. He left a promising career as an art dealer and studied to be a teacher.

Among those included under the title of neighbor, none deserve it more than those of our own household. . . . They ought to be one of the principal objects of our love.

—Francis de Sales

Failing in this pursuit, he turned to evangelism (of sorts). But he isolated himself from all of his friends and failed in his "religious pursuit." Van Gogh's ideals of isolationism and rugged individualism caused him to abandon virtually all of his relationships, and he almost starved himself to death in the poverty-stricken coal town of Borinage.

His relationship with Theo was kept alive by a fragile thread. Theo kept insisting that Vincent devote himself to expressing his artistic gifts. Despite Vincent's refusal to respond to his advice, and despite the pain that his caring concern for his brother caused him, Theo persisted. There came a moment when Vincent wrote to Theo, "I said to myself, In spite of everything I shall rise again: I will take up my pencil, which I have forsaken in my great discouragement, and I will go on with my drawing. From that moment everything has seemed transformed for me." Vincent had found his calling—but it is doubtful that this would ever have happened had it not been for the ongoing love and persistence of his brother Theo.

Psychologists and psychiatrists agree that family is the most powerful influence in a person's life. Francis de Sales cast our responsibility for family members in the context of Jesus' call to love our neighbor.

To have that love for our neighbor which is commanded by the Lord, we must entertain good and amiable feelings towards him, especially when he is disagreeable and annoying to us on account of any defect, natural or moral; for then we find nothing in him to love, except in God. . . . In performing works of charity and kindness, we ought to consider not the person who receives them, but Him for whose sake they are done. Nor let us be discouraged if we sometimes feel repugnance; for an ounce of this solid and reasonable love is of much greater value than any amount of that tender and sensitive love which we share with the animals, and which often deceives and betrays our reason. (*A Year with the Saints*, 323)

Among all those who are included under the title of neighbor, there are none who deserve it more, in one sense, than those of our own household. They are nearest of all to us, living under the same roof and eating the same bread. Therefore they ought to be one of the principal objects of our love, and we should practice in regard to them all the acts of a true charity, which ought to be founded not upon flesh and blood, or upon their good qualities, but altogether upon God. (*A Year with the Saints*, 328)

How easy it is to disregard the needs of our own family! How careless we can be in regard to them. We forget that when we listen to a family member, we meet that person's need for attention. When we affirm another, we meet his or her need for significance. When we protect a spouse or sibling or parent, we meet the need for security.

Every relationship has the potential of providing something we need, and every relationship provides the possibility for us to meet someone else's need. The family is the primary setting for living together in a caring relationship. The family becomes a body when its members function in harmony. The meeting of each individual's needs happens through the dynamic process of love.

Every family seems to have a member who needs more attention than other family members. Many families have a "black sheep," one who feels he or she doesn't belong. Or, there may be a rebel, the prodigal son or daughter. Many families have persons with unusual physical or mental problems or exceptional emotional needs. "Loving our neighbor" who also happens to be a family member is up close and personal. Proximity keeps the issue of need glaring. It's next to impossible to escape.

Tragically, most dysfunctional families are the result of family members' refusing to honestly share their needs, to admit inadequacy, fear, and weakness—refusing to trust each other, to mutually "bear one another's burdens," to assist one another in finding the support and security needed.

De Sales says that we are to practice acts of true charity toward family members "founded not upon flesh and blood, or upon their good qualities, but altogether on God." Christians, especially ministers, need to heed this guidance. As a minister, I have been guilty of paying more attention to congregational needs than to the needs of my own family. I have had to repent of my sin with great sorrow and tears.

Christians in every kind of work or profession are vulnerable to this temptation: finding our primary meaning in work, thinking that earning a living is our highest responsibility; using work as an escape from the burdens and problems of family; allowing work to steal time, energy, and interest that rightly belongs to our family. We end up trivializing what should be most important to us. We make other family members into a kind of collateral accessory. We treat them as possessions or extensions of ourselves instead of as individuals who have their own particular needs. In terms of time and attention, the family becomes subordinate.

Jesus was clear about the meaning and significance of marriage:

> *Some Pharisees came to him, and to test him they asked, "Is it lawful for a man to divorce his wife for any cause?" He answered, "Have you not read that the one who made them at the beginning 'made them male and female,' and said, 'For this reason a man shall leave his father and mother and be joined to his wife, and the two shall become one flesh'? So they are no longer two, but one flesh. Therefore what God has joined together, let no one separate." (Matthew 19:3-6)*

In another setting, though Jesus was speaking of children in general, his word should have special meaning in the family:

> *Whoever welcomes one such child in my name welcomes me.*
> *If any of you put a stumbling block before one of these little ones who believe in me, it would be better for you if a great millstone were fastened around your neck and you were drowned in the depth of the sea. (Matthew 18:5-6)*

Paul, the writer of scripture who most expansively and clearly defined the Christian life, spoke powerfully about the meaning of marriage:

> *Wives, be subject to your husbands as you are to the Lord. For the husband is the head of the wife just as Christ is the head of the church, the body of which he is the Savior. Just as the church is subject to Christ, so also wives ought to be, in everything, to their husbands.*
> *Husbands, love your wives, just as Christ loved the church and gave himself up for her, in order to make her holy by cleansing her with the washing of water by the word, so as to present the church to himself in splendor, without a spot or wrinkle or anything of the kind—yes, so that she may be holy and without blemish. In the same way, husbands should love their wives as they do their own bodies. He who loves his wife loves himself. For no one ever hates his own body, but he nourishes and tenderly cares for it, just as Christ does for the church, because we are members of his body. "For this reason a man will leave his father and mother and be joined to his wife, and the two will become one flesh." This is a great mystery, and I am applying it to Christ and the church. Each of you, however, should love his wife as himself, and a wife should respect her husband. (Ephesians 5:22-33)*

Unless we view the "big picture" of Paul's teaching on marriage, its power is diminished. We should not isolate Paul's word about wives being submissive to their husbands and focus only on that admonition without looking further to see what Paul says about husbands' responsibilities. Submission is an ethical theme that runs throughout the New Testament. It needs to be the posture of all Christians because we are to follow the crucified Lord, who emptied himself to become the servant of all. Submission is the "cross lifestyle" to which we are called. Jesus not only died a cross-death; he also lived a cross-life of submission and service.

When we come to Paul's passage about wives being submissive to their husbands, we need to see it as a commentary, in the context of the family, on the revolutionary teachings of the New Testament. "Be subject to one another out of reverence for Christ" (Eph. 5:21) is the general guiding principle for all Christians. We are commanded (not just women, but all persons—men and women, parents and children, masters and slaves) to live lives of submission, not because of our station in life but because Jesus lived a life of submission and showed that such a lifestyle is the only way to "find life."

In a previous book I addressed the issue of submission and Paul's teaching in Ephesians 5:22-33:

> It is almost impossible for us to understand the radical nature of this teaching because we are so far removed from the world of Paul's day. In that day—and this persists in some cultures even now—persons were bound into a certain "station." The Greeks held that this was the way the gods had created things; persons had no choice. This was especially true of women. Women were seen as chattel, things to be used at whim and fancy, without rights, little more than slaves.
>
> Those to whom first-century culture afforded no choice were addressed by Paul as *free*; they could decide. This was revolutionary. Why would he call wives, children, and slaves to submission? That was their lot already. But something had happened to them. The gospel had freed them from a subordinate station in society. Second-, third-, and fourth-class citizenship was challenged by the gospel, and those *condemned* to those classes knew it. Paul, then, is not calling for submission on the basis of the way things were, the station in which the gods had ordered matters. No New Testament writer did that. All contemporary customs of superordinate and subordinate were completely ignored. Everyone was "to count others better than themselves" (Phil. 2:3) and to be subject to one another out of reverence for Christ.
>
> Wives were to be subject to their husbands not because that was a part of the natural order, but because submission is the style of all Christians. When wives and others began to live this way, the status quo was deprived of its divine sanction, of its inherent rightness and permanence, and a revolution of *mutual respect, affirmation, and service* began. (Maxie D. Dunnam, *The Communicator's Commentary*, vol. 8, 231–32, italics mine)

Paul followed his admonition to wives with a radical call to husbands (Eph. 5:28-33). He instructed husbands to love their wives as Christ loved the church and gave himself for it. In this Ephesians passage we see that there are no "high" or "low" positions in Christian marriages and homes, or in the entire Christian family. A new order had been born in which all participants could regard themselves as servants of one master, Jesus Christ, and give themselves in mutual service to one another because of him.

But Paul did not speak powerfully just about the meaning of marriage. He also continued his teaching in chapter 6 of Ephesians by speaking about family and family relationships:

> *Children, obey your parents in the Lord, for this is right. "Honor your father and mother"—this is the first commandment with a promise: "so that it may be well with you and you may live long on the earth."*
>
> *And, fathers, do not provoke your children to anger, but bring them up in the discipline and instruction of the Lord. (Ephesians 6:1-4)*

It is clear from this passage that in a Christian family, *reciprocal respect* between parents and children is absolutely necessary. Children need love and respect, affirmation and support, and if they don't find that in their family, they will meet this need in all sorts of destructive and distorted ways.

REFLECTING AND RECORDING

Who in your family most needs to receive your love, your *neighborly* care and concern? Spend some time reflecting on your failure in relation to that person—perhaps you have treated him or her with negligence, impatience, even contempt. Ask God to forgive your shortcomings in regard to this person. Then pray for this family member, and seek God's guidance for changing your attitudes toward him or her. Pray for your relationship, and plan ways to demonstrate your concern and love for this person.

DURING THE DAY

Put into practice the plan you have just prayed about.

Group Meeting for Week 7

INTRODUCTION

Last week you may have discussed whether your group wants to continue meeting. If so, here are some possibilities to consider.

1. Select two or three weeks of the workbook that were especially difficult or meaningful. Repeat those weeks in more depth to extend your time together.

2. Decide to continue meeting as a group, using another resource. Appoint two or three members to bring resource suggestions to the group next week.

   If this workbook style is meaningful, there are several others in the series:

   > *The Workbook on Living Prayer*
   > *The Workbook on Intercessory Prayer*
   > *The Workbook on Spiritual Disciplines*
   > *The Workbook on Becoming Alive in Christ*
   > *The Workbook on Coping As Christians*
   > *The Workbook on the Christian Walk*
   > *The Workbook on Christians under Construction and in Recovery*
   > *The Workbook on Loving the Jesus Way*
   > *The Workbook on the Seven Deadly Sins*
   > *The Workbook on Virtues and the Fruit of the Spirit*
   > *The Workbook on Keeping Company with the Saints*

3. One or two persons may decide to recruit and lead another group through this workbook. Many people are looking for a small-group experience, and this is a way to respond to their need.

SHARING TOGETHER

1. You have only one more group meeting. Invite a couple of volunteers to share what this experience has meant to them thus far.

2. John Wesley, in one way or another, always connected God's love for us and our love for God to our love for others. Ask everyone to turn to the Reflecting and Recording section of Day 1 of this week.

    a. Invite a couple of persons to describe an experience in which someone was merciful to them in a way that might be a response to Jesus' call, "Be merciful, just as your Father is merciful" (Luke 6:36).

    b. Now invite a couple of persons to share an experience when they sought to be merciful to someone else.

3. Turn to the Reflecting and Recording section of Day 2 of this week. Invite volunteers to share lessons they learned from comparing the words of Luther and Tammy.

4. On Day 3 we focused on being instruments in the hands of God. De Caussade's direction for being instruments in God's hands may surprise you. Spend eight to ten minutes discussing those directions (listed here). Do they fit your understanding? In what way do they challenge your stereotype of what it means to be an instrument of God? Are you exercising these directions? Which directions are most difficult for you to follow?

   • act quietly

   • act without anxiety

   • act without hurry

   • act without uneasiness about the future

   • act without troubling about the past

5. Luther spoke a penetrating word of judgment: "I cannot turn my neighbour away without turning God away: and that is to fall into unbelief." Spend eight to ten minutes discussing this idea. Is Luther right? Does scripture support him? Does your church teach and preach this? Is anyone willing to confess an experience in which he or she turned a neighbor away and, in retrospect, realized that he or she was turning God away?

6. On Day 5, we concentrated on the theme of serving incognito. I named three persons who were not "set high on the candlestick of the Church" but had a lasting impact on me. Invite two group members to name and describe such a person in their lives who for them was a "burning and shining light."

7. In light of this sharing, spend four to five minutes discussing Luther's challenge, "We are to be Christs to our neighbour."

8. On Day 6, an Alcoholics Anonymous group was described as a setting of fellowship among people from all walks of life, as well as different ethnic groups. AA meetings demonstrate the dynamics of humility and trust. Discuss this as a model for the church. What characteristics of AA should describe the church? What are the limitations? What prevents these dynamics from being present in the church? What are the primary essentials for the church to be experienced as a place of welcome?

9. Spend four to five minutes considering and discussing this thought: Any contempt or condemnation we have for another person reflects at least a degree of arrogance on our part.

10. Spend what time you have left for sharing discussing the issues raised today (Day 7) about family members being our neighbors. Concentrate at least for a few minutes on this claim: Every relationship has the potential for providing something we need, and every relationship provides the possibility for us to meet someone else's need.

PRAYING TOGETHER

Structure your prayer time in the following way. Invite one person to offer a prayer for the following concerns; before each category, ask if anyone has special requests.

- the unlovely—those we all know who are not lovable
- the difficult to love—those who may be gifted and have a lot going for them but are selfish, arrogant, cold, or antagonistic to our efforts to relate to them
- our families—members who have special needs, broken relationships, illness
- saints incognito—thanksgiving for those who have loved us and contributed to our wholeness, success, and total well-being

WEEK 8

THEY KNEW
PEACE AND JOY
THAT
TRANSCENDED
CIRCUMSTANCES

DAY
1

The Inheritance of the Saints

For this reason, since the day we heard it, we have not ceased praying for you and asking that you may be filled with the knowledge of God's will in all spiritual wisdom and understanding, so that you may lead lives worthy of the Lord, fully pleasing to him, as you bear fruit in every good work and as you grow in the knowledge of God. May you be made strong with all the strength that comes from his glorious power, and may you be prepared to endure everything with patience, while joyfully giving thanks to the Father, who has enabled you to share in the inheritance of the saints in the light. He has rescued us from the power of darkness and transferred us into the kingdom of his beloved Son, in whom we have redemption, the forgiveness of sins. (Colossians 1:9-14)

The saints were confident that the entirety of our lives is in God's hands, so they knew peace and joy that transcended circumstances. It was as though the prayer of Paul for the Colossians had been answered in their lives: "being strengthened with all power according to his glorious might so that you may have great endurance and patience, and joyfully giving thanks to the Father, who has qualified you to share in the inheritance of the saints in the kingdom of light" (Col. 1:11-12, NIV).

The imagery in this passage from Paul is powerful and suggestive. The contrast between light and darkness, common with Paul as well as with the Gospel writer John, was more than figurative. The pervasive idea, which Paul propounded often, was that people are subject to the powers of the universe, "the potentates of the dark present" (Eph. 6:12, MOFFATT), the rulers of darkness. By his death and resurrection Christ has overcome these powers and rescued us from their tyranny.

The saints gave witness to their struggles and doubts. Many of them knew dark nights of the soul that seemingly would never end.

There are two important lessons here. One, there are two kingdoms: light and darkness, flesh and spirit, good and evil. The saints constantly talked about this, expressing the fact that they had to wrestle with these two kingdoms. Paul says that we have been rescued from the darkness and brought into the kingdom of light.

> If Paul's terminology is archaic, or if his understanding of the system of angelic powers that rule in the elements seems outdated, the truth of his message is not less relevant, or the power of the promised deliverance any less needed.

How impotent we feel in a technological society—how helpless in the clutches of mechanical law, scientific determinism! How often do we give in to the overwhelming feeling that we have no control—that everything is determined by heredity, environment, natural powers, economic and social forces. How ominous is the power of sin! We move along as best we can, propelled by the forces around us, bobbing erratically along the torrential river of life as though we were Ping-Pong balls in a mountain stream. Paul says no! We have been delivered into a kingdom of light, of freedom. We have a destiny about which we can decide, and we have access to the power of Christ to live against the tide of determinism. We are "*saints of the light*," and the darkness will never prevail against the light (John 1:4–5).(*The Communicator's Commentary,* vol. 8, 337–38)

Along with the first lesson from this passage—that there are two kingdoms, light and darkness, flesh and spirit, good and evil, and that we have been rescued from the darkness and brought into the kingdom of light—there is a second lesson: We are now residents of the new kingdom; it is not something that is ours in some distant future—we claim it now. We have been delivered from a world that is subject to evil forces into a realm in which Christ is King. Jesus is Lord, and he alone has ultimate authority over us. No darkness can overcome us, no power can overwhelm us, and no experience can completely devastate us. Sin cannot hold sway in our lives. We belong to Christ; his is the kingdom, the power, and the glory. The Father has qualified us to share in "the inheritance of the saints in the kingdom of light" (Col. 1:12, NIV).

The saints with whom I have kept company give witness to their struggles and doubts. Many of them knew dark nights of the soul that seemingly would never end. Many of them suffered immense physical disability and pain. Some experienced extreme mental anguish, while all knew some degree of emotional struggle and spiritual doubt. Margery Kempe shared a part of her struggle, speaking metaphorically of a journey.

I asked the Lord if I should go on a journey; he said, "Go in my name. I will go with you and bring you back in safety."

The Lord sent storms so fierce that we expected to be shipwrecked and commended ourselves and our ship to the care of the Lord.

Lord, I came on this journey for love of you and you have promised that I shall be safe. Remember your promises and show me that it was you who directed me to come and not some evil spirit who has led me astray.

The Lord answered me, "Why are you afraid? Why do you not trust me? I am as powerful on the sea as on the land."

"I will keep my promises to you. Wait patiently and trust me. Do not waver in your faith, for without faith you grieve me. If you trust and do not doubt, you will gain peace of mind and strength to comfort those with you who are in fear and sorrow." (*The Joy of the Saints,* 276)

The saints accepted the witness of scripture—witness like that of God to Gideon as Gideon was commanded to battle the Midianites: "Go in the strength you have and save Israel . . . Am I not sending you? . . . I will be with you, and you will strike down all the Midianites together" (Judg. 6:14, 16, NIV) Or witness like that of Jesus as he sent the disciples into the world, saying, "Remember, I am with you always" (Matt. 28:20).

There is a paradox and a promise in these witnesses. Like Gideon, we will be called on to face a battle, and many times the battle is for us alone. But we will never be alone. Mark Trotter, my California preacher friend, now retired, illustrated this wonderful paradox with a lovely story by Robert Drake, a Tennessean who writes stories about growing up in small towns in that state. He wrote about a piano teacher named Miss Caroline Walker, who had taught piano for as long as anybody could remember and was a legend in her town.

> She had two goals in teaching. One was to teach her girls to be ladies, so she introduced them to manners as much as she did to music. And the other was to enable them to play their selection perfectly at the May recital. She drilled them all year for that one piece to make sure that they would get it perfect.
>
> She taught them "presence," how to be a lady on stage. How, when they sat down, to spread their skirt around the piano stool. How to stand straight with hands held at [their] waist to announce, "I will play such-and-such by so-and-so." And then describe what everybody is supposed to hear, like "the tiny feet of deer splashing in a mountain stream," or "fairies gliding through a mountain glen."
>
> The night of the recital came. It was held in the high school auditorium. There were ten pupils to give their recital that night. It came Anne Louise's turn, and she nearly fainted. She forgot what she was supposed to say. She knew she couldn't get through it. But it was her turn, so she had to go. She walked to the wings where Miss Caroline was standing waiting for her. She was really nervous now. Her body stiffened so she couldn't even move. Miss Caroline stood behind her, put her hands on Anne Louise's shoulders, and bent down to whisper in her ear, "You have worked very hard and you know your piece. You have nothing to fear. And remember, I am counting with you all the way." Then with a little shove she pushed Anne Louise out onto the stage.
>
> All of a sudden she was looking at the audience made up of the relatives of all the people who were in the recital, including her own. She launched into her speech, "I shall play such-and-such by so-and-so." Then she spread her skirt and sat down at the keyboard like a lady, just as she had been taught.
>
> She noticed now that she was not as nervous as she thought she would be. She knew that Miss Caroline was in the wings. And she remembered the last words that Miss Caroline said to her just before she went out on the stage, "Remember, I am counting with you all the way." And she felt that they were held together now by something that was greater than both of them. Teacher and disciple were one. And she realized that this was what she had been preparing for all year long, for this test.
>
> Then [Anne Louise] began to play. The music at her command came cascading out of the baby grand, filling that darkened hall, so full of joy, so full of life, and right on cue. ("You're Not in Charge Here," sermon preached by Mark Trotter on May 15, 1988, at First United Methodist Church, San Diego, CA)

Mark used that story to illustrate the meaning of Jesus' ascension. He summed up his explanation, saying: "It means we're on stage now. [Jesus is] gone. He's ascended into heaven. We're on stage now, but he's in the wings."

From the wings we hear Jesus' promptings as he spoke to Kempe, "Do not waver in your faith, for without faith you grieve me. If you trust and do not doubt, you will gain peace of mind and strength to comfort those with you who are in fear and sorrow."

Reflecting and Recording

Recall and record here an experience when you were called to do something, to go in a certain direction, or to relate to a particular circumstance for which you felt totally incapable and/or unprepared. Your only assurance was God's promise, "I am with you." Get in touch with your reservations and fears—but also the confidence and strength that was yours as you moved through that experience. Make enough notes to enable you to relive it.

Spend the rest of your time reflecting on Paul's double lesson: (1) there are two kingdoms, light and darkness, flesh and spirit, and (2) we have been rescued from the darkness and brought into the kingdom of light. We are now citizens of the new kingdom.

DURING THE DAY

Here is Eugene Peterson's paraphrase of Colossians 1:10-14:

> *We pray that you'll live well for the Master, making him proud of you as you work hard in his orchard. As you learn more and more how God works, you will learn how to do your work. We pray that you'll have the strength to stick it out over the long haul—not the grim strength of gritting your teeth but the glory-strength God gives. It is strength that endures the unendurable and spills over into joy, thanking the Father who makes us strong enough to take part in everything bright and beautiful that he has for us.*
>
> *God rescued us from dead-end alleys and dark dungeons. He's set us up in the kingdom of the Son he loves so much, the Son who got us out of the pit we were in, got rid of the sins we were doomed to keep repeating.* (THE MESSAGE)

This passage is also printed on page 243. Cut it out and carry it with you this week, keeping it in a place where you can read it three or four times each day.

DAY
2

Christ Is a God of Joy

"A little while, and you will no longer see me, and again a little while, and you will see me." Then some of his disciples said to one another, "What does he mean by saying to us, 'A little while, and you will no longer see me, and again a little while, and you will see me'; and 'Because I am going to the Father'?" They said, "What does he mean by this 'a little while'? We do not know what he is talking about." Jesus knew that they wanted to ask him, so he said to them, "Are you discussing among yourselves what I meant when I said, 'A little while, and you will no longer see me, and again a little while, and you will see me'? Very truly, I tell you, you will weep and mourn, but the world will rejoice; you will have pain, but your pain will turn into joy. When a woman is in labor, she has pain, because her hour has come. But when her child is born, she no longer remembers the anguish because of the joy of having brought a human being into the world. So you have pain now; but I will see you again, and your hearts will rejoice, and no one will take your joy from you. On that day you will ask nothing of me. Very truly, I tell you, if you ask anything of the Father in my name, he will give it to you. Until now you have not asked for anything in my name. Ask and you will receive, so that your joy may be complete.

"I have said these things to you in figures of speech. The hour is coming when I will no longer speak to you in figures, but will tell you plainly of the Father. On that day you will ask in my name. I do not say to you that I will ask the Father on your behalf; for the Father himself loves you, because you have loved me and have believed that I came from God. I came from the Father and have come into the world; again, I am leaving the world and am going to the Father."

His disciples said, "Yes, now you are speaking plainly, not in any figure of speech! Now we know that you know all things, and do not need to have anyone question you; by this we believe that you came from God." Jesus answered them, "Do you now believe? The hour is coming, indeed it has come, when you will be scattered, each one to his home, and you will leave me alone. Yet I am not alone because the Father is with me. I have said this to you, so that in me you may have peace. In the world you face persecution. But take courage; I have conquered the world!" (John 16:16-33)

Who isn't impressed by this word of Jesus? He was with his disciples in the upper room, at the very threshold of Calvary. He was warning them of his coming death and witnessing about the resurrection and his return to the Father. He confirmed his promise of peace and joy for them by displaying that spirit of peace and joy.

In the next chapter of John's Gospel (chapter 17), in what has become known as his High Priestly Prayer, Jesus prays for himself, for his disciples, and for all believers. Though it took place on the eve of the cross, the prayer is punctuated with joy, peace, and thanksgiving. The reason this was possible is clear in the prayer itself:

I ask not only on behalf of these, but also on behalf of those who will believe in me through their word, that they may all be one. As you, Father, are in me and I am in you, may they also be in us, so that the world may believe that you have sent me. (John 17:20-21)

Jesus was one with the Father. Martin Luther fairly shouted it: "Christ is a God of joy. . . . A Christian should be and must be a [person] of joy." He continued,

The devil is the spirit of sadness, but God is the Spirit of joy, and he is our salvation.

We have more occasion for joy than sadness. The reason is we believe in the living God, and Christ lives, and we shall live also.

God can make himself known only through those works of his which he reveals in us, which we feel and experience within ourselves. When the experience is to learn that he is a God who looks into the depths and helps principally the poor, despised, afflicted, miserable, forsaken and those who are of no account, at that very moment a love for him is created and surges up from the heart's core. The heart overflows with gladness, and leaps and dances for the joy it has found in God.

In this experience the Holy Spirit is active, and has taught us in the flash of a moment the deep secret of joy.

You will have as much joy and laughter in life as you have faith in God. (*The Joy of the Saints*, 119)

I am a graduate of the University of Southern Mississippi. A classmate, Aubrey Lucas, some years later became the president of Southern and led the school to national prominence. Many graduates of the school have received fame and fortune; some have known national prominence. Perhaps the most celebrated person connected with Southern was not a graduate—in fact, she was never a student of Southern or any college. She was pulled out of the sixth grade, never to continue formal schooling, to care for an ailing family member and to help her mama with the laundry.

The saints took joy in believing and putting their faith into action. Their joy resulted from accepting Jesus' promise, "Be of good cheer, I have overcome the world."

—John 16:33, NKJV

I first heard about her from my friend, President Lucas. He was ecstatic, telling me about the $150,000 gift he had received for the school. I was surprised because I knew that he had received million-dollar, even multimillion-dollar gifts, and countless others exceeding this one. Why such excitement over $150,000? The gift was from Oseola McCarty, and her generosity became known across America.

Oseola McCarty never married. At age eighty-seven, she had done one thing all her life: laundry. She became famous, not for her laundry business, but for the $150,000 she gave to the University of Southern Mississippi. She had saved $250,000 by washing the dirty clothes of wealthy bankers and merchants in her hometown of Hattiesburg, Mississippi.

In the beginning, she earned between $1.50 and $2.00 a bundle for washing and ironing, but the price rose with inflation. Miss McCarty said, "When I started making $10 a bundle—I don't remember when . . . sometime after the war—I commenced to save money. I put it in savings. I never would take any of it out." When the time came to lay down her old-fashioned washboard, she decided to check with her banker to see how much money she had stowed away. She learned the astonishing figure. Realizing that she had more money in the bank than she could ever use, she decided to give it away—to her church, to several relatives, and the bulk of it to the University of Southern Mississippi.

To the surprise of my friend, President Lucas, this soft-spoken African-American laundry woman gave a $150,000 scholarship to help African-American young people attend college. Miss McCarty explained her gift to the college like this: "I want to help somebody's child go to college. I just want [the money] to go to someone who will appreciate it and learn. I'm old and I'm not going to live always. . . . I can't do everything, but I can do something to help somebody. And what I can do I will do. I wish I could do more."

The news of her philanthropy spread. Barbara Walters, each of the major network news programs, CNN, and *People* magazine interviewed her, and her story was carried in other newspapers and magazines across America in the summer of 1995.

Prior to her gift giving, Oseola McCarty had never traveled out of the South, but after news of her generosity spread, she was invited to the White House, where President Clinton awarded her the Presidential Citizens Medal, the second highest award given to U.S. civilians.

Miss McCarty once said that she read her Bible every morning and prayed on her knees every evening, and she rarely missed attending Friendship Baptist Church. She never looked for, nor did she expect, the kind of publicity she received. In report after report she simply said that she was grateful for the chance to help others gain what she never had the opportunity to take advantage of. In one television report I saw, when the interviewer asked why she didn't spend the money on herself, she responded: "It is more blessed to give than to receive; I've tried it."

It was obvious to people who knew Miss McCarty—and to all of us who read her story in magazines and newspapers and saw her talk with interviewers on television—that she was a person of deep faith. As a result, she was a person of joy. Her joy overflowed in her generosity.

Likewise, the saints took joy in believing and in putting their faith into action. By their lives, they affirmed Luther's contention that "a Christian should be . . . a [person] of joy." The saints' joy resulted from their acceptance of Jesus' promise: "In the world you will have tribulation; but be of good cheer, I have overcome the world" (John 16:33, NKJV).

REFLECTING AND RECORDING

Think of someone who exhibits joy in the midst of trial and tribulation. Make enough notes about that person's situation, circumstances, attitudes, and responses to help you remember his or her story.

Name three characteristics of this person.

Spend the rest of your time reflecting on this question: What characteristics of this person are missing from your life?

DURING THE DAY

Continue reading Peterson's paraphrase of Colossians 1:10-14 (page 212).

Check out the joy factor in the persons you meet. Is joy present in their lives? What inhibits or makes joy possible?

DAY
3

"Good Is the Will of God"

But we appeal to you, brothers and sisters, to respect those who labor among you, and have charge of you in the Lord and admonish you; esteem them very highly in love because of their work. Be at peace among yourselves. And we urge you, beloved, to admonish the idlers, encourage the fainthearted, help the weak, be patient with all of them. See that none of you repays evil for evil, but always seek to do good to one another and to all. Rejoice always, pray without ceasing, give thanks in all circumstances; for this is the will of God in Christ Jesus for you. Do not quench the Spirit. Do not despise the words of prophets, but test everything; hold fast to what is good; abstain from every form of evil.

May the God of peace himself sanctify you entirely; and may your spirit and soul and body be kept sound and blameless at the coming of our Lord Jesus Christ. The one who calls you is faithful, and he will do this. (1 Thessalonians 5:12-24)

John Wesley could not preach or write letters without quoting scripture. If you did not know scripture and if many of his sentences were not bounded by quotation marks, you would think they were his own words. He immersed himself in scripture so much that it was his natural language. He had a ready grasp of the Bible's content and was able to quote New and Old Testament phrases and sentences to express what he wanted to say. As you read the following passage from Wesley, underline the phrases that come from scripture.

> He who hath this hope [in Christ], thus "full of immortality, in everything giveth thanks;" as knowing that this (whatsoever it is) "is the will of God in Christ Jesus concerning him." From him, therefore, he cheerfully receives all, saying, "Good is the will of the Lord;" and whether the Lord giveth or taketh away, equally "blessing the name of the Lord." For he hath "learned, in whatsoever state he is, therewith to be content." . . . Whether in ease or pain, whether in sickness or health, whether in life or death, he giveth thanks from the ground of his heart to Him who orders it for good; knowing that as "every good gift cometh from above," so none but good can come from the Father of Lights, into whose hand he has wholly committed his body and soul, as into the hands of a faithful Creator. He is therefore "careful" [anxiously or uneasily] "for nothing;" as having "cast all his care on Him that careth for him," and "in all things" resting on him, after "making his request known to him with thanksgiving." (*The Works of John Wesley*, vol. 8, 342–43)

Wesley stacked words on words and phrases on phrases to make the case that God's will is always good, that we can have peace and be content in all circumstances, and that we can be free of anxiety because we can cast all our cares on God and rest in God. An old gospel chorus also captures this conviction:

Got any rivers you think are uncrossable?
Got any mountains you can't tunnel through?
God specializes in things thought impossible,
He does the things no other power can do.

In Week 4, we gave a good bit of attention to the will of God. We considered why we are so resistant to, or fearful of, the will of God. Is our problem that we don't believe God's will is good? We need to remember C. S. Lewis's sober declaration: "There are only two kinds of people in the end; those who say to God, 'Thy will be done,' and those to whom God says, in the end, '*Thy* will be done'" (*The Great Divorce*, 69).

We wouldn't admit it, and certainly we have not concluded intellectually, that God's will is not good. But where are we practically? And emotionally? Do we order our lives, make our decisions, pursue a life of obedience and holiness in the sure confidence that "good is the will of the Lord," as John Wesley said?

> *We can never know peace until we rest in the assurance that God has a plan for our lives, that God is working that plan, and that God's will for us is good.*

Christians through the ages have given witness to the fact that we can never know peace, fulfillment, and a sense of security and joy until we rest in the assurance that God has a plan for our lives; that the Almighty is working that plan; and that God's will for us is good.

Donald Grey Barnhouse has a wonderful story that relates to this idea. An elderly minister friend of his carried in his Bible a bookmark made of silk threads woven into a motto. The back of the bookmark was a tangled web of crossed threads that seemed to have no reason or purpose. When the pastor visited a home where there was trouble, sorrow, or death, he would often show this bookmark to the people he was visiting. He would present it to them with the reverse side facing up, showing all of its unintelligible tangle. When the bereaved or troubled one had examined the bookmark without finding any explanation for the seeming disorder, the pastor would invite the person to turn over the bookmark. There, clearly visible against the white silk background, was the phrase, in colored threads, "God is love."

The wise pastor would then talk about the tangled patterns of life, and how God takes those tangled, confusing, frustrating circumstances and weaves them into something good that eventually will bring peace and meaning and fulfillment and joy (*Expositions of Bible Doctrines*, vol. 3, 148).

REFLECTING AND RECORDING

We will continue considering this issue tomorrow as we think about our need to be content to wait on God. For now, enter a period of "examination of conscience." Move deliberately through the following questions, spending enough time with each one to make this period an earnest and honest time with God.

Do you honestly believe that God's will is good?

Have you experienced a time during the past six months when you resisted God's will and questioned whether it was good?

Are you pursuing a life of obedience and holiness, knowing that this is God's will for you? Or, are you resisting obedience and holiness, because you are hesitant or uncertain that God's will is good for you?

During the past year, have you known an unexplainable joy even in the midst of trial, suffering, or uncertainty? Have you identified the source of that joy?

Are you currently experiencing a lack of peace, fulfillment, security, or joy? What might be causing this lack in your life?

DURING THE DAY

Yesterday we considered a quotation from Luther that concluded with this word, "You will have as much joy and laughter in life as you have faith in God." Remember this as you move through the day. Continue reading Peterson's paraphrase of the word from Colossians (page 212) and checking out the joy factor in the persons you meet.

DAY
4

The Tough Business of Waiting

Yesterday I suggested that while we have not concluded intellectually that God's will and plan for our life is not good, practically and emotionally we act as though that were true. We asked the question: Do we order our lives, make our decisions, and pursue a life of obedience and holiness in the sure confidence that God's will is good? We also observed that Christians through the ages have borne witness to the fact that we can never know peace, fulfillment, and a sense of security and joy until we rest in the assurance that God has a plan for our life, that the Almighty is working that divine plan, and that God's will for us is good.

The apostle Paul makes it clear that not only you and I, but also all creation, cannot rest until God's plan has been fulfilled and until we Christians come to the full birth of the new life that God promises.

> *I consider that the sufferings of this present time are not worth comparing with the glory about to be revealed to us. For the creation waits with eager longing for the revealing of the children of God; for the creation was subjected to futility, not of its own will but by the will of the one who subjected it, in hope that the creation itself will be set free from its bondage to decay and will obtain the freedom of the glory of the children of God. We know that the whole creation has been groaning in labor pains until now; and not only the creation, but we ourselves, who have the first fruits of the Spirit, groan inwardly while we wait for adoption, the redemption of our bodies. For in hope we were saved. Now hope that is seen is not hope. For who hopes for what is seen? But if we hope for what we do not see, we wait for it with patience.*
>
> *Likewise the Spirit helps us in our weakness; for we do not know how to pray as we ought, but that very Spirit intercedes with sighs too deep for words. And God, who searches the heart, knows what is the mind of the Spirit, because the Spirit intercedes for the saints according to the will of God.*
>
> *We know that all things work together for good for those who love God, who are called according to his purpose. (Romans 8:18-28)*

On Day 2 of this week we quoted Luther as saying, "You will have as much joy and laughter in life as you have faith in God." At the center of our faith is our trust in the fact of a divine plan, and specifically, that God's will for our life is good. Paul gives a singing, poetic witness to this concept:

> *Blessed be the God and Father of our Lord Jesus Christ, who has blessed us in Christ with every spiritual blessing in the heavenly places, just as he chose us in Christ before the foundation of the world to be holy and blameless before him in love. He destined us for adoption as his children through Jesus Christ, according to the good pleasure of his will, to the praise of his glorious grace that he freely bestowed on us in the Beloved. In him we have redemption through his blood, the forgiveness of our trespasses, according to the*

riches of his grace that he lavished on us. With all wisdom and insight he has made known to us the mystery of his will, according to his good pleasure that he set forth in Christ, as a plan for the fullness of time, to gather up all things in him, things in heaven and things on earth. In Christ we have also obtained an inheritance, having been destined according to the purpose of him who accomplishes all things according to his counsel and will, so that we, who were the first to set our hope on Christ, might live for the praise of his glory. (Ephesians 1:3-12)

God has not promised us a life free of confusion, frustration, grief, tragedy, pain, or suffering. God has promised a life free of desperation if we trust in God and in God's deliverance. This faith and trust often requires waiting—painful, trying, challenging, demanding waiting. De Caussade presents a perspective on such waiting:

Abandonment to God is for you just now the one thing necessary. When you go to prayer you must be resigned to suffer exactly as God pleases.

When distraction, aridity, temptations and weariness overwhelm you, say: "You are welcome, cross of my God; I embrace you with a resigned will; make me suffer until my self-love becomes crucified and dead." Then remain in God's presence like a beast of burden weighed down by its load and almost ready to perish, but expecting succour and help from its master.

If you could but throw yourself in spirit at the foot of the cross of Jesus Christ, humbly kiss his sacred wounds, and remain there at his divine feet, steadfast and motionless, and do nothing else but wait patiently in silence and peace as a poor beggar waits for hours at a time at the gates of a great king, hoping to receive an alms!

But, before all things, do not dream of making any more efforts, either in prayer or in anything else, trying to be more recollected than God wishes you to be. Be satisfied to know that this state of dissipation displeases you, and that you have a great desire to be recollected; but only when it pleases God, and as much as it pleases him, neither more nor less. (*The Joy of the Saints*, 264)

I have shared previously about my friend Tammy, who ministers to homeless children in Bangalore, India. In a recent e-mail, she shared with her prayer partners the threat and danger she was facing. The government had shut down three children's homes in the greater Bangalore area—all operated by Christians, with foreigners involved. The general anti-Christian sentiment of the government, coupled with problems in these homes, was bringing widespread investigation, threats, and harassment. Tammy wrote:

God did not promise a life free of confusion, frustration, grief, tragedy, pain, or suffering. God did, however, promise to be with us in times of trouble and to deliver those who love the Lord.

The danger is real. The threat is real. But God's power is much MORE REAL. He has shown us this in recent days. Of course, He has shown us this all along, I guess we have just been reminded of this in recent days. I can't explain the shift in our outlook, nothing on the outside has changed. But . . . Jesus has spoken to us, encouraged us, and challenged us in the middle of the threats. I gotta be honest, I wouldn't trade that for anything. It is worth it. One verse He has continually shown the staff and me is Psalm 91. The whole passage has encouraged us. Specifically, He spoke to us in "1,000 may fall at your side, 10,000 at your right hand, but it will not come near you." We sense His presence, His encouragement, and His pleasure these days more than ever. We know that He is leading, guiding, and protecting. Not in some obscure, 'God is leading me' kinda way, but in a realistic tangible way. He is LEADING, GUIDING, AND PROTECTING. (Tammy Hutchins, e-mail, December 30, 2000)

Tammy and her colleagues can wait and not be desperate over the threat of investigation and closing because they are trusting God.

REFLECTING AND RECORDING

Psalm 91, to which Tammy referred, is printed below. Read the psalm slowly and meditatively, allowing it to speak to you. Put a check mark by the phrases that speak personally to you today:

> *You who live in the shelter of the Most High,*
> *who abide in the shadow of the Almighty,*
> *will say to the Lord, "My refuge and my fortress;*
> *my God, in whom I trust."*
> *For he will deliver you from the snare of the fowler*
> *and from the deadly pestilence;*
> *he will cover you with his pinions,*
> *and under his wings you will find refuge;*
> *his faithfulness is a shield and buckler.*
> *You will not fear the terror of the night,*
> *or the arrow that flies by day,*
> *or the pestilence that stalks in darkness,*
> *or the destruction that wastes at noonday.*
>
> *A thousand may fall at your side,*
> *ten thousand at your right hand,*
> *but it will not come near you.*
> *You will only look with your eyes*
> *and see the punishment of the wicked.*
> *Because you have made the Lord your refuge,*
> *the Most High your dwelling place,*
> *no evil shall befall you,*
> *no scourge come near your tent.*
> *For he will command his angels concerning you*
> *to guard you in all your ways.*
> *On their hands they will bear you up,*
> *so that you will not dash your foot against a stone.*
> *You will tread on the lion and the adder,*
> *the young lion and the serpent you will trample*
> *under foot.*
>
> *Those who love me, I will deliver;*
> *I will protect those who know my name.*
> *When they call to me, I will answer them;*
> *I will be with them in trouble,*
> *I will rescue them and honor them.*
> *With long life I will satisfy them,*
> *and show them my salvation. (Psalm 91)*

Now go back and examine the phrases you checked. In the space beside each one, write a one- or two-sentence prayer of thanksgiving, commitment, or petition in response to God speaking to you through the Word.

During the Day

Do you know someone like Tammy who is facing a big problem, a trying ordeal—someone who is up against a genuine trial and needs assurance of God's presence and promised power? Pray for that person today and find some way—a letter, a telephone call, maybe even a financial contribution—to express your love and concern.

Continue reading the word from Colossians and checking out the joy factor in the persons you meet.

DAY
5

Content Despite Circumstances

Doris Hier tells a story about her daughter, who worked in Chicago before she was married. One day she got off the commuter train to go to her job when a scruffy-looking panhandler stopped her, asking for a quarter. This young woman was never one to cast judgment or ignore need, but she was absolutely penniless and couldn't help the fellow. Looking him straight in the eye, she said, "I'm sorry I don't have a quarter. I don't have any money to take the bus to work today." She couldn't believe what happened then. Without saying a word, the fellow reached into his pocket and gave her a quarter (Doris Hier, *Christian Reader*, vol. 33, no. 5).

Wouldn't you like to visit with that man—to know his story, to discover how he learned generosity, to lay your heart up against his and discover some of the same beatings of care and concern?

The saints teach us that because of the cross and Christ's resurrection, we can be content and even know deep joy despite our circumstances.

I would not even hint that the fellow was content to be in his situation, but there is something about his spontaneous expression of generosity that reminded me of Paul's testimony:

I rejoice in the Lord greatly that now at last you have revived your concern for me; indeed, you were concerned for me, but had no opportunity to show it. Not that I am referring to being in need; for I have learned to be content with whatever I have. I know what it is to have little, and I know what it is to have plenty. In any and all circumstances I have learned the secret of being well-fed and of going hungry, of having plenty and of being in need. I can do all things through him who strengthens me. (Philippians 4:10-13)

The saints learned for themselves, and taught us, that the contentment Paul talked about was no shallow, superficial thing. Jesus had made clear that his peace was different from the peace the world affords: "Peace I leave with you, My peace I give to you; I do not give to you as the world gives. Do not let your hearts be troubled, and do not let them be afraid" (John 14:27).

Martin Luther urged his "dear father prior," a fellow priest with whom he corresponded, to seek this peace Christ gives:

You do indeed "seek peace and ensue it," but altogether in the wrong way. You seek the peace the world gives, not the peace Christ gives.

Are you not aware, my dear father prior, how God is so wonderful among his people that he has set his peace where there is no peace, that is in the midst of all our trials? As he says, "Rule thou in the midst of thine enemies."

It is not, therefore, that man whom no one bothers who has peace. That kind of peace is the peace the world gives. It is that man whom everyone disturbs and everyone harasses, and yet, who joyfully and quietly endures them all.

You are saying with Israel, "Peace! Peace!" when there is no peace. Say, rather, with Christ, "Cross! Cross!" and there is no cross. For the cross ceases to be a cross the moment you say gladly, "Blessed cross! Of all the trees that are in the wood there is none such as thee!"

Seek this peace and you will find peace. Seek for nothing else than to take on trials with joy. Seek them as you would holy relics. You will never find this peace by seeking and choosing what you feel and judge to be the path of peace. (*The Joy of the Saints*, 71)

One of the most memorable and challenging demonstrations of the peace that comes only through Christ was my preacher friend Doyle Masters. In early November 1978, doctors informed Doyle that he had inoperable cancer and that drug treatment did not look promising.

Doyle wrote an open letter to his congregation. The letter sings with confidence and joy in the sufficiency of Christ despite the circumstances. Here are parts of the letter:

The options open to me medically are minimal and at best do not promise renewed energy nor longevity. The other option is to turn this over to God in faith for His healing and ultimate will. This we have been directed to do by God after much prayer and spiritual surrender. What the future holds we do not know, but we know God holds it.

. . . .

These past few days have rolled over us like an avalanche, leaving in their wake some central certainties which make up my Thanksgiving list. Out of the dark night of the soul has come the sunlight of God's love. I am thankful for God who is real and personal, for a Christ who is present in power, and for the Holy Spirit who is by our side in every struggle.

My gratitude overflows for a faith that is unwavering in the face of seemingly insurmountable obstacles, and for the personal practice of prayer that brings all God's promises to bear in any situation.

. . . .

My Thanksgiving list is made this year not from what I have but from who has me—a God who is able to do exceedingly abundantly above all I ask or think. (Dunnam, *The Communicator's Commentary*, vol. 8, 321)

Doyle knew, with Paul, the all-sufficient Christ. . . . He died at the too-early age of forty-eight. As I sat in his memorial service seeking comfort for my grief, I reflected upon my friend's life and our relationship.

I had heard him preach only once. The outline of that sermon, obviously present deep in my consciousness because of its simplicity and profoundness, came vividly to my mind. His theme was "One Day at a Time." He made three points:

1. Today is all you have.
2. Today is all you need.
3. Today is all you can handle.

What powerful thoughts! What a legacy to leave his friends.

We can live with greater intention and purpose if we keep in mind that this day is all we have. We can only live *now*, and so we must make the most of it.

To know that today is all we need helps us to focus our lives creatively. There are many things we can do and need to do today. Even in relation to our larger plans and life goals, there are some steps that we can take today—and those are the only steps we need to take.

Today is all we can handle—*but we can handle today*. What freedom comes when we take our anxious eyes off the future, when we cease anticipating all the problems and difficulties of tomorrow and focus our energy on the present! We know that Christ's power is sufficient for every day, but that power is available only moment by moment.

My reflections on my friend's life and death were interrupted by a nudge from another friend who had sat down beside me. He handed me a note. Through blurring tears I read, "Maxie, I'm so glad on this day that we share a resurrection faith." (*The Communicator's Commentary*, vol. 8, 321–22)

The saints, who grounded themselves in scripture, teach us that because of the cross and resurrection of Christ, we can be content, even know deep joy, despite the circumstances.

REFLECTING AND RECORDING

Spend some time considering what it would mean if you accepted each point from my friend Doyle's sermon. Don't rush. Let the truth of each statement enliven and capture your reflections.

Today is all you have.

Today is all you need.

Today is all you can handle.

DURING THE DAY

These three claims are printed on page 243. Cut them out, and put them in a place where you will see them often during the day. Live by their wisdom.

DAY
6

Satan Is the Author of Uneasiness

One reason the saints knew joy and peace that transcended circumstances was because they were careful to discern the work of Satan in their lives—to recognize his efforts to divert them from single-minded devotion to and trust in God. On Day 2 we quoted Luther's word, "The devil is the spirit of sadness, but God is the Spirit of joy, and he is our salvation." De Caussade warned about Satan's labor and cunning devices to deprive us of peace:

The great principle of the interior life is the peace of the soul, and it must be preserved with such care that the moment it is attacked all else must be put aside and every effort made to try and regain this holy peace.

Peace and tranquillity of mind alone give great strength to the soul to enable it to do all that God wishes, while anxiety and uneasiness make the soul feeble and languid, and as though sick.

Then one feels neither taste for, nor attraction to virtue, but, on the contrary, disgust and discouragement of which the devil does not fail to take advantage. For this reason he uses all his cunning to deprive us of peace, and under a thousand specious pretexts, at one time about self-examination, or sorrow for sin, at another about the way we continually neglect grace, or that by

our own fault we make no progress; that
God will, at last, forsake us.

This is why masters of the spiritual life
lay down this great principle to distinguish
the true inspirations of God from those that
emanate from the devil; that the former are
always sweet and peaceful, inducing to confidence and humility, while the latter are
intense, restless and violent, leading to discouragement and mistrust, or else to presumption and self-will.

(*The Joy of the Saints*, 146)

Paul knew the wiles of the devil, so he called Christians to be free of anxiety, to rejoice and
praise God, and to concentrate on prayer and thanksgiving.

*Rejoice in the Lord always; again I will say, Rejoice. Let your gentleness be known to everyone. The Lord
is near. Do not worry about anything, but in everything by prayer and supplication with thanksgiving let
your requests be made known to God. And the peace of God, which surpasses all understanding, will
guard your hearts and your minds in Christ Jesus. (Philippians 4:4-7)*

It is fascinating that hundreds of years before modern psychology, de Caussade recognized how fear and anxiety can be debilitating and lead to dysfunction. Also, it is amazing that he was spiritually
sensitive enough to recognize how Satan can use our anxiety and
uneasiness to deprive us of peace, cause us to question our relationship to God, and thus "make the soul feeble and languid, and as
though sick."

In his study of self-actualizing people, psychologist Abraham
Maslow found that they shared, in varying degrees, certain attitudes.
One of these was tolerance for uncertainty. Self-actualizing people,
according to Maslow, seemed to know how to live with the un-

> *Satan can use our anxiety
> and uneasiness to deprive
> us of peace, cause us to
> question our relationship
> to God, and thus make
> the soul sick.*

known without feeling threatened or frightened. Uncertainty and ambiguity—not knowing
about the future, and a confusion about values and things as they are—are facts of life. How we
need to appropriate Paul's word, "Be anxious for nothing" (Phil. 4:6, NKJV).

Anxiety, in the way Paul used the term, and the way we most often experience it, is the
futile, frustrating, debilitating attempt to bear the burdens of life, and especially of the future, by
ourselves. The Christian answer to anxiety is confident prayer, which has its source in "the
peace of God, which surpasses all understanding" (v. 7).

This is no glib word, no pious cliché, no easy moralizing about complex issues.
Remember, Paul was in prison. Ponder for even a minute the immediate circumstances out of
which this word came, and let the movement of his life be flashed, however quickly, upon the
screen of your mind. At every step of his Christian journey, the hound of anxiety was snapping
at his heels. And even when the hound was not within biting distance, its howl must have
sounded loud in his ears. Fears, uncertainty about the future, persecution, physical disease,

mental anguish—again the list could become a catalog. Paul's word comes from the sweaty arena of life where his word needs to be heard, and from a person who has experienced the answer he is offering.

Paul's advice to pray rather than worry is not an easy solution. He offers no magic formula here, no bedtime or morning rote repetition of words that we have labeled prayer. He is talking about the serious business of bringing our lives before God, examining our dependence upon God, placing our lives in God's hands to be used, remembering and celebrating what God has already done, confessing our needs and dedicating our gifts, and committing ourselves and all that we are to God's kingdom. When we view prayer in that fashion, then it is not glib to say that anxiety is an attempt to carry the burden of the present and the future by ourselves. Prayer is yielding our burden to and leaving it in the safe hands of God.

This is not a one-time, once-and-for-all, well-it's-done-now kind of thing. It is a life process, and its power is cumulative. I saw evidence of this in Nelson Mandela. As one of the presidents of the World Methodist Council, I had the privilege of sharing with my wife in a service when we officers of the Council gave Mandela the World Methodist Peace Award for the year 2000. The service was held in Cape Town's Central Methodist Mission on September 21, 2000. Dr. Mandela's entire life is a witness to God's guidance and support as he gave himself courageously in the fight against apartheid. It is also the witness of community and the mutual support of persons committed to the same purpose.

In his presence and witness, as he responded to receiving the peace award, there was the added confirmation to what he said in his autobiography, *Long Walk to Freedom*. Mandela said that "no epiphany, no singular revelation, no moment of truth" shaped his life purpose. Rather, he said,

> A steady accumulation of a thousand slights, a thousand indignities, a thousand unremembered moments, produced in me an anger, a rebelliousness, a desire to fight the system that imprisoned my people. There was no particular day on which I said, From henceforth I will devote myself to the liberation of my people; instead, I simply found myself doing so, and could not do otherwise. (*Long Walk to Freedom*, 109)

Mandela proved that as he walked to his car from Central Mission, where he had received the award. A small child with one leg and a crutch hobbled toward him. The security people were there to turn away that little one and others who pressed in. But Dr. Mandela motioned for the child to come to him. Almost immediately, at least twenty-five other street children pressed against him and his car. I will never forget the light on the faces of those children as they talked to this great man and felt the warmth of his welcome and smile.

REFLECTING AND RECORDING

Spend a few minutes pondering this word from Luther: "The devil is the spirit of sadness, but God is the Spirit of joy, and he is our salvation." Can you identify occasions when your sadness was the result of the devil's seeking to control your life?

Read again de Caussade's quotation on page 226 and translate the first three paragraphs into your own words in the space provided beside it.

Now reread de Caussade's last paragraph. Examine your own experience, seeking to identify feelings and inspiration that have come from God and those that may have emanated from Satan.

DURING THE DAY

Ponder the wisdom of my friend Doyle's sermon (see Day 5) and seek to apply it today.

DAY
7

Death Has No Victory

What I am saying, brothers and sisters, is this: flesh and blood cannot inherit the kingdom of God, nor does the perishable inherit the imperishable. Listen, I will tell you a mystery! We will not all die, but we will all be changed, in a moment, in the twinkling of an eye, at the last trumpet. For the trumpet will sound, and the dead will be raised imperishable, and we will be changed. For this perishable body must put on imperishability, and this mortal body must put on immortality. When this perishable body puts on imperishability, and this mortal body puts on immortality, then the saying that is written will be fulfilled:

"Death has been swallowed up in victory.
Where, O death, is your victory?
Where, O death, is your sting?"

The sting of death is sin, and the power of sin is the law. But thanks be to God, who gives us the victory through our Lord Jesus Christ.

*   Therefore, my beloved, be steadfast, immovable, always excelling in the work of the Lord, because you know that in the Lord your labor is not in vain. (1 Corinthians 15:50-58)*

In his commentary on this passage from First Corinthians, William Barclay says that we must read it "as we would read great poetry, rather than as we would dissect a scientific treatise."

Paul is dealing with things that defy language and baffle expression. He first insists that we are not fit to inherit the kingdom of God; we must undergo a change before we can enter the kingdom. So, the change will come—"in the twinkling of an eye"—when the dead will be raised imperishable.

Paul then declares that Christians do not need to fear this change—because death has been defeated—it has no victory. Paul closes his teaching by putting forth a challenge: If we have this victory, and if we know the victory is ours, then we are to let nothing move us, giving ourselves always fully to the work of God, "because [we] know that [our] labor in the Lord is not in vain" (v. 58).

Though not preoccupied with death, the saints did not shy away from reflecting on it, and facing it as a reality that shaped their living. Luther said,

> When I feel the dread of death, I say, "O death, you have nothing to do with me, because I have another death which kills my death." And the death which kills is stronger than that which is killed." (*The Joy of the Saints*, 307)

Thérèse of Lisieux sounds almost playful, certainly unreserved, in her reflection on death.

> It seems to me that nothing stands in the way of my going to heaven. I no longer have any great desires, beyond that of loving till I die of love. I am free, and I fear nothing, not even what I once dreaded more than anything else, a long illness which would make me a burden to the community.
>
>   Should it please God, I am quite content to have my sufferings of body and soul prolonged for years. I do not shrink from a long life: I do not refuse the battle. The Lord is the rock upon which I stand—"who teaches my hands to fight, and my fingers to war. He is my protector and I have hoped in him" (Psalm 144:1-2).
>
>   I have never asked God to let me die young, but I have always thought that this favour will be granted me.
>
>   Very often God is satisfied with our wish to labour for his glory, and how immense are my desires to do so. (*The Joy of the Saints*, 80)

Christians do not need to fear death because God has given us victory over death through Christ Jesus.

The saints knew that that their entire lives rested in God's hands. When we realize that death is one of those large issues taken care of by God's grace, we are enabled to deal with smaller issues and concerns and to know joy despite circumstances.

Leah Koncelik Lebec, a mother and writer, wrote a deeply moving, probing reflection on the stillbirth of her son when she was seven months pregnant. She talked honestly about the emotional roller-coaster she experienced, the confusion, the inability to know what to do once she and her husband discovered the baby was dead in the womb.

That first night, we went to bed, and neither one of us knew what to do. There was the lump that used to be "the baby," but it wasn't the baby anymore. We didn't have the words to talk about it. But as I lay back against the pillow, and turned quietly away from him, my heart started beating fast. There was something looming on the edges of my consciousness, but I didn't want it to come any closer.

Suddenly a whisper rose unbidden from my heart: "Good night, baby." I wanted silence. Stonily, I turned to fitful, fearful sleep. But the whisper rose again, even as my mind tried to crush the words: "Good night, little one." And then, with a thrill of fear: "Farewell, beloved."

The next day, we went to a church. We were vaguely wondering what we should do when the baby was born. Should we bury it? Should we baptize it? We talked to a priest. We didn't know him and he didn't know us. We were not rooted in any religious community then. We stumbled into his church, and demanded that he say the right words to us at a time when neither he nor we could know how heavily these decisions would weigh.

"Don't think of it as anything but an operation," he said. "Don't bury it or baptize it. It will only increase the pain." He's right, I thought, even as a more cynical thought nudged its way in: an "operation"? What does this guy know about childbirth? But Alain and I decided to agree with him. We didn't really care one way or another about burial or ritual. The fetus was dead. The sooner its body was taken care of the better. ("Stillbirth," *First Things*, June/July 2000, 42)

It was a tragic story in many ways. After the baby was born, Leah held him.

I took the baby into the crook of my elbow, and felt the weight of his body against me.

I raised one hand, and cupped it around his tiny head. There was a kind of downy hair on his head. I touched the swirling soft pattern with the tips of my fingers. I caressed his head, then his check. I stared into a perfect face.

His eyes were closed. I touched the lids, then bent to kiss them: first one, then the other. He looked asleep. There was a dimple in his chin; the little mouth was shaped like his father's. A rosebud mouth, so still and quiet.

No cry, no sound, my son? (*First Things*, 42)

A nurse took the baby away, and after a long day in which Leah was treated for some other medical problems, she was alone.

It is dark. There are no machines, no doctors, no nurses, no one to be polite to, no heart problem to talk about and explain, no husband to hover worriedly over my bed, no tests, no monitors.

There is no baby.

There, in the dark, it hits me. The grief is a physical thing. It comes in waves—wave after wave, shocking my spirit, shattering my heart. I curl my body around its emptiness. Its center is gone. Its womb is empty. My arms are empty.

But you were here! I held you! Where have you gone, beloved? Where are you, my little son?

There is no one in the room with me, but even so, I try to muffle the wrenching sobs. His vulnerability, his fragility, his weight are more than I can bear. I feel him in my arms, but he is not here. My son. I am a mother, but my child is gone. Where are you? He is not here, but I cannot let him go. Who is holding that hand? On what breast are you cradled tonight? Are you afraid, wherever you are? Are you crying? Is someone there to hold you? Please God, hold him, rock him, cradle him, soothe him, whisper to him, caress him. Love him for me, please God.

The storm passes, but I am changed forever. It sufficed to hold him, to look into his face, and he entered my heart forever. I am a mother, and my son has died. Where there was no knowledge of him before, now there is a river, coursing through my mind and heart, bearing the memory and the loss of him forever. (*First Things*, 43)

Leah and her husband named their son Damien. She said they learned too late that the rituals of death are important and healing. They attempted to find the baby's body so that they could have him baptized and buried.

> . . . but . . . the hospital staff had lost the baby's body and had no records of where he had been taken. "Where are you?" became both a literal and a figurative cry. My dreams were dominated for months by desperate searches, through darkness, through strange lands, with empty arms stretched out in front of stumbling feet. (*First Things*, 43)

In time Leah and her husband, Alain, were blessed with three other children. But she says that Damien was the one who "changed the landscape of my hopes and my dreams and my thoughts."

> My children speak of him naturally and happily, without the embarrassment or fear that so many adults feel in hearing his name. They expect to see him one day, "on that mountain," where every tear is washed away. He is not here, yet he is with us. I bear him forever, my first-born son, and my children speak his name.
>
> "Stillbirth." There is such paradox in the word, such death. The first syllable cancels out the second. All that newness, that unfurling life, is canceled out already, from the beginning. All that sweet force, gathering, gathering, month after month, now silent, still.
>
> And yet, triumphing over that tragic paradox, I have found an astonishing, infinitely more paradoxical joy, embedded even in that memory of my first child, unmoving in my arms.
>
> What possible joy? The realization, for me, of how strongly God loves us. Yes, loves us, all six billion—whatever—of us, teeming over the earth. I have come to understand the love for Damien that pierced my heart as a dim reflection of God's love for us. Such love is instantaneous, it is absolute, it has no care for how many of us there are or what we have accomplished. It has no care for how long we have been alive. Young or old, sick or well, we are lovely in His sight, worthy to His heart. The love that overwhelmed me, even for a seven-month-old stillborn baby, also deepened my understanding, comforted me, and in the end, held up for me a mirror of the divine. Our capacity to grasp the humanity, the luminous beauty, of every child who comes into being is our capacity to love as God loves—with a strength that is primal, unreasonable, and unshakable.
>
> God loves us as a mother loves her child—because we are there, because we are His, because we are ourselves: irreplaceable, forever unique, never, ever to be forgotten. "The Lord called me from the womb, from the body of my mother he named my name" (Isaiah 49:1). (*First Things*, 44)

REFLECTING AND RECORDING

Has the death of a family member or friend left you with unresolved frustration and pain? Spend some time processing that loss in light of the witnesses of scripture, Luther, Thérèse, and Leah Koncelik Lebec.

Are you, a family member, or a loved one facing what appears to be imminent death? Acknowledge your feelings about this and offer them to God. Ask God to help you deal with these feelings in light of these witnesses we have considered today.

Spend whatever time you have left reflecting on the weeks you have spent with this workbook and the persons who have shared the journey with you. Make this a time of prayerful thanksgiving and commitment.

DURING THE DAY (AND ALL COMING DAYS)

Claim your relationship as a citizen of God's kingdom in company with the saints of the ages, and offer yourself as the presence of Christ to all you meet.

Group Meeting for Week 8

INTRODUCTION

Today is the last meeting designed for this group. You have talked about the possibility of continuing to meet. Conclude those plans. Whatever you choose to do, determine the actual time line so that participants can make a clear commitment. Assign some persons to follow through with decisions that are made.

SHARING TOGETHER

Your sharing during this session should reflect on the entire eight-week experience. Leader, be sure to save enough time for responses to suggestion 10.

1. Begin your sharing by discussing Paul's teaching that (1) there are two kingdoms—light and darkness, flesh and spirit—and (2) we have been rescued from the darkness and brought into the kingdom of light. We are now citizens of the new kingdom. How do those two kingdoms express themselves? What are the signs of the new kingdom?

2. Looking back at our "lessons from the saints," what are some of the lessons they teach us about these two kingdoms and how we are to live in the new kingdom?

3. Invite two persons to name and describe the person of joy they named in the Reflecting and Recording time of Day 2.

4. What were the primary characteristics of those persons? What was the source of their joy? Do their lives confirm Paul's teaching about "two kingdoms" and Christians being rescued from the kingdom of darkness and being citizens of the kingdom of light?

5. Invite a couple of persons in the group to give a two- or three-minute response to Luther's statement, "You will have as much joy and laughter in life as you have faith in God." (Allow them to express disagreement if they feel it.)

6. Spend ten to fifteen minutes discussing the suggestion that while we may have not concluded intellectually that God's will is not good, practically and emotionally we act as though that is the case.

7. Turn to Psalm 91 in the Reflecting and Recording period of Day 4 (page 222). Invite three to four persons to share a point at which the psalm spoke personally to them—and the prayer they wrote in response.

8. Invite individuals who wish to share a personal response to each of the affirmations of Doyle Masters on Day 5. Urge them to address only one of the affirmations—an experience when it became clear that

> Today is all you have.
> Today is all you need.
> Today is all you can handle.

Allow enough sharing for all the affirmations to be addressed.

9. Invite someone to read his or her paraphrase of de Caussade's word in Day 6, then spend eight to ten minutes discussing this teaching. Include responses to Luther's word, "The devil is the spirit of sadness, but God is the Spirit of joy, and he is our salvation." Take note of personal occasions when your sadness, anxiety, and lack of peace may have been caused by the devil seeking to control your life.

10. Spend the remaining time sharing what these eight weeks have meant to individuals in the group—new insights, challenges, disciplines they will have to work on.

PRAYING TOGETHER

Saint Teresa of Avila said the following about prayer:

In prayer it is well to occupy ourselves sometimes in making acts of praise and love to God; in desires and resolutions to please Him in all things; in rejoicing at His goodness and that He is what He is; in desiring His honor and glory; in recommending ourselves to His mercy; also in simply placing ourselves before Him, beholding His greatness and His mercy, and, at the same time, our own vileness and misery, and then to let Him give us what He pleases, whether it be showers or aridity; for He knows better than we what is most suitable for us. (*A Year with the Saints*, 266)

1. Since on this day, Day 7, we have focused on death—we have recalled that death has no victory—begin your prayer time by inviting persons to share concerns about death, such as the recent loss of a loved one or someone who is facing death. As these concerns are named, pray for each one.

2. Spend two or three minutes in silence, thinking and praying for individuals about whom you are concerned and to whom you may need to speak.

3. Invite each group member to share a commitment he or she has made or prayer requests. As each person shares, have a time of prayer—silent or oral, preferably oral—so that each person will be prayed for specifically.

4. Now ask two or three people to offer general prayers of thanksgiving for the eight-week experience and petitions for further growth and guidance.

5. A benediction is a blessing or greeting shared with another person or by a group in parting. A variation on the traditional "passing of the peace" can serve as a benediction. Form a circle with group members. The leader takes the hand of the person next to him/her, looks into his or her eyes, and says, "The peace of God be with you." That

person responds, "And may God's peace be yours." Then that person takes the hand of the person next to him or her and says, "The peace of God be with you," and receives the response, "And may God's peace be yours." Continue passing the peace around the circle until everyone has had the opportunity to participate.

6. After the passing of the peace, speak to one another more spontaneously. Move around to different individuals in the group, saying whatever you feel is appropriate for your parting blessing to each person. Or simply embrace the person and say nothing. In your own unique way, bless each person who has shared this journey with you.

Acknowledgments

The publisher gratefully acknowledges the following copyright holders for permission to use copyrighted material:

Barry P. Boulware for excerpt from his sermon "You've Got to Be Kidding," 23 February 1992.

First Things for excerpt from "Stillbirth" by Leah Koncelik Lebec. Copyright © 2000 *First Things* (June/July 2000).

Denise George for her story "Debbie Morris: Forgiving the 'Dead Man Walking.'"

HarperCollins, Publishers, Inc. for excerpts from *Streams of Living Water* by Richard J. Foster. Copyright © 1998 by Richard J. Foster.

Tammy Hutchins for excerpts from her e-mail correspondence.

Multnomah Publishers for excerpt from *The Prayer of Jabez: Breaking through to the Blessed Life.* Copyright © 2000 by Bruce H. Wilkinson.

Norman Neaves for excerpt from his sermon "Living Down in the Valley," 2 December 1990.

Scribner, a division of Simon & Schuster, Inc., for excerpts from *A Dairy of Readings* by John Baillie. Copyright © 1955 by John Baillie; copyright renewed © 1983 by Ian Fowler Baillie.

Seedsowers Publishing House for excerpts from *The Seeking Heart.* Copyright © 1992 by Christian Books Publishing House.

Simon & Schuster, Inc. for excerpts from *On the Love of God*, translated by W. J. Knox Little.

Templegate Publishers for excerpts from *The Joy of the Saints.* Introduction and arrangement copyright © 1988 by Robert Llewelyn.

Time, Inc. for excerpt from "How the Best Golfer in the World Got Better." © 2000 Time, Inc.

Mark Trotter for excerpt from his sermon "You're Not in Charge Here," 15 May 1988.

Upper Room Books for excerpts from *A Longing for Holiness: Selected Writings of John Wesley*, ed. by Keith Beasley-Topliffe. Copyright © 1997 by Upper Room Books, and for excerpts from *Making Life a Prayer: Selected Writings of John Cassian*, ed. by Keith Beasley-Topliffe. Copyright © 1997 by Upper Room Books.

BIBLIOGRAPHY

Albom, Mitch. *Tuesdays with Morrie: An Old Man, a Young Man, and Life's Greatest Lesson.* New York: Doubleday, 1997.

Baillie, John. *A Diary of Readings.* New York: Charles Scribner's Sons, 1955.

Barclay, William. *The Letter to the Romans.* Rev. ed. Philadelphia: The Westminster Press, 1975.

Barnhouse, Donald Grey. *Expositions of Bible Doctrines: God's Grace, God's Freedom, God's Heirs.* Vol. 3. Grand Rapids, Mich.: Wm. B. Eerdmans Publishing Company, 1959, 1961, 1963.

Bell, Jarrett. "The Morning After: What It Really Feels Like to Play Pro Football Every Sunday." *USA Today* (Dec. 7, 2000).

Bernard of Clairvaux. *Selections from the Writings of Bernard of Clairvaux.* Edited by Douglas V. Steere. Nashville: The Upper Room, 1961.

Bouknight, William R. *The Authoritative Word: Preaching Truth in a Skeptical Age.* Nashville: Abingdon Press, 2001.

Bowen, Barbara M. *Strange Scriptures That Perplex the Western Mind.* 2nd ed. Grand Rapids, Mich.: Wm. B. Eerdmans Publishing Co., 1940.

Caretto, Carlo. Foreword to *Two Dancers in the Desert: The Life of Charles de Foucauld,* by Charles Lepetit. MaryKnoll, N.Y.: Orbis Books, 1983.

Carson, D. A. *For the Love of God: A Daily Companion for Discovering the Treasures of God's Word,* vol. 2. Wheaton, Ill.: Crossway Books, 1999.

Cassian, John. *Making Life a Prayer: Selected Writings of John Cassian.* Edited by Keith Beasley-Topliffe. Nashville: Upper Room Books, 1997.

Chambers, Oswald. *The Psychology of Redemption.* London: Marshall, Morgan and Scott, 1930.

Coppedge, Allan, and William Ury. *In His Image: A Workbook on Scriptural Holiness.* Franklin, Tenn.: Providence House Publishers, 2000.

Dunnam, Maxie. *Alive in Christ.* Nashville: Abingdon Press, 1987.

Dunnam, Maxie D. *Galatians, Ephesians, Philippians, Colossians, Philemon.* Vol. 8 of *The Communicator's Commentary,* edited by Lloyd J. Ogilvie. Waco, Tex.: Word Books, Publisher, 1982.

Fénelon, François. *Christian Counsels: Selected from the Devotional Works of Fénelon, Archbishop of Cambrai.* Translated by A. M. James. London: Longmans, Green, and Co., 1872.

_____. *Letters and Reflections of François de Fénelon.* Edited by Thomas S. Kepler. New York: World Publishing Company, 1955.

_____. *The Seeking Heart.* Sargent, Ga.: The SeedSowers Christian Books Publishing House, 1992.

_____. *Selections from the Writings of François Fénelon.* Edited by Thomas S. Kepler. Nashville: The Upper Room, 1962.

Flavel, John. *Keeping the Heart.* Grand Rapids, Mich.: Sovereign Grace Publishers, 1971.

_____. *The Works of John Flavel,* vol. 5. London: The Banner of Truth Trust, 1968.

Foster, Richard J. *Streams of Living Water: Celebrating the Great Traditions of Christian Faith.* San Francisco: HarperSanFrancisco, 1998.

Francis of Assisi. *The Little Flowers of St. Francis.* Translated by Raphael Brown. Garden City, N.Y.: Image Books, 1958.

Goodgame, Dan. "The Game of Risk: How the Best Golfer in the World Got Even Better." *Time* (August 14, 2000), 57–62.

Harnish, James A. *Passion, Power and Praise: A Model for Men's Spirituality from the Life of David.* Nashville: Abingdon Press, 2000.

The Joy of the Saints: Spiritual Readings Throughout the Year. Introduced and arranged by Robert Llewelyn. Springfield, Ill.: Templegate Publishers, 1989.

Kempis, Thomas à. *The Imitation of Christ.* Edited by Douglas V. Steere. Nashville: The Upper Room, 1950.

Kepler, Thomas S. *A Journey with the Saints.* Nashville: The Upper Room, 1951.

King, Martin Luther, Jr. *A Testament of Hope: The Essential Writings and Speeches of Martin Luther King, Jr.* Edited by James Melvin Washington. New York: HarperCollins, 1991.

Law, William. *The Works of the Reverend William Law.* 9 vols. London: J. Richardson, 1762.

Lebec, Leah Koncelik. "Stillbirth." *First Things* (June/July 2000) 104:40–44.

Lepetit, Charles. *Two Dancers in the Desert: The Life of Charles de Foucauld.* MaryKnoll, N.Y.: Orbis Books, 1983.

Lewis, C. S. *The Great Divorce.* New York: The Macmillan Company, 1946.

_____. *Mere Christianity.* Rev. ed. New York: Collier Books, 1960.

Luther, Martin. *Commentary on the Epistle to the Galatians.* Translated by Theodore Graebner. Grand Rapids, Mich.: Zondervan Publishing House, 1949.

_____. *Daily Readings with Martin Luther.* Edited by James Atkinson. Springfield, Ill.: Templegate Publishers, 1987.

_____. *The Table Talk of Martin Luther.* Edited by Thomas S. Kepler. Grand Rapids, Mich.: Baker Book House, 1979.

Mandela, Nelson. *Long Walk to Freedom: The Autobiography of Nelson Mandela.* Boston: Little, Brown and Company, 1994.

McCourt, Frank. *Angela's Ashes: A Memoir.* New York: Scribner, 1996.

Murray, Andrew. *The Believer's Secret of Obedience*. Minneapolis, Minn.: Bethany House Publishers, 1982.

Norris, Kathleen. *The Cloister Walk*. New York: Riverhead Books, 1996.

Nouwen, Henri J. M. *Making All Things New: An Invitation to the Spiritual Life*. San Francisco: Harper and Row, Publishers, 1981.

Palmer, Phoebe. *Phoebe Palmer: Selected Writings*. Edited by Thomas C. Oden. New York: Paulist Press, 1988.

Peck, M. Scott. *The Road Less Traveled: A New Psychology of Love, Traditional Values and Spiritual Growth*. New York: Simon and Schuster, 1978.

Peterson, Eugene H. *Subversive Spirituality*. Grand Rapids, Mich.: William B. Eerdmans Publishing Company, 1997.

Ridenour, Fritz, ed. *I'm a Good Man, But* . . . Glendale, Calif.: G/L Publications, 1969.

Sales, Saint Francis de. *Introduction to the Devout Life*. Translated and edited by John K. Ryan. New York: Image Books, 1972.

_____. *The Love of God: A Treatise*. Translated by Vincent Kerns. Westminster, Md.: The Newman Press, 1962.

Selzer, Richard. *Mortal Lessons: Notes on the Art of Surgery*. New York: Simon and Schuster, 1976.

Steere, Douglas. *On Beginning from Within*. New York: Harper and Brothers, 1943.

Teresa of Avila. *The Complete Works of Saint Teresa of Jesus*. Vol. 1. Translated and edited by E. Allison Peers. London: Sheed and Ward, 1946.

Thérèse of Lisieux. *The Story of a Soul: The Autobiography of Saint Thérèse of Lisieux*. Translated by Michael Day. London: Burns & Oates, 1951.

Wesleyan Theological Journal: Bulletin of the Wesleyan Theological Society. Full text of articles dating back to 1966 available online at wesley.nnu.edu/theojrnl/.

Wesley, John. *A Longing for Holiness: Selected Writings of John Wesley*. Edited by Keith Beasley-Topliffe. Nashville: Upper Room Books, 1997.

Wesley, John. *A Plain Account of Christian Perfection*. London: The Epworth Press, 1952.

Wesley, John. *The Works of John Wesley*. 14 vols. Grand Rapids, Mich.: Zondervan Publishing House, n.d.

Wilkinson, Bruce H. *The Prayer of Jabez: Breaking Through to the Blessed Life*. Sisters, Ore.: Multnomah Publishers, 2000.

Willard, Dallas. *The Spirit of the Disciplines: Understanding How God Changes Lives*. New York: Harper & Row Publishers, 1988.

A Year with the Saints: Twelve Christian Virtues in the Lives and Writings of the Saints. Translated by A Member of the Order of Mercy. Rockford, Ill.: TAN Books and Publishers, 1891.

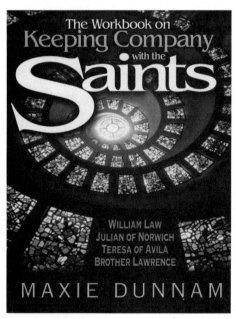

Affirmation Cards

Today is all you have.
Today is all you need.
Today is all you can handle.

[WEEK 8, DAY 5]

We pray that you'll live well for the Master, making him proud of you as you work hard in his orchard. As you learn more and more how God works, you will learn how to do your work. We pray that you'll have the strength to stick it out over the long haul—not the grim strength of gritting your teeth but the glory-strength God gives. It is strength that endures the unendurable and spills over into joy, thanking the Father who makes us strong enough to take part in everything bright and beautiful that he has for us.

God rescued us from dead-end alleys and dark dungeons. He's set us up in the kingdom of the Son he loves so much, the Son who got us out of the pit we were in, got rid of the sins we were doomed to keep repeating. (Colossians 1:10-14, THE MESSAGE)

[WEEK 8, DAY 1]

Jesus said. . . . "I am the bread of life. Whoever comes to me will never be hungry, and whoever believes in me will never be thirsty" (John 6:35).

[WEEK 2, DAY 2]

Divine love, enlightening our soul and making us pleasing to God, is called grace. Giving us power to do good, it is called charity. When it reaches the point of perfection where it makes us earnestly, frequently and readily do good, it is called devotion.

—Francis de Sales
[WEEK 2, DAY 2]

All to Jesus I surrender;
all to him I freely give;
I will ever love and trust him,
in his presence daily live.
I surrender all, I surrender all,
all to thee, my blessed Savior,
I surrender all.

From "I Surrender All," words by J. W. Van Deventer, 1896
[WEEK 6, DAY 5]

Mold me and make me after thy will,
While I am waiting, yielded and still.

From "Have Thine Own Way, Lord,"
words by Adelaide A. Pollard, 1902
[WEEK 5, DAY 1]

[The Holy Spirit's word to Margery Kempe]
Go in the name of Jesus. I will go with you to help and support you in all you do. Trust me, you have never found me wanting. I will never ask you to do anything that is unacceptable to God.

I am your God and I delight in you, and we shall never be parted. All the promises I have made to you will come true at the right time.

[WEEK 1, DAY 5]

[God's word to Margery Kempe]
Rejoice and be happy! If you knew how much pleasure I get from speaking to you, you would never do anything else.

[WEEK 1, DAY 3]

Lord, give me the grace to be wholly yours.
[WEEK 1, DAY 1]

ABOUT THE AUTHOR

Dr. Maxie Dunnam became president of Asbury Theological Seminary in 1994 after twelve fruitful years of ministry as senior minister at the 6,000-member Christ United Methodist Church in Memphis, Tennessee. From 1975 to 1982 he was world editor of *The Upper Room* daily devotional guide, and prior to that he was Director of Prayer Life and Fellowship for The Upper Room.

Dr. Dunnam holds a bachelor's degree from the University of Southern Mississippi, a master's degree in theology from Emory University, and a doctor of divinity degree from Asbury Theological Seminary. He served recently as one of the presidents of the World Methodist Council and currently chairs the World Evangelism Committee. He is also an elected member of the University Senate of The United Methodist Church and serves on the executive committee of The Association of Theological Schools.

A prolific writer, Dr. Dunnam has authored more than thirty books, including the widely used *Workbook on Living Prayer, This Is Christianity, Unless We Pray,* and two volumes in the Communicator's Commentary series.

Dr. Dunnam and his wife, Jerry, have three adult children: Kim, Kerry, and Kevin.

Upper Room Spiritual Classics, Series 2

With this second set of devotional classics, Upper Room Books® offers selections from more great Christian writers—Francis and Clare of Assisi, Julian of Norwich, Evelyn Underhill, Toyohiko Kagawa, and Thomas à Kempis. ISBN# 0-8358-0853-X $24.00 (5 titles in slipcase)

Titles in Series 2:

Encounter with God's Love - *Selected Writings of Julian of Norwich*
Revealing insights from a lifetime of prayer, the writings of this late fourteenth-century nun and mystic offer some of the most moving discussions of God's love in all of Christian literature. ISBN# 0-8358-0833-5 $5.00

The Riches of Simplicity - *Selected Writings of Francis and Clare*
Perhaps no one has captivated the hearts of such a wide spectrum of Christians as Francis and Clare. These thirteenth-century saints are depicted through biographical vignettes as well as in prayers, letters, and other writings. ISBN# 0-8358-0834-3 $5.00

A Pattern for Life - *Selected Writings of Thomas à Kempis*
From the time of its appearance around 1420, à Kempis' *The Imitation of Christ* has perhaps had more influence on Christian spirituality than any other book except the Bible. ISBN# 0-8358-0835-1 $5.00

The Soul's Delight - *Selected Writings of Evelyn Underhill*
This twentieth-century British writer and retreat leader has been widely known for her compelling exploration of the spiritual life. Her work introduced many readers to the spiritual classics and offered profoundly simple advice on opening oneself to God. ISBN# 0-8358-0837-8 $5.00

Living Out Christ's Love - *Selected Writings of Toyohiko Kagawa*
Often cited as a model of how to blend prayer, compassion, and social action, Kagawa worked in the period between the two world wars to establish settlement houses, labor unions, and peasant unions and carry on evangelistic campaigns. His writings include autobiographical reflections and thoughts about the Lord's Prayer. ISBN# 0-8358-0836-X $5.00

Upper Room Spiritual Classics, Series 3

This third set of devotional classics includes wisdom from spiritual leaders who strove to devote their lives totally to the will of God: John of the Cross, the Desert Mothers and Fathers, John Law, John Woolman, and Catherine of Siena. ISBN# 0-8358-0905-6 $24.00 (5 titles in slipcase)

Titles in Series 3:

Loving God Through the Darkness - *Selected Writings of John of the Cross*
Loving God alone requires detachment from other things, a process of moving through the "dark night of the soul." John of the Cross elegantly expresses this process of seeking divine union in his poems and books on the spiritual life. A Carmelite monk and a close associate of Teresa of Avila, John lived during the religious turmoil of sixteenth-century Spain. ISBN# 0-8358-0904-8 $5.00

Seeking a Purer Christian Life - *The Desert Mothers and Fathers*
In the third, fourth, and fifth centuries, thousands of men and women moved into the deserts of Egypt and Syria to seek a simple way of living. Their sayings about prayer, spiritual disciplines, and living in community spread throughout the Christian world and became the foundation of monasticism. ISBN# 0-8358-0902-1 $5.00

Total Devotion to God - *Selected Writings of William Law*
In these selections from his book *A Serious Call to a Devout and Holy Life*, Law calls for a total devotion to God. Responding to the religious moderation of 18th-century England, Law writes that the truly devout must live their lives in utter accordance with the will of God. ISBN# 0-8358-0901-3 $5.00

Walking Humbly with God - *Selected Writings of John Woolman*
Woolman's journal reveals the development of a Christian soul seeking to know and do God's will in all things. A devout Quaker, Woolman lived simply, in solidarity with the poor and oppressed. He traveled throughout the American colonies in the mid-1700s, urging other Quakers to free their slaves and to stand with him against slavery. ISBN# 0-8358-0900-5 $5.00

A Life of Total Prayer - *Selected Writings of Catherine of Siena*
In seeking to submit her will completely to God, Catherine of Siena practiced extreme self-sacrifice fueled by prayer so intense that she often lost awareness of the world around her. She expressed these experiences in letters and writings that address the turbulent times of fourteenth-century Italy in which she lived. ISBN# 0-8358-0903-X $5.00